Hiking Waterfalls Northern California

A Guide to the Region's Best Waterfall Hikes

Second Edition

Tracy Salcedo

FALCONGUIDES

ESSEX, CONNECTICUT

FALCONGUIDES®

An imprint of Globe Pequot, the trade division of
The Rowman & Littlefield Publishing Group, Inc.
4501 Forbes Blvd., Ste. 200
Lanham, MD 20706
www.rowman.com

Falcon and FalconGuides are registered trademarks and Make Adventure Your Story is a trademark of The Rowman & Littlefield Publishing Group, Inc.

Distributed by NATIONAL BOOK NETWORK

British Library Cataloguing in Publication Information available

Library of Congress Cataloging-in-Publication Data

Names: Salcedo, Tracy author.
Title: Hiking waterfalls Northern California : a guide to the region's best waterfall hikes / Tracy Salcedo.
Description: Second edition. | Essex, Connecticut : Falcon Guides, [2023] |
  Includes bibliographical references and index. | Summary: "Hiking Waterfalls Northern California
  includes detailed hike descriptions, maps, and color photos for the area's most scenic waterfall hikes.
  Hike descriptions also include history, trivia, and GPS coordinates. This book takes you through state and
  national parks, forests, monuments, and wilderness areas, and from city parks to the most secluded
  corners of the area, to view the most spectacular waterfalls"—Provided by publisher.
Identifiers: LCCN 2022051708 (print) | LCCN 2022051709 (ebook) | ISBN 9781493067015 (paperback)
  | ISBN 9781493067022 (epub)
Subjects: LCSH: Hiking—California, Northern—Guidebooks. | Waterfalls—California, Northern—
  Guidebooks. | Trails—California, Northern—Guidebooks. | Natural history—California, Northern—
  Guidebooks. | California, Northern—Guidebooks.
Classification: LCC GV199.42.C2 S255 2023 (print) | LCC GV199.42.C2 (ebook) | DDC
  796.5109794—dc23/eng/20221031
LC record available at https://lccn.loc.gov/2022051708
LC ebook record available at https://lccn.loc.gov/2022051709

♾™ The paper used in this publication meets the minimum requirements of American National Standard for Information Sciences—Permanence of Paper for Printed Library Materials, ANSI / NISO Z39.48-1992.

Contents

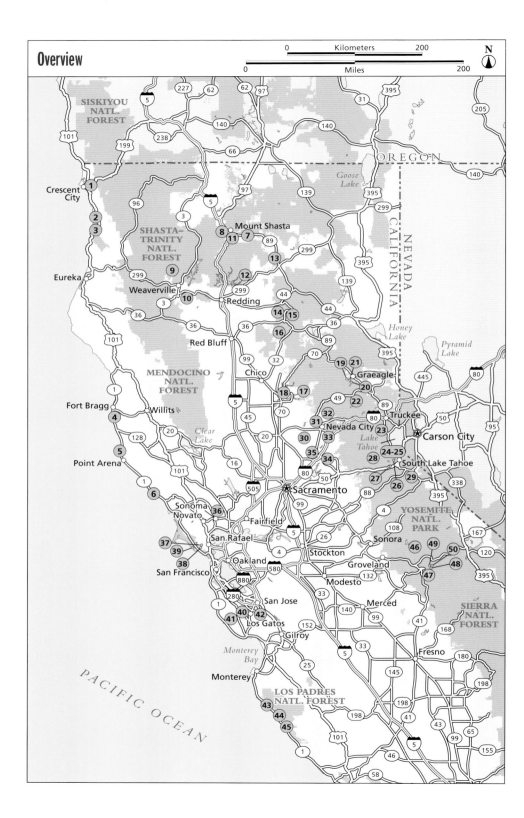

Overview

Kilometers
0   200

Miles
0   200

N

SISKIYOU
NATL.
FOREST

OREGON

CALIFORNIA   NEVADA

Crescent
City

Eureka

SHASTA–
TRINITY
NATL.
FOREST

Weaverville

Mount Shasta

Goose
Lake

Honey
Lake

Pyramid
Lake

Redding

Red Bluff

MENDOCINO
NATL.
FOREST

Chico

Clear
Lake

Graeagle

Fort Bragg

Willits

Truckee

Carson City

Nevada City

Point Arena

Lake
Tahoe

Sacramento

South Lake Tahoe

Sonoma
Novato

Fairfield

YOSEMITE
NATL.
PARK

San Rafael

Sonora

Stockton

San Francisco

Oakland

Groveland

Modesto

San Jose

Merced

SIERRA
NATL.
FOREST

Los Gatos

Gilroy

Monterey
Bay

Fresno

Monterey

LOS PADRES
NATL. FOREST

PACIFIC OCEAN

Acknowledgments

I must start by thanking the waterfall explorers and writers who've come before me. It turns out that a number of folks out there with waterfall obsessions have created fabulous resources for those who seek to find and explore Northern California's waterfalls. My hat is off to them: I cannot hope to catalog what they already have. I have included their books and websites as resources at the end of this guide.

Just as crucial to the production of this guide is the work and input of those who serve as stewards of public lands. All of the waterfalls in this guide are accessible via trails on public lands, whether in national forests, national parks, state parks, or local parks and open space preserves. My thanks to the land managers who oversee these public resources, both for the hard work they do every day and for taking the time to review hike descriptions within this guide.

I am also grateful to friends and colleagues who supported me while I hiked and wrote. Thanks also to the editors and mapmakers at FalconGuides who ushered the guide through production. Finally, thanks to friends and family, including Alison Pimentel, Mike Witkowski, Julianne Roth, Bettina Hopkins, Kerin McTaggart, Mitchell and Karen Friedman, Rita Friedman, Deb and Kern Rodman, Tory Rodman Traver, Samantha and Callie Friedman, Ned Farnkopf, Jesse and Judy Salcedo, Nick and Nancy Salcedo, Chris Salcedo and Angela Jones, the late, great Sarah Chourré, Martin Chourré, and last but never least, my sons, Jesse, Cruz, and Penn Chourré.

Mount Tamalpais and San Francisco Bay from the trail to Carson Falls (hike 37).

Introduction

When I wrote the first edition of this guide, finding and visiting Northern California's waterfalls became the obsession I suspected it would. One waterfall led to the next, and then to another, and even as I put this second guide to bed, my mind spins with the possibilities. By one waterfall blogger's count, more than 1,400 waterfalls await exploration in the state. This guide covers just a fraction of those—the ones I consider the best. This meant culling the "almosts," which I couldn't bear, so additional options for my fellows in waterfall wanderlust are briefly described as Honorable Mentions at the end of geographic sections in this guide.

It still holds true that hiking NorCal waterfalls is like sailing or skiing: You won't see them if the conditions aren't right. California has a rainy season and a dry season, which means many falls are ephemeral, running for only a handful of months before evaporating. Thus, winter and spring are optimal for waterfall hiking, with watercourses filled by either rainfall or snowmelt.

But prime conditions for seeing waterfalls in full flow go deeper than that. Climate matters. Unfortunately, as was the case when I researched the first edition of this guide, drought continues to wither streams throughout the Golden State. Even in winter, instead of waterfalls, I hiked to NorCal's water-streaked cliffs. Then there were the wildfires. In recent years the forests surrounding many of the north state's falls have burned, sometimes in epic fashion.

All of these conditions—these extremes—are tragic and frustrating, enervating and painful. For a walker in the woods, the standing dead in burn scars, the fallen grandmother trees in drought zones, and the dry cliffs where water should be falling are difficult to reconcile, even as nature heals around them. The trails endure, but capturing the lushness of a waterfall in full flow, either in photographs or in the mind's eye, has become elusive.

Still, we are talking about hiking. And hiking is what sets this guide apart from other waterfall compendiums. Regardless of the weather, the state of the falls, whether the forest is untouched or painted by the mosaic of fire, these trails are worth taking—the best waterfall trails California has to offer. More than ever, in these days of human-caused climate change, the journey matters just as much as the destination. The hike to Carson Falls in Marin County exemplifies the thought-provoking juxtaposition of sustaining waterfalls in drought, the destination a stagnant pool at the base of a black-streaked cliff reached via a trail where views open gloriously onto Mount Tamalpais slowly drawing a blanket of fog over its wooded ridgelines. The hike to Kings Creek Falls in Lassen Volcanic National Park reveals the unexpected beauty that follows wildfire: Ravaged by the Dixie Fire in 2021, even in the first season after the fire, the land along the route was blooming again, wildflowers watered by a snow-fed stream born on a volcano.

The Merced River churns below the bridge atop Nevada Fall (hike 50).

The spirit of the unexpected qualifies every hike in this guide. I've given each waterfall a beauty rating (up to five stars), but these are more than ratings of the falls themselves: They also take into account the quality of the hike. The fifty hikes in this guide are a drop in the proverbial bucket, but they represent the best waterfall hikes I've taken in the part of the state I call home. I hope these hikes will inspire you, as they have inspired me, to head out on the route less traveled, and to find loveliness wherever you roam.

How to Use This Guide

Mileages

Original research for this guidebook was done in 2013, 2014, and the beginning of 2015, and it was updated in 2021 and 2022. Trails were hiked using modern GPS technology, but exact mileages may differ from what appears on park maps. Distances listed on trail signs don't necessarily mesh with maps or GPS readings. I have recorded the mileages logged on my GPS unit for consistency's sake. Discrepancies seldom exceeded 0.5 mile and shouldn't affect a hiker's ability to gauge the difficulty or duration of a given hike.

Difficulty Ratings

The hikes are rated easy, moderate, or strenuous. In assigning a label, I took into account elevation gains and losses, hiking surfaces, and distances. Generally speaking, easy hikes are short and relatively flat. Moderate hikes involve greater distances and (perhaps) greater elevation changes. Strenuous hikes include steep ascents, long-distance loops, and routes that include challenging trail surfaces.

Keep in mind that every trail is only as difficult as you make it. If you keep a pace within your level of fitness, drink plenty of water, and stoke up on good, high-energy foods, you can make any trail easy.

Route Finding

Trails in this guide are generally well marked and maintained. All highlighted trails are on public land.

Using GPS

GPS coordinates are provided for trailheads in this guide, but be warned: Blindly plugging these coordinates into the navigation system of your car may not provide you with the best driving directions to the trailhead. Using GPS navigation to reach trailheads in Yosemite National Park, for example, is notorious for recommending travel on historic roads that now are trails or no longer exist. The coordinates provided are useful for locating trailheads in relationship to other amenities, like highways and towns, and for confirming you are starting your hike in the right place. To navigate to any of these trailheads, follow the written directions provided, or refer to a reliable mapping source, whether paper or electronic.

Likewise, be cautious when using GPS or an application on your smartphone to navigate on these trails. Cell signal can be spotty or nonexistent. You should also make sure your device is fully charged, and carry extra batteries or a battery charger.

Creative trail construction makes crossing deadfall a snap on the trail.

Maps

The USGS topographic maps that pertain to each route are listed in the hike descriptions. If a trail map is available from another source, either from the land management agency or online, that resource is listed. In the case of California state parks, search for the park name on the agency website to go to the park's home page. Click on "Brochures," then on "Park Brochure." A PDF of the printed brochure for each state park in this guide includes a basic but adequate map. Park partners may also be listed on the state park site; additional resources may be available online from these nonprofits.

How the Hikes Were Chosen

All of the hikes in this guide are day hikes and, with only one exception, do not exceed 10 miles out and back or as a loop.

Additionally, all trailheads can be reached using passenger vehicles, though some of the roads are gravel or dirt. Conditions on unpaved roads vary with season, use, weather, and maintenance schedules; contact the land manager listed for each destination for the most current road status.

Hiking Essentials

Hiking waterfalls in Northern California often means venturing into the backcountry. While all of these excursions are day hikes, no matter the length of your hike, you should be prepared.

For starters, every hiker should carry survival and first-aid materials, layers of clothing for all kinds of weather, a compass, and a good topographic map—and know how to use them.

The next-best piece of safety advice is to hike with a partner or in a party. If you choose to hike alone, tell somebody where you're going, your route, and when you plan to return.

Finally, before you set out on any hike, consider physical conditioning. Being fit makes wilderness travel more fun and much safer.

Here are a few more tips:

- Check the weather forecast. Be careful not to get caught at high altitude in a bad storm or along a stream in a flash flood. Watch cloud formations so you don't get stranded on a ridgeline during a lightning storm. Avoid traveling for prolonged periods in cold weather.
- Keep your party together; move only as fast as your slowest companion.
- Before you leave for the trailhead, find out as much as you can about the route, especially the potential hazards.
- Don't wait until you're confused to look at your map, whether paper or on an electronic device. Follow it as you go, maintaining a continual fix on your location.
- If you get lost, don't panic. Sit down, relax, check your map, and get your bearings. Confidently plan your next move. If necessary, retrace your steps until you find familiar ground, even if that lengthens your trip. If you calmly and rationally determine a plan of action, you'll be fine.
- If you are genuinely lost, stay put. It is easier for authorities to locate a lost hiker when that hiker is not on the move.
- Your pack should contain backcountry essentials, including water, an emergency blanket and/or emergency bivy, and a whistle, which will help ensure your safety if you become lost or can't make it back to the trailhead for another reason.
- Stay clear of all wild animals. Make sure you know how best to deal with encounters with a black bear, mountain lion, or other animal in the backcountry.

Play It Safe

Hiking is generally a safe endeavor, but common sense dictates that when venturing into the wild, travelers should take precautions. Education is the best protection, but a day pack loaded with everything you need to stay safe if you get held up on the trail, for whatever reason, is good insurance.

Carry a good first-aid kit that includes, at a minimum: aspirin or over-the-counter pain reliever, antihistamine tablets (Benadryl), antibacterial ointment, antiseptic swabs, butterfly bandages, adhesive tape, adhesive strips, two triangular bandages, two inflatable splints, moleskin or Second Skin for blisters, 3-inch gauze, rubber gloves, a sewing needle and thread, and lightweight first-aid instructions.

Pack a survival kit that includes, at a minimum, the following: compass and map (a GPS unit will do, but be sure to carry extra batteries), whistle, signal mirror, flashlight, water purification tablets or filter, space blanket and/or lightweight bivy, a warm hat, gloves, and a layer that is weather resistant (rain jacket and/or windbreaker).

Critters

You will share most trails in Northern California with a variety of wild creatures, many of which will go unseen and undetected. Some will come right up to you, like that adorable ground squirrel who wants to share your granola bar. Some will pester you, like horseflies, bees, and wasps. Some you may only catch fleeting glimpses of, such as mule deer and pileated woodpeckers. And some you may only encounter by way of what they leave behind: footprints and scat.

For the most part, animal encounters on the trail are benign. Abide by two basic rules for both your safety and that of the animals:

- Do not feed any wild animal, no matter how cute or how much it begs. Acclimating chipmunks, deer, birds, and larger mammals like bears to human food is not only dangerous for people, but also reduces the animals' ability to survive when the people have gone home.
- Keep your distance. Approaching a wild creature not only increases the chance that you might get bitten (or worse), it also increases anxiety levels for the animals.

The ultimate in harmless woodland creatures: the banana slug.

Black Bears

Though black bears generally stay clear of humans, they can be encountered just about anywhere in Northern California, especially in the high Sierra Nevada, in the foothills of Gold Country, and in the forests of the North Coast.

Black bears do not, as a rule, attack humans, but they may pose a danger if you handle food improperly, if you startle them, or if you get between a mother bear and her cub.

Food is the primary instigator of bear-human interactions. Keep in mind that letting a bear get human food is contributing—directly—to the eventual destruction of that bear. Think of proper bear etiquette as protecting the bears as much as yourself.

Avoid bear encounters while hiking by making noise. If you travel with a group, talking is an effective bear deterrent. If traveling alone, carry a bear bell or make noise by singing or talking to yourself. If nothing else, holler "Hey, bear" now and then to let them know you're around.

If you encounter a black bear, remember the following:

- Keep your distance. Maintain a separation of at least 300 feet from any black bear.
- Do not run. Running may initiate a predatory response from the bear.
- Back away. Turning your back may trigger a predatory response.
- Don't climb a tree, as black bears can climb them too.
- If you are with small children, pick them up without bending over. If you are a group, band together.
- If attacked, defend yourself. Try to remain standing. Do not feign death. Use bear spray if you have it. Teach others in your group how to behave in a black bear encounter.
- Respect any warning signs posted by agencies. Report encounters, including location, to park rangers, who may want to post education/warning signs.
- If physical injury occurs, leave the area. Do not disturb the site of an attack. Black bears who have attacked people must be killed, and an undisturbed site is crucial for effectively locating the dangerous animal.

Mountain Lions

Mountain lion sightings are relatively rare, and attacks on humans are extremely rare, but it's wise to educate yourself before heading into mountain lion habitat—which includes most of the territory covered in this guide.

To stay as safe as possible when hiking in mountain lion country, follow this advice:

- Travel with a friend or in a group, and stay together.
- Don't let small children wander away by themselves.
- Avoid hiking at dawn and dusk, when mountain lions are most active.
- Know how to behave if you encounter a mountain lion.

The vast majority of mountain lions exhibit avoidance, indifference, or curiosity that never results in human injury. But it's natural to be alarmed if you have an encounter. Keep your cool by remembering the following:

- If a mountain lion is more than 50 yards away and directs its attention to you, it may be only curious. Back away, keeping the animal in your peripheral vision. Look for rocks, sticks, or something to use as a weapon, just in case. Keep small children close. It's best to choose another route or time to hike through the area.

- If a mountain lion is crouched less than 50 yards away and staring at you, it may be assessing the chance of a successful attack. Slowly back away, but maintain eye contact. Do not run; running may stimulate a predatory response. Make noise, talking and yelling loudly and regularly. Try not to panic. Shout to make others in the area aware of the situation. Raise your arms above your head and make steady waving motions, or raise your jacket or another object above your head to make yourself appear larger. Do not bend over, as this will make you appear smaller and more prey-like.

- If you are with small children, pick them up without bending over. If you are in a group, band together.

- Defend yourself and others. If attacked, fight back. Try to remain standing. Do not feign death. Pick up a branch or rock; pull out a knife, pepper spray, or other deterrent device. Teach others in your group how to behave in the event of a mountain lion encounter.

- Respect any warning signs posted by agencies. Report encounters, including location, to park rangers, who may want to visit the site and, if appropriate, post education/warning signs.

- If physical injury occurs, leave the area. Do not disturb the site of an attack. Mountain lions who have attacked people must be killed, and an undisturbed site is crucial for effectively locating the dangerous mountain lion.

Rattlesnakes

Most regions covered in this guide are rattlesnake country. Rattlesnakes typically are not aggressive toward humans—we are too big to be prey. Most snakebites occur when hikers startle or attempt to handle a rattlesnake. To avoid a nasty encounter, watch where you put your hands and feet when you are stepping over logs or climbing on rocks. If you see a rattler, back away and let it pass.

Ticks

Hiking waterfalls means hiking in tick season. Though not all species are carriers, some ticks in Northern California can transmit Lyme disease. After traveling through brush, check your clothing for the arachnids. If one latches on, remove it carefully, making sure to get the mouthparts. You can have the creature tested to see if it might have transmitted the disease.

Let's face it: If you hike all of these waterfalls, you are going to encounter every kind of weather, from snow to blistering sunshine. Insulate yourself from the potential consequences of weather extremes by keeping yourself properly hydrated, carrying high-energy snacks, wearing a hat, applying sunscreen, and packing layers of clothing that you can add or shed depending on the conditions.

Hiking in extreme weather—extreme heat, heavy or freezing rain or snow—can lead to weather-related illness. Knowing the symptoms of, and how to treat, both hypothermia and heat-related illnesses can be life-saving.

Hypothermia is a condition in which the body's internal temperature drops below normal. It is caused by exposure to cold; is aggravated by wetness, wind, and exhaustion; and can be life-threatening. Given NorCal waterfalls may be most vigorous during and after rainstorms, hypothermia is a real possibility for hikers who don't take precautions.

To defend against hypothermia, stay dry. Choose rain clothes that cover your whole body and provide good protection against wind-driven rain. If your party is exposed to wind, cold, and wet, watch yourself and others for uncontrollable fits of shivering; vague, slow, slurred speech; memory lapses; incoherence; fumbling hands; frequent stumbling or a lurching gait; drowsiness; exhaustion; and inability to get up after a rest. When a member of your party has hypothermia, he or she may deny any problem. Believe the symptoms, not the victim. Even mild symptoms demand the following treatment:

- Get the victim out of the wind and rain.
- Strip off all wet clothes and get the victim into warm clothes.
- If the victim is mildly impaired, provide warm drinks.
- Get off the trail and seek medical attention as quickly as possible.

Heat-related illnesses can be avoided by not hiking in the heat of the day and staying hydrated. Selecting clothing that breathes, which allows perspiration to evaporate and cool the skin, and wearing a lightweight, brimmed hat will help. Applying sunscreen to all exposed parts of the body is always a good idea.

Warning signs of heat-related illness include nausea and/or vomiting; headache, light-headedness, and/or fainting; weakness, fatigue, and/or a lack of coordination; loss of concentration; and flushed skin. Symptoms of heat exhaustion include all of the above, coupled with low blood pressure, heavy sweating, and a rapid pulse. If you or a member of your party exhibits these symptoms, seek shade, lie down and elevate the feet and legs, apply a wet cloth to the head and neck (and other parts of the body, if you can), and drink cool liquids.

Sunset burnishes the Merced River copper.

Heatstroke is life-threatening. Hikers who lose consciousness, vomit, have red, hot skin (moist or dry), and have a weak pulse and shallow breathing are in danger of convulsions, coma, and death. Cool the victim by any means possible, as quickly as possible, and call for emergency medical aid.

Wildfires

Fortunately, waterfall season doesn't generally coincide with fire season in Northern California (though human-caused climate change is altering that dynamic). That said, some of these hikes follow trails in burn zones, where hikers may encounter widow-makers (falling trees), ankle-twisting stump holes, mudslides, and route-finding challenges. If a waterfall is in a region that has burned in recent years, I've included that information in the hike description. The hazards change with time, so it's important to check with land managers before your hike.

If you plan to hike during fire season, stay tuned to the weather forecasts and be prepared to change your plans should a fire erupt near your planned route. Smoke is another concern: You can wear a mask rated for wildfire smoke while you walk, but generally it's safer, and more pleasant, to hike when the air is clear and you can enjoy the views.

The same sun that parches California's annual grasses also may parch hikers. Stay hydrated.

Hydration

No matter the weather conditions or the difficulty of the hike, hikers need to drink plenty of water. Hydrate before, during, and after your hike. Whether you prefer a hydration bladder or a water bottle (or two), make sure you are carrying more than what you think you might need.

That said, as far as quantity is concerned, there are no hard-and-fast rules. Drink as much as you can. Drink even when you are not thirsty. But at a minimum, plan on consuming 32 ounces of water for every 2 hours on the trail. That may mean carrying a filter or purification tablets so that you can refill water bottles or bladders from streams and lakes, even on day hikes (all backpackers should carry these).

Unless it's an emergency, do not drink untreated or unfiltered water from any water source.

Leave No Trace

Most of us know better than to litter—in or out of the backcountry. Be sure you leave nothing, regardless how small, along the trail or at a campsite. Pack everything out, including your orange peel and apple core. Also pick up any trash that others leave behind.

Other important Leave No Trace ethics:

- Follow the main trail. Avoid cutting switchbacks and walking on vegetation beside the trail.
- Don't pick up "souvenirs," such as rocks, antlers, or wildflowers. The next person wants to see them too, and collecting souvenirs universally violates park regulations.
- Avoid making loud noises on the trail (unless you are in bear country) or in camp. Be courteous—remember, sound travels easily in the backcountry, especially across water.
- Carry a lightweight trowel to bury human waste 6 to 8 inches deep and at least 200 feet from any water source. Pack out used toilet paper in a ziplock bag.
- Go without a campfire if you can't find an established fire pit. Carry a stove for cooking and a flashlight, candle lantern, or headlamp for light.
- Camp in obviously used sites when they are available. Otherwise, camp and cook on durable surfaces such as bedrock, sand, gravel bars, or bare ground.

Leave no trace. Put your ear to the ground and listen carefully. Thousands of people coming behind you are thanking you for your courtesy and good sense.

For more information visit https://LNT.org.

Looking at the back side of Half Dome from the Panorama Trail to Illilouette Fall in Yosemite National Park (hike 48).

Map Legend

Symbol	Description	Symbol	Description
80	Interstate Highway	■	Building/Point of Interest
101	US Highway	Λ	Campground
93	State Highway	▲	Campsite
D2 / FR 21N35Y	County/Forest Road	⊛	Capital
	Local Road	⌒	Cave
	Unpaved Road	⌐⌐⌐⌐⌐	Cliffs
	Railroad	—	Dam
	Featured Trail	⚈	Gate
	Trail	▬	Lodging
	Paved Trail	Ⓟ	Parking
IIIIIIIII	Boardwalk	⤳	Pass/Gap
	State Line	▲	Peak/Summit
	Small River/Creek	⊞	Picnic Area
	Intermittent Stream	×	Point Elevation
	Body of Water	⛺	Ranger Station
	Marsh/Swamp	⚍	Restrooms
	Sand	⬕	Scenic View/Viewpoint
	National/State Forest/Park	⟋	Spring
	National Wilderness/Reserve/Preserve	⛐	Stables
	State/County Park	☎	Telephone
	Recreation Area	○	Town
	Miscellaneous Area	⑩	Trailhead
	Bench	⊐⊏	Tunnel
	Boat Ramp	❓	Visitor/Information Center
	Bridge	≋	Waterfall
		♿	Wheelchair Accessible

North Coast

This region stretches south along the California coastline and includes waterfalls in Del Norte, Humboldt, and Mendocino Counties. You can reach these beauties from Crescent City, Eureka and Arcata, Fort Bragg, and Gualala. The landscape is rugged from coastline to coastal mountains, and stands of old-growth coast redwoods, the signature species of the North Coast, tower over most of these waterfall hikes. Be prepared for fog, wind, and rain: You're not always in sunny California when you're rambling the North Coast.

On the trail to Fern Falls in Jedediah Smith Redwoods State Park (hike 1).

1 Fern Falls

Hike through a stunning old-growth redwood forest to a perennial waterfall on Jordan Creek.

Height: About 30 feet
Beauty rating: ★ ★ ★ ★ ★
Start: Boy Scout Tree Trailhead
Distance: 5.8 miles out and back
Difficulty: Moderate due only to distance
Hiking time: 3 hours
Seasons/schedule: Year-round; sunrise to sunset
Fees and permits: None
Trail contact: Jedediah Smith Redwoods State Park, 1111 2nd St., Crescent City, CA 95531; (707) 464-6101; www.parks.ca.gov
Canine compatibility: Dogs not permitted on trail.
Trail surface: Dirt singletrack

Land status: Jedediah Smith Redwoods State Park. *Note:* When Redwood National and State Parks were created in 1968, the boundary encircled three California state parks. Jedediah Smith, Del Norte Coast, and Prairie Creek Redwoods are embedded inside the national park. The state of California and the National Park Service operate the parks in partnership.
Nearest town: Crescent City
Other trail users: None
Maps to consult: USGS Hiouchi CA and Crescent City CA; park map available at the visitor center and online
Water availability: None
Amenities available: None
Cell service: None
Trail conditions: The trail is well maintained.

Finding the trailhead: From the Pacific Coast Highway (CA 1/US 101) in Crescent City, take Elk Valley Road east for 1.1 mile to the junction with Howland Hill Road. Turn right onto Howland Hill Road and follow the narrow road for 3.5 miles, winding through tremendous redwood groves, to the signed Boy Scout Tree Trail parking pullout. The one-lane road is paved for the first mile and is a good gravel road after that. There is parking for about twenty-five cars. If you must park outside the pullout, be sure you are safely clear of Howland Hill Road. Trailhead GPS: N41 46.139' / W124 06.602'

The Hike

From the second you set out on the Boy Scout Tree Trail, you will be enchanted. Lit by the slanting rays of a midwinter sun, the furrowed bark of the massive redwoods alongside the trail shimmers gray and green. Touch the bark: It feels light and alive, its pores open to the mist and the filtered sunshine. The term "magical" is overused in the voluminous literature praising California's redwoods, but really, there's no more accurate way to describe the old-growth forests of the North Coast. This one is quintessential.

Thankfully, you'll have ample time to reset the awe meter, because Fern Falls lies far down the winding path. With plenty of opportunities to contemplate the girths of the trunks, crick your neck gazing into the canopy, and sneak a hug or two, by the

Fern Falls tumbles into a clear pool at trail's end.

time you reach the waterfall, with its flanking ferns and shallow pool, you should be primed and open to yet another sublime setting.

To begin, the Boy Scout Tree Trail climbs gently away from the trailhead. The trees along this stretch are stunning—among the largest you'll see along the route. Perhaps it is the orientation of the slope, perhaps the angle of the sun, but the huge silvery trunks are illuminated with artistic perfection. The trail is artful as well, looping easily up the slope through fern gardens, under fallen giants, and over picturesque footbridges.

The other remarkable thing about the outset of the trail is how sounds of the sea, far out of sight, filter into the woods. The lonesome sigh of a buoy, the cry of a gull, the moans of foghorns all drift up into the stillness. The resonant quietness seeps into the bones.

Climb over a sloping ridge and begin to drop; the trees here are slightly—only slightly—diminished in size and grandeur. A long, rolling descent leads into a creek drainage; use the bridge to ford the stream, and then climb out of the ravine. The route drops through several more drainages beyond, with bridges spanning the waterways. Watch carefully for the spur trail to the Boy Scout Tree, which breaks right at about the 2.5-mile mark.

Fern Falls is at trail's end. The waterfall fans out across a short, low-angle rock face and drops into a clear pool, with a gravel beach of sorts on the far side of the creek at its base. Return as you came.

Fern Falls (Jedediah Smith Redwoods State Park)

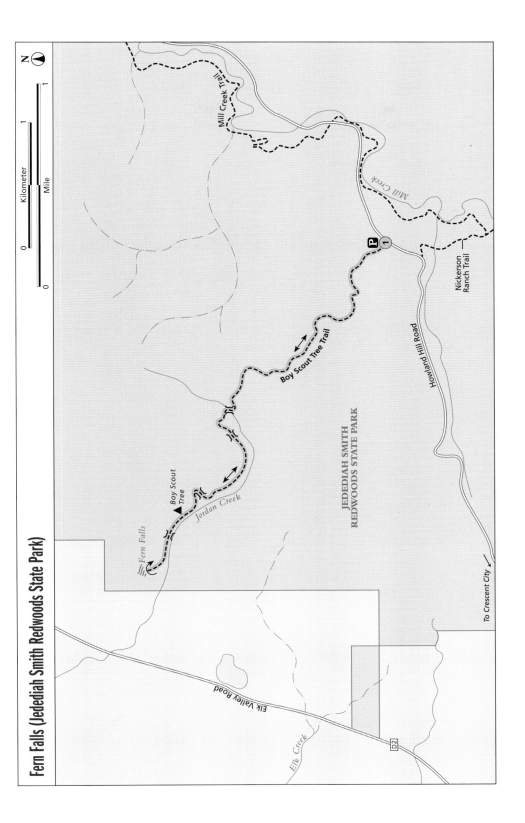

N

0 1 Kilometer 1

0 Mile 1

Mill Creek Trail

Mill Creek

Boy Scout Tree Trail

Nickerson Ranch Trail

Howland Hill Road

JEDEDIAH SMITH
REDWOODS STATE PARK

Boy Scout Tree

Jordan Creek

Fern Falls

Elk Valley Road

Elk Creek

D2

To Crescent City

The trail to Fern Falls passes through a luminous redwood forest.

Miles and Directions

0.0   Start by heading uphill on the Boy Scout Tree Trail.

0.2   Cross a footbridge.

1.6   Drop down switchbacks and cross a footbridge.

1.9   A set of stairs leads through another stream drainage and to a second footbridge.

2.5   Switchback down to a bridge over a streamlet. The side trail to the Boy Scout Tree breaks right.

2.6   Cross another bridge; the trail parallels a stream.

2.9   Reach Fern Falls. Retrace your steps.

5.8   Arrive back at the trailhead.

2 Gold Bluffs Beach Falls

Follow a spectacular stretch of California's Coastal Trail to a secluded waterfall.

Height: About 250 feet

Beauty rating: ★★★★

Start: Trailhead in the Gold Bluffs Beach Day Use Area

Distance: 3.2 miles out and back

Difficulty: Easy

Hiking time: About 2 hours

Seasons/schedule: Year-round; sunrise to sunset

Fees and permits: An entrance fee is charged. You will need to secure a free permit to access the trailhead, which also serves the popular Fern Canyon Loop, from May 1 to Sept. 30. Permits can be accessed online through the Redwood Parks Conservancy website at www .redwoodparksconservancy.org/permits/ fern-canyon-permits.

Trail contact: Prairie Creek Redwoods State Park, 127011 Newton B. Drury Pkwy., Orick, CA 95555; (707) 464-6101 or (707) 488-2039; www.parks.ca.gov

Canine compatibility: Leashed dogs permitted on Gold Bluffs Beach; no dogs allowed on trails.

Trail surface: Dirt, mud, sand; singletrack

Land status: Prairie Creek Redwoods State Park. *Note:* When Redwood National and State Parks were created in 1968, the boundary encircled three California state parks. Jedediah Smith, Del Norte Coast, and Prairie Creek Redwoods State Parks are embedded in the national park. The state of California and the National Park Service operate the parks in partnership.

Nearest town: Orick

Other trail users: None

Maps to consult: USGS Fern Canyon CA; park map available at the entrance station or online

Water availability: None

Amenities available: Restrooms, trash cans, and information signboards

Cell service: None

Trail conditions: The trail is muddy in the rainy season, which is pretty much year-round.

Finding the trailhead: From Eureka head north on US 101 for about 45 miles, through the hamlet of Orick, to the signed junction with Davison Road (also signed for Gold Bluffs Beach). The junction is about 3 miles north of Orick. Turn left onto Davison Road and travel 6.6 miles to the trailhead at the end of the road. The entrance station, where fees are paid, is at 3.5 miles; pass a gate, which closes at sunset, at 5.5 miles. The gravel road is negotiable by passenger cars, but several stream crossings and the overall roughness of the surface are easier to navigate in a high-clearance vehicle. Trailhead GPS: N41 24.039' / W124 03.949'

The Hike

Gold Bluffs Beach Falls tumbles over a high bluff on the east side of the California Coastal Trail and is screened from the trail by sedges, willows, and the interlocking boughs of evergreens. You'll hear the fall before you see it—a slender but significant horsetail arcing hundreds of feet from the tree-topped summit of the gold-hued bluff. Enveloped in the dense shade and surrounded by steep cliffs, with the sound of falling

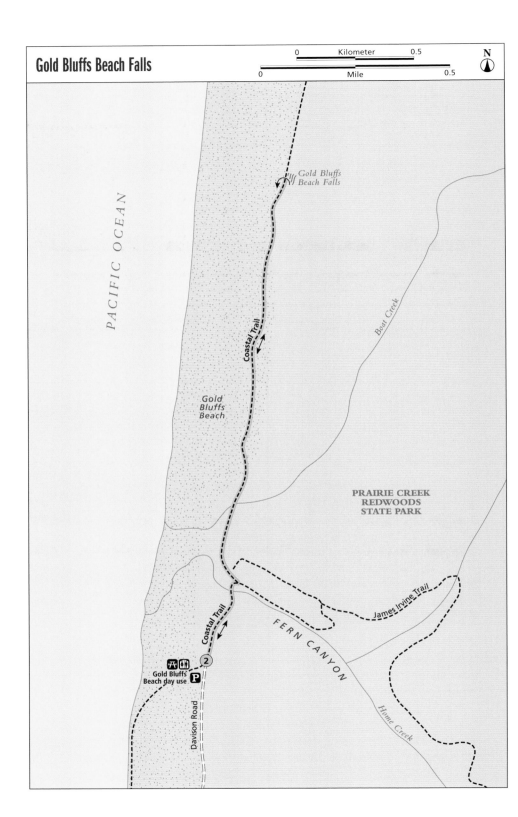

Gold Bluffs Beach Falls

0   Kilometer   0.5

0   Mile   0.5

N

PACIFIC OCEAN

Gold Bluffs Beach Falls

Coastal Trail

Boat Creek

Gold Bluffs Beach

PRAIRIE CREEK REDWOODS STATE PARK

James Irvine Trail

Coastal Trail

FERN CANYON

2

Gold Bluffs Beach day use

P

Davison Road

Home Creek

Gold Bluffs Beach Falls hide behind thick foliage near the Pacific shoreline.

water muffling the beat of the surf on the Pacific shoreline, the site seems distant from the nearby strand.

The short first section of the Coastal Trail, to the mouth of Fern Canyon, is easy. Home Creek, which spills out of the canyon, is the biggest obstacle: Depending on the season and recent rainfall, the crossing can be tricky. Pick up the Coastal Trail on the north side of the creek, left of the signed junction with the James Irvine Trail/

The scenic Coastal Trail leads north to Gold Bluffs Beach Falls.

Fern Canyon Loop Trail, and continue through willow and alder stands flourishing in the riparian zone. This patch of trail can be profoundly mucky: In one wild moment my boot was completely sucked off my foot by sticky mud. Wet feet precluding the need to find rocks or logs to hop across soggy patches, staying on the trail became much more straightforward after that misstep.

After a half mile, the Coastal Trail breaks out into a narrow swath of meadowland, with towering bluffs on the east and a break of dunes on the west. The steady thumping of surf crashing onto Gold Bluffs Beach forms a backbeat for the next easy mile of hiking. The bluffs are truly impressive, in places more than 500 feet high, capped by flattop of forest with occasional ephemeral cascades tumbling down toward the sea. Seabirds and raptors soar overhead, riding columns of air that rise up the vertical faces.

The falls are the turnaround point. Return as you came, unless you plan to continue on the Coastal Trail to the Oregon border.

Miles and Directions

0.0 Start on the wide, flat Coastal Trail toward Fern Canyon.

0.2 Ford Home Creek at the mouth of Fern Canyon. At the signed junction with the James Irvine/Fern Canyon Loop Trail on the far side of the creek, stay left on the Coastal Trail.

0.8 Break out of the woods. The trail winds through grasses at the base of the bluffs.

1.6 Reach the base of Gold Bluffs Beach Falls. Punch through the foliage to check out the plunge, and then retrace your steps.

3.2 Arrive back at the trailhead.

3 Trillium Falls

A shady loop links the bridge overlooking Trillium Falls to Elk Meadow, where odds are good you'll see a member of California's largest herd of Roosevelt elk.

Height: 25 feet
Beauty rating: ★★★★
Start: Elk Meadow Picnic Area trailhead
Distance: 2.7-mile lollipop
Difficulty: Easy
Hiking time: About 1.5 hours
Seasons/schedule: Year-round; sunrise to sunset
Fees and permits: None
Trail contact: Prairie Creek Redwoods State Park, 127011 Newton B. Drury Pkwy., Orick, CA 95555; (707) 464-6101 or (707) 488-2039; www.parks.ca.gov
Canine compatibility: No dogs allowed.
Trail surface: Dirt singletrack

Land status: Prairie Creek Redwoods State Park. *Note:* When Redwood National and State Parks were created in 1968, the boundary encircled three California state parks. Jedediah Smith, Del Norte Coast, and Prairie Creek Redwoods are embedded inside the national park. The state of California and the National Park Service operate the parks in partnership.
Nearest town: Orick
Other trail users: None
Maps to consult: USGS Orick CA; park map available at the entrance station or online
Water availability: None
Amenities available: Restrooms, picnic sites, trash cans, and information signboards
Cell service: Marginal but possible
Trail conditions: The trail is well maintained.

Finding the trailhead: From Eureka head north on US 101 for about 45 miles, through the hamlet of Orick, to the signed junction with Davison Road (also signed for Gold Bluffs Beach). The junction is about 3 miles north of Orick, with Elk Meadow sprawling along the west side of the highway. Turn left onto Davison Road and travel 0.2 mile to a left turn into the paved Elk Meadow parking lot and trailhead. Trailhead GPS: N41 19.387' / W124 02.732'

The Hike

Trillium Falls, a 25-foot cascade in a redwood-shaded canyon, lies only a half mile from the trailhead, but the loop that winds through the surrounding forest, with views across the valley to the east and brief passage alongside Elk Meadow, is worth following all the way around.

Not the least of the attractions are the Roosevelt elk who frequent the meadow. These giant creatures were once nearly extinct in the state, along with the tule elk found farther south. Conservation efforts have resulted in the return of both subspecies in protected areas of their former ranges. Don't approach the elk; view from a distance and take only pictures.

Trillium, on the other hand, you can examine up close. It's a striking, low-growing member of the lily family, with three bracts that look like leaves and flowers with

Trillium Falls is one highlight along this trail loop; the other is the chance to see Roosevelt elk.

three petals. The flowers can be red, purple, white, or yellow, depending on the species. They bloom along the trail from midwinter through spring.

To reach the falls, follow the paved path from the parking lot. At the junction go right on the paved, multiuse Davison Trail toward the Trillium Falls Trail. A signboard marks the start of the trail proper; climb away from the open meadowlands into the redwood forest above.

At the half-mile mark, after passing through the Redwood Volunteers Grove, cross the bridge overlooking the falls. It's the perfect vantage point, with the modest cataract tumbling down and under the span. You can return as you came, but this route continues beyond the falls, following a modest traversing climb along the base of the coastal ridge, winding in and out of ravines thick with ferns and shaded by redwoods.

Pass a number of named groves as the path begins to descend and then hooks back north toward the trailhead above Elk Meadow. Views open along this stretch; in the afternoon, while the trail is in deep shadow, the ridgetops across the valley glow in the light of the sinking sun.

DEFENDING THE NORTH COAST REDWOODS

Redwood National and State Parks, which encompass Prairie Creek Redwoods, Del Norte Coast, and Jedediah Smith Redwoods State Parks, protect about 45 percent of the remaining old-growth redwood forest in California. Within these boundaries the remnants of a coast redwood forest that once sprawled over 2 million acres towers into the clouds.

Protection of California's redwood forests, particularly stands of old-growth, has been no small feat. The trees' preservation has spurred passion and conflict throughout the region from the latter part of the twentieth century through today.

One ongoing threat to the trees is the timber industry. The durable heartwood is highly valued as a building material and fuels lumbering enterprises, which have been the economic backbone of towns and cities along the North Coast for more than a century. My link to this give-and-take is intimate: My father was a warrior in several nonviolent skirmishes between loggers and environmentalists. He traveled into redwood country on numerous occasions as a young man, working to preserve the Headwaters Redwood Grove, an old-growth stand slated for harvest by the Pacific Lumber Company. He was, on one occasion, arrested for his defiance—along with so many other peaceful protestors that buses were needed to transport them away from the site. As he tells the story, officers used zip ties in lieu of handcuffs because there weren't enough handcuffs to go around.

Another ongoing threat to healthy redwood forests is the cultivation of marijuana. Growing weed for recreational and medical use is another bulwark of the North Coast economy, and the social and economic battlegrounds that surround its cultivation and marketing have shifted public focus from saving the redwoods to securing marijuana as an economic stronghold.

The third threat: human-caused climate change. Redwoods thrive on the fog that perennially blankets the North Coast, able to siphon moisture from the marine layer. Scientists theorize that the redwoods' symbiosis with fog has resulted in the trees' attaining such spectacular heights, as being tall enables them to take advantage of all the moisture in a thick fog bank. But with climate change has come a decrease in the height and density of the marine layer, which in turn threatens the ability of the redwoods to survive. This battle is being engaged on a number of fronts . . . and I have no doubt my father would again submit to a zip-tie arrest if that would make a difference.

Trillium Falls

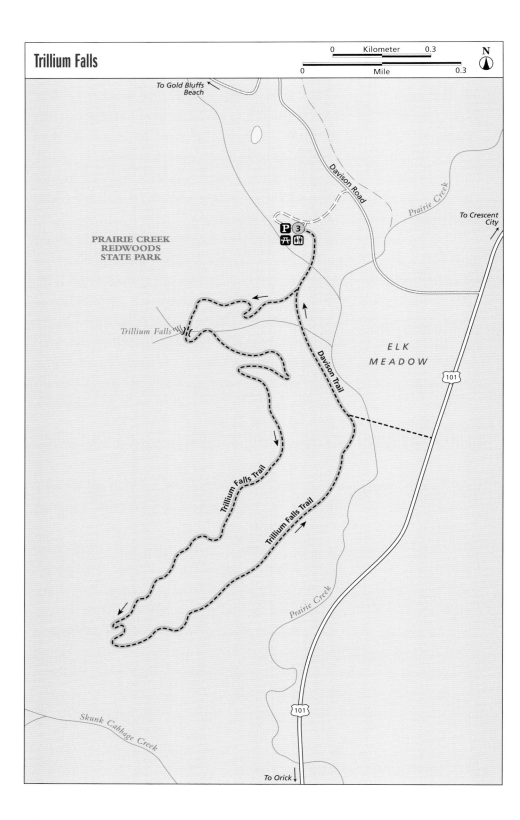

0   Kilometer   0.3

0   Mile   0.3

N

To Gold Bluffs
Beach

Davison Road

Prairie Creek

To Crescent
City

PRAIRIE CREEK
REDWOODS
STATE PARK

Trillium Falls

Davison Trail

ELK
MEADOW

101

Trillium Falls Trail

Trillium Falls Trail

Prairie Creek

Skunk Cabbage Creek

101

To Orick

The route finally drops back onto the paved Davison Trail, which traces the west side of Elk Meadow as it heads north toward the trailhead. If the willows are bare, you can see into the meadow, where Roosevelt elk may be grazing. Follow the Davison Trail back to the trailhead.

Miles and Directions

0.0 Follow the paved path down to the paved Davison Trail. Turn right on the Davison Trail.

0.1 The Trillium Falls Trail breaks right. Follow the footpath up into the woods.

0.4 Switchbacks lead up to the Redwood Volunteers Grove.

0.5 Reach Trillium Falls. Cross the bridge and continue climbing.

0.9 Arc westward into a fern-lined alley, and then climb a threesome of switchbacks.

1.1 Pass a bench in the first of several named groves to follow; this is the Doris and Richard Leonard Grove.

1.4 Cross a roadway, following the trail signs. A series of named redwood groves follows, with the trail winding down through carpets of fern.

2.1 Cross a bridge. The trail continues north, stretching back toward the trailhead.

2.5 Back alongside Elk Meadow, pass two trail junctions, staying left at each and following the flat, wide Davison Trail.

2.6 Close the loop at the junction with the Trillium Falls Trail. Retrace your steps.

2.7 Arrive back at the trailhead.

4 Russian Gulch Falls

Cruise inland from the sea through a fern canyon and into a wooded gulch that hosts a perennial waterfall.

Height: 40 feet

Beauty rating: ★★★★

Start: Either the parking area near the campground, or the day-use parking area for the Fern Canyon Trail. Parking can be full on weekends, so your starting point for the hike may vary.

Distance: 5.6 miles out and back

Difficulty: Moderate due only to distance

Hiking time: About 3 hours

Seasons/schedule: Year-round; sunrise to sunset

Fees and permits: An entrance fee is charged.

Trail contact: Russian Gulch, Mendocino Headlands, and Van Damme State Parks, 12301 North CA 1, Mendocino, CA 95460; (707) 937-5804; www.parks.ca.gov

Canine compatibility: No dogs permitted on trail; dogs allowed west of CA 1 on the beach.

Trail surface: Pavement, dirt

Land status: Russian Gulch State Park

Nearest town: Mendocino

Other trail users: Cyclists

Maps to consult: USGS Mendocino CA; park map available at the entrance station and online

Water availability: Water is available at the trailhead.

Amenities available: Restrooms, trash cans, picnic facilities, and campsites

Cell service: Marginal at the trailhead; none in the canyon

Trail conditions: The paved portion is broad and multiuse; the dirt sections may be muddy.

Finding the trailhead: From Fort Bragg head south on CA 1 for about 8 miles to the signed entrance to Russian Gulch State Park; from Mendocino, head north about 3 miles to the entrance. Pass the entrance station, and then follow the park road down and under the scenic highway bridge to the day-use parking area at the rec hall and campground. If the gate is open, you can continue through the campground to the parking area at the gated trailhead proper. Trailhead GPS (parking at the camp entrance): N39 19.829' / W123 48.122'

The Hike

Despite its proximity to the Pacific Ocean, all the water you'll encounter along the trail through Fern Canyon and up to Russian Gulch Falls is fresh, filtering out of gullies and ravines into the main stream, and the sound that fills the bottomland is not that of pounding surf but of falling water.

The route to the falls follows a flat multiuse trail that traces the north side of the stream. Willows and oaks line the waterway, with redwoods and pines on the ridges, and an understory of ferns creeps up the canyon walls in places, forming alleys of verdant green. The path is easily shared by all users and invites walking and talking, making it a family favorite.

Ferns, moss, and redwoods crowd the trail to Russian Gulch Falls.

The route begins at the entrance to the campground (though if the gate is open and parking is available, you may shave 1 mile off the round-trip distance by starting at the Fern Canyon trailhead proper). Follow the road through the sites, then through the parking area, to the gate at the beginning of Fern Canyon. A long, easy walk lies ahead, punctuated by streamlets filtering down and under the path, fern-clad rock outcroppings, and trees adorned with lace lichen and bursts of fern and moss on their trunks.

North Trail and the Falls Loop Trail intersect about 2 miles up the paved trail. Though you can take the loop trail either way, the most direct path to the falls (the Waterfall Trail) climbs straight ahead up a narrow dirt track. The going is more difficult, with the trail climbing steps and crossing wooden footbridges as it traverses

Russian Gulch Falls

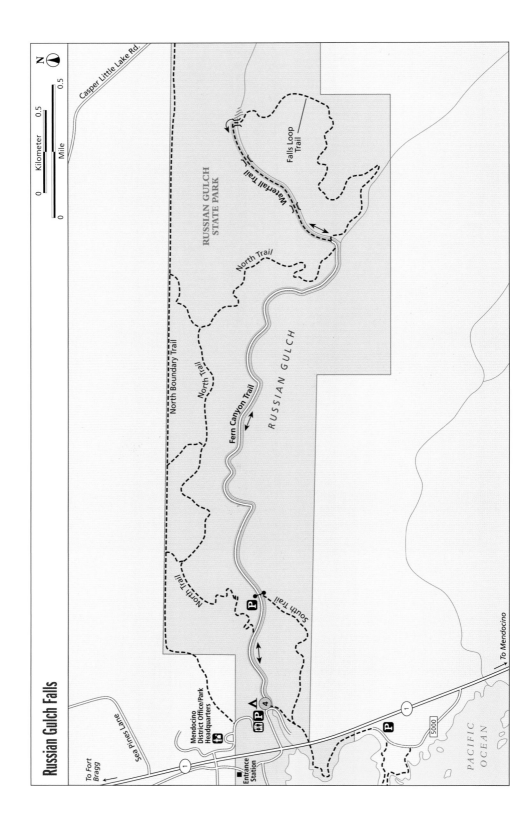

N

Kilometer

0   0.5

0   0.5
Mile

To Fort Bragg

Sea Pines Lane

Casper Little Lake Rd.

Mendocino District Office/Park Headquarters

Entrance Station

North Boundary Trail

North Trail

North Trail

North Trail/

North Trail

Fern Canyon Trail

South Trail

RUSSIAN GULCH

RUSSIAN GULCH STATE PARK

Waterfall Trail

Falls Loop Trail

PACIFIC OCEAN

To Mendocino

5000

Russian Gulch Falls fans out across a rock wall in a deep coastal canyon.

above the steepening waterway. A final descent drops you onto the bridge below the falls, which sprawl over a rock face that bulges like the belly of a Buddha. Redwoods tower overhead, and ferns cluster on the steep slopes.

The bridge is a perfect overview, but it'll possibly be clotted with other hikers. Wide patches on the trails above the falls also provide nice vantage points. Return as you came.

Miles and Directions

0.0 Walk up the campground road toward the trailhead proper.

0.5 Follow the paved Fern Canyon path into the gulch.

1.7 The stream forms a small cataract.

2.2 Reach the end of the paved trail and the junctions of the Waterfall Trail, North Trail, and Falls Loop Trail. Follow the Waterfall Trail, a dirt track that climbs directly up the gulch.

2.4 Climb a set of stairs and cross a footbridge over a side stream.

2.6 Climb another set of steps to another footbridge.

2.8 Reach Russian Gulch Falls. Check out the sights from the bridge or from viewpoints on trails just above the falls. Retrace your steps.

5.6 Arrive back at the trailhead.

Options: You can stretch your hike and your exploration of Russian Gulch by continuing past the waterfall to pick up the Falls Loop Trail. Another option is to follow the hiker's-only North Trail, which departs from the campground and meets up with Fern Canyon Trail where the pavement ends.

5 Stornetta Falls

Walk along the edge of the continent to a seasonal waterfall that spills over a steep bluff into the Pacific.

Height: About 50 feet

Beauty rating: ★★★★

Start: Bend in the Road trailhead on Lighthouse Road

Distance: 1.8 miles out and back

Difficulty: Easy

Hiking time: About 1 hour

Seasons/schedule: Year-round; sunrise to sunset

Fees and permits: None

Trail contact: Bureau of Land Management, Ukiah Field Office, 2550 N. State St., Ukiah, CA 95482; (707) 468-4000; www.blm.gov/visit/point-arena-stornetta-unit

Canine compatibility: Leashed dogs permitted.

Trail surface: Dirt singletrack

Land status: Point Arena–Stornetta Unit of the California Coastal National Monument

Nearest town: Point Arena

Other trail users: None

Maps to consult: USGS Point Arena CA; map on the Point Arena–Stornetta Public Lands site online

Water availability: None

Amenities available: Parking, portable toilets, and information signboard

Cell service: Marginal

Trail conditions: The trail is narrow and rustic, riding the bluff top. Erosion may cause closures. Avoid the edges.

Finding the trailhead: From Point Arena head north on CA 1 for about 2.5 miles to Lighthouse Road. Turn left (west) onto Lighthouse Road and go 1.3 miles to the roadside trailhead and parking pullout on the left. About ten cars can park in the pullout, with additional parking available alongside the road (be sure to pull clear of the traffic lane). Trailhead GPS: N38 56.421' / W123 43.780'

The Hike

Point Arena–Stornetta Public Lands, which stretch along the coastline north of the seaside village of Point Arena, is a relatively new addition to California's parklands. It's part of the California Coastal National Monument, established in 2000 to protect islands and rocks along the state's coastline; the unit was added to the monument in 2014. Development of this pocket of the monument, administered by the Bureau of Land Management, is minimal, with a singletrack wandering along the edges of bluffs that drop several hundred feet into the Pacific Ocean. It's an edge-of-the-continent extravaganza, with views stretching north to the Point Arena Lighthouse, south into Point Arena, east into the coastal ranges, and west—oh, west—over Sea Lion Rocks to the endless horizon.

The Stornetta waterfall is fed by a slender, perennial stream that pours off the edge of the bluffs near trail's end. Rainfall charges the watershed, so time your visit for the winter or after a healthy springtime rainstorm. The stream pours through a cleft in

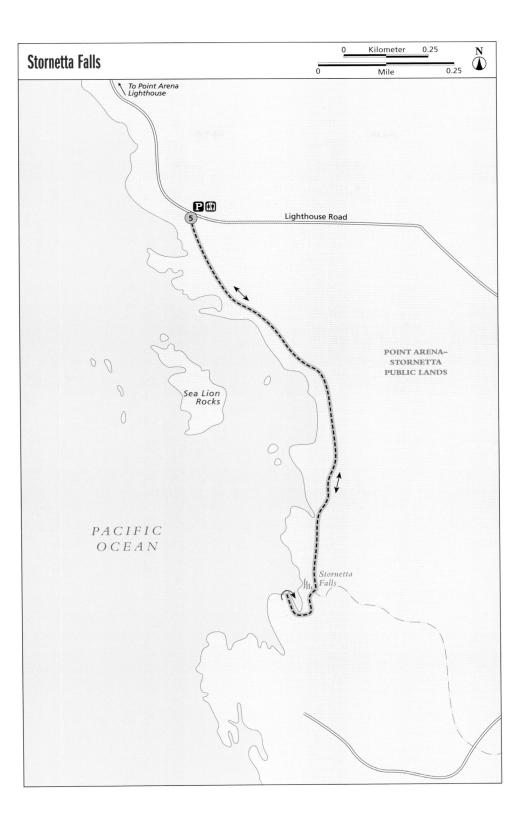

Stornetta Falls

To Point Arena
Lighthouse

Lighthouse Road

POINT ARENA–
STORNETTA
PUBLIC LANDS

Sea Lion
Rocks

PACIFIC
OCEAN

Stornetta
Falls

Kilometer

Mile

N

Water flows gently over the edge of the bluffs at Stornetta Falls.

the bluff top, and the fall, which spills into that cleft, is best viewed by circling around on the bluff arcing west (seaside) of the stream.

The waterfall is about a mile from the trailhead and reached via a rough, flat path beaten into the grass by hikers' boots and delineated with 4-foot-high brown trail markers. Watch for sinkholes, which form when the tides erode the bluffs. Avoid the holes, and avoid getting too close to the edges of the bluffs themselves, which are also prone to erosion. Take in the falls, take in the vistas, take in the wind, and then return as you came. **Note:** Erosion on the bluff and other geologic shifts have changed the aspect of the waterfall over time, so bear in mind that what you see in any given winter, and where you see it, may vary.

Miles and Directions

0.0 Pass through the stile at the trailhead and head off across the bluffs, following the track beaten into the turf and the widely spaced trail markers.

0.5 Pass a cluster of wind-whipped cypresses.

0.7 Cross the stream above the waterfall.

0.9 Curl around on the bluff west of the waterfall, looking back east to view. Retrace your steps.

1.8 Arrive back at the trailhead.

6 Sea Ranch Falls

Short walks lead to a pair of falls that spill over cliffs onto seaside beaches.

Height: About 50 feet for both Stengel and Pebble Beach waterfalls

Beauty rating: ★ ★ ★ ★

Start: The Stengel Beach trailhead is at the junction of Wild Iris Road and CA 1; the Pebble Beach trailhead is off CA 1 about 1 mile south of the Stengel Beach access.

Distance: 0.6 mile out and back for the Stengel Beach waterfall; 1.5 miles out and back for Pebble Beach waterfall

Difficulty: Easy

Hiking time: Less than 1 hour for each trail; about 2 hours including driving time

Seasons/schedule: Year-round; sunrise to sunset

Fees and permits: Parking fees are charged at both trailheads, but if you purchase a pass at one, it's good for the other on the same day.

Trail contact: Sonoma County Regional Parks, 2300 County Center Dr., Suite A120, Santa Rosa, CA 95403; (707) 565-2041; parks@sonomacounty.org

Canine compatibility: Leashed dogs permitted.

Trail surface: Dirt, staircases

Land status: Bureau of Land Management; the trailheads are within the Sea Ranch subdivision and link to private trails.

Nearest town: Gualala

Other trail users: None

Map to consult: USGS Stewarts Point CA

Water availability: None at either trailhead

Amenities available: Toilets, fee stations, trash cans, and information signboards at both trailheads; parking for about 10 cars at Stengel Beach; parking for about 4 cars at Pebble Beach

Cell service: Marginal

Trail conditions: Both trails are short and well maintained but involve staircases and are subject to erosion.

Finding the trailhead: To reach both trailheads from Gualala, head south on CA 1. The Wild Iris junction and Stengel Beach parking lot is 5.9 miles south of Gualala. The Pebble Beach parking area is on the west side of CA 1 about 7.5 miles from town. Trailhead GPS: Stengel Beach N38 43.006' / W123 27.454'; Pebble Beach N38 42.012' / W123 26.188'

The Hikes

Like Stornetta Falls, the bluff falls in Sea Ranch are ephemeral, changeable, and best viewed in winter. They are also in magical settings, with views opening up and down the rugged Sonoma County coastline south of Gualala and out across the Pacific.

Both falls are accessible through the exclusive Sea Ranch subdivision via public beach access trails. To reach Stengel Beach waterfall (and Stengel Beach), the single-track path crosses the private Bluff Trail twice before passing under the canopy of a cluster of Monterey cypress. The stream that feeds the fall runs alongside the last 25 yards of trail, then plunges over the bluff to the sea, as does the staircase leading down to the beach. **Note:** The staircase was closed for repair in 2024. Check with Sonoma County Regional Parks for updates on beach access.

From trail's end on the blufftop, you can view the head of the Pebble Beach waterfall.

Reaching the Pebble Beach waterfall (and Pebble Beach) requires a longer and prettier blufftop walk, with houses sprouting like well-appointed gray mushrooms from Sea Meadow, and spectacular ocean views.

The first junction with a private Sea Ranch trail is not far from the trailhead. Cross the private Bluff Trail at about 0.3 mile; signs keep you on the public beach access trail. The trail arcs right (north) through a low copse of Monterey cypress; the most accessible waterfall, a fine little cascade, is best viewed from above by slipping off-trail before the stand of trees, walking out toward the edge of the bluff, and looking inland. A second cascade is only visible from the public beach below, and only at low tide.

To reach the dark sands of Pebble Beach, return to the stand of cypress and go right, cross the bridge over the no-name stream feeding the first fall, then descend a wooden staircase. The last step, as they say, is a doozy. If the tide is out, go left on the strand, along the bases of the cliffs, to catch sight of the falls. Watch the sea; don't turn your back. Return as you came.

The Stengel Beach waterfall begins its tumble onto the strand.

Miles and Directions

Stengel Beach Waterfall

0.0   Start at the Stengel Beach trailhead.

0.1   The trail crosses the private Bluff Trail twice as it approaches the staircase to the beach.

0.2   Pass under the cypress to the beach staircase and the top of the fall.

0.3   Descend to the beach. Enjoy, then return as you came.

0.6   Arrive back at the trailhead.

Pebble Beach Waterfall (includes short beach walk)

0.0   Start at the Pebble Beach Trailhead. Cross an intersection with a private Sea Ranch trail, staying on the Pebble Beach Trail.

0.3   Cross the private Bluff Trail, staying on the Pebble Beach Trail.

0.5   Where the trail bends under a stand of cypress, go left across the bluff to view the top of the waterfall. To reach the beach, return to the trail and continue right, crossing a footbridge.

0.75 Descend the staircase to the beach. Take in the sights, then return as you came.

1.5   Arrive back at the trailhead.

Honorable Mentions

Smith River Waterfalls

The rains that soak California's North Coast fuel a number of waterfalls in the Smith River drainage along CA 199. Most drop right next to the highway and don't require a hike to view; many are seasonal, so travel in late winter and spring will ensure the best flow. One of the prettiest is east of Gasquet and best viewed from the westbound lane; it tumbles about 70 feet down an exposed talus slope. The curves along CA 199 should slow you down enough to see what can be seen, but don't hold up traffic for the sake of viewing—use turnouts and pullouts.

A marginal "hike" to falls on the Middle Fork of the Smith River can be reached off Knopki Creek Road. The unmaintained path is short and, frankly, scary, skittering down a steep hillside to an "overlook" on a root ball. The 40-foot cascade, heavily screened by trees, is split by a buttress of dark rock, and debris is scattered both in the flow and alongside the pool below.

A scary informal track offers sketchy access to a waterfall on the Middle Fork Smith River.

Fern Canyon

In the height of the rainy season, you can spy waterfalls running down between the ferns of this storied North Coast canyon. As a waterfall hike, it's a bit of a stretch: The ephemeral waterfalls you may spy play second fiddle to the wallpaper of ferns that flocks the cliffs from floor to top. It's a fairy tale in the wilderness—a realm of forest sprites and wood nymphs. The sounds of the surf, the burbling of Home Creek flowing over its gravelly bed, and the occasional low voice of a visitor expressing awe or catching their breath as icy water flows over their boot tops add to the spell.

The wide, gravel Coastal Trail leads up to the canyon mouth (the same approach as for Hike 2: Gold Bluffs Beach Falls), then follow Home Creek into the canyon as far as you can. Be prepared to get wet. Follow the canyon out and back, or make a loop by hitching up with the John Irvine Trail to return along the top of the canyon to the mouth of Home Creek.

Ephemeral falls can be spotted in Fern Canyon after winter rains, but the headliners are the fern-flocked walls of the gorge.

Dora Falls

Located just north of the Standish-Hickey State Recreation Area, the "gateway to tall trees country," Smithe Redwoods State Natural Reserve protects a stand of coast redwoods on the site of a former resort. The redwood grove is on the banks of the South Fork Eel River; step out of the trees onto the riverbank, and the sunlight can be blinding . . . if the fog hasn't rolled up the river valley.

Dora Falls is across the highway from the redwood grove. Carefully cross the two-lane roadway, hop over the guardrail near the bridge spanning Dora Creek, and pick up the narrow footpath that climbs along the right (south) side of the stream. The 60-foot seasonal waterfall, best viewed when fed by winter rains, begins as split streams and then fans down the cliff face, forming a curtain about 20 feet wide before settling into a pool and feeding into the mouth of a culvert (the culvert's tail is at the highway bridge). Linking a walk to the falls with a cruise through the Smithe reserve redwood grove totals about 0.5 mile.

Waterfalls and redwoods: an enchanting pairing along trails on the North Coast.

Chamberlain Falls

Secluded but easy to reach, 40-foot Chamberlain Falls has the feel of a secret hide-away. Located in a dense stand of old-growth redwoods at the head of a steep ravine, with limited parking and no amenities, its appeal is its remoteness. The waterfall is in the Jackson Demonstration State Forest, managed by the California Department of Forestry and Fire Protection. Beginning in the 1860s, logging removed most of the old-growth redwoods and firs from this part of the Coast Range; the Demonstration Forest, established in 1949, hosts sustainable timber harvests and promotes research, restoration, and recreation. The 0.6-mile out-and-back route is engaging and family friendly, descending a couple of flights of wooden stairs and quick switchbacks to the base of the falls.

To reach the trailhead from Fort Bragg, follow CA 20 east for 17 miles to the Chamberlain Creek Conservation Camp. Cross the highway bridge over Chamberlain Creek at mile marker 17.3 and turn immediately left onto FR 200. Follow FR 200 for 1.1 miles to a junction; stay left on FR 200, signed for Camp Mendocino. Follow the good but winding road for 3.2 miles to where a simple fence line framing a staircase marks the trailhead. Park alongside the roadway, where there is room for four or five cars.

Chamberlain Falls captivates even when diminished by drought.

Shasta-Trinity

Between the remote and lovely Trinity Alps and Mount Shasta, the 14,180-foot composite volcano that towers over the upper Sacramento River valley, recreational opportunities in the north-central part of the state abound. These waterfall hikes are found in the watersheds surrounding Redding, Dunsmuir, Mount Shasta City, and Weaverville.

Middle Falls on the McCloud River (hike 7).

7 McCloud Falls

A lovely trail through woodland and canyon links three distinctive falls on the McCloud River.

Height: 15 feet (Lower Falls), 50 feet (Middle Falls), 30 feet plus cascades (Upper Falls)
Beauty rating: ★★★★★
Start: Lower Falls Trailhead in the picnic area
Distance: 4.2 miles out and back
Difficulty: Moderate due only to distance and the climb from Middle Falls to the overlook above
Hiking time: About 2.5 hours
Seasons/schedule: Year-round; sunrise to sunset
Fees and permits: None
Trail contact: US Forest Service, Shasta-Trinity National Forest, McCloud Ranger Station, PO Box 1620, McCloud, CA 96057; (530) 964-2184; www.fs.usda.gov/main/stnf

Canine compatibility: Leashed dogs permitted.
Trail surface: Pavement, dirt singletrack, stone staircases
Land status: Shasta-Trinity National Forest
Nearest towns: McCloud; Mount Shasta City
Other trail users: None
Map to consult: USGS Lake McCloud CA
Water availability: Water is available in the campground near the trailhead.
Amenities available: Restrooms, picnic sites, trash cans, and information at the trailhead; Fowlers Campground with additional facilities is nearby
Cell service: None
Trail conditions: The singletrack trail is well maintained and remote.

Finding the trailhead: From I-5 as it passes Mount Shasta City, follow CA 89 east for about 14.7 miles, past the town of McCloud, to the McCloud River Loop Road/FR 40N44 (signed for Fowlers Camp and Lower Falls). Turn right onto the McCloud River Loop Road and go 0.6 mile to the junction with Fowler Public Camp Road. Stay right on the camp road, following signs for Lower Falls. Continue 0.5 mile to the Lower Falls picnic area and trailhead. Trailhead GPS: N41 14.422' / W122 01.490'

The Hike

This tour of the three waterfalls on the McCloud River near Mount Shasta begins at Lower Falls, literally steps from the trailhead picnic area. Lower Falls can be viewed either from the picnic area itself or by walking down short staircases to the riverside, where a shelf of water-sculpted rock provides a viewing platform. Lower Falls is diminutive compared to what lies upstream, but it makes a lovely starting and ending point.

From Lower Falls a paved trail leads through the mixed evergreen woodland that thrives alongside the McCloud River, rounding easy switchbacks into Fowlers Campground. Interpretive signs describe how the indigenous people, the Winnemem Wintu, called these "the Falls Where the Salmon Turn Back," as well as the more modern history of the area, which has served as a tourist attraction since the 1800s.

Middle McCloud Falls is inarguably the most spectacular of the three waterfalls on the McCloud River.

Locals have long hunted and fished near the McCloud, and the river also provided water for the town that shares its name.

The trail turns to dirt as it leaves the campground. Follow the easy route along the river to the second waterfall, where the McCloud pours over a 50-foot rock escarpment into a broad pool, feathering across a face that stretches about 100 feet from canyon wall to canyon wall. This substantial block of whitewater would definitely turn a salmon back.

Climb switchbacks out of the canyon, the most strenuous part of the hike but nicely graded. Views of Middle Falls make the ascent easier. The path becomes paved on the canyon rim, with railings protecting overlooks of the falls below.

The route reverts to dirt as it continues upstream, now high above the river. Slip under a mossy cliff face that overhangs on the north, and then cross a slide, where the path is narrow and exposed. The route ends at overlooks near Upper Falls, a tiered waterfall with cascades above a final horsetail that shoots clear of the rock before plunging into a pool below. Upstream of the final drop, the whorls and eddies of the waterway have sculpted huecos in the bedrock; the empty pockets are polished and dark, while the river pools and cycles in others, deepening them before moving on. When it's time for you to do the same, backtrack to the trailhead.

McCloud Falls

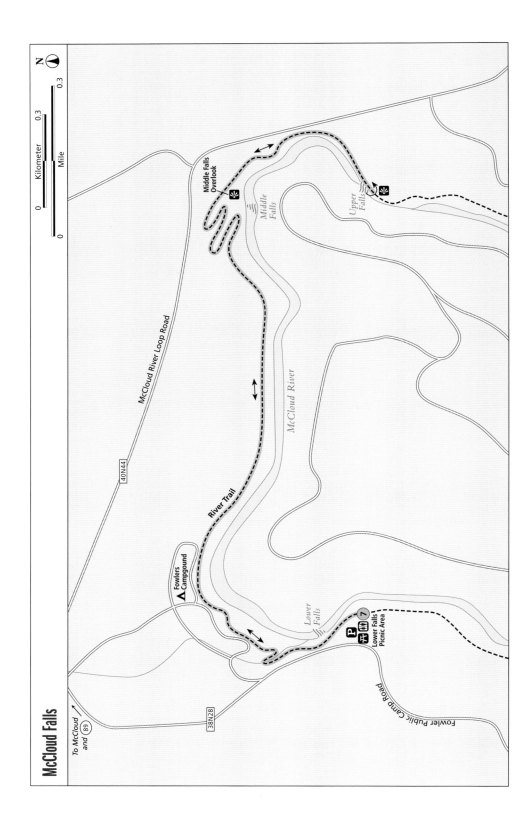

To McCloud and (89)

McCloud River Loop Road

40N44

38N28

River Trail

Fowlers Campgound

McCloud River

Lower Falls

Lower Falls Picnic Area

Fowler Public Camp Road

Middle Falls Overlook

Middle Falls

Upper Falls

N

Kilometer
0   0.3

0   0.3
Mile

The McCloud River churns in a hueco above the Upper Falls.

Miles and Directions

0.0 Begin by heading through the picnic area toward the river. Take the staircase down to the riverside. Follow the paved path upstream.

0.3 Reach Fowlers Campground. Stay right (riverside) on the paved River Trail, ignoring spur trails leading left into the camp.

0.6 Leave the camp at the sign for Middle Falls; the trail turns to dirt.

1.3 Reach Middle Falls. Climb switchbacks up toward the rim.

1.6 Climb a wooden staircase onto the canyon rim. Follow the trail, now paved, past an overlook of Middle Falls.

2.1 Reach the overlooks of Upper Falls. Retrace your steps.

4.2 Arrive back at the trailhead.

8 Faery Falls

Follow a remote forest road alongside Ney Springs Creek to a secluded waterfall.

Height: About 40 feet

Beauty rating: ★★★★

Start: Faery Falls Trailhead at parking area on Ney Springs Road

Distance: 2.0 miles out and back

Difficulty: Easy, with one short, steep pitch

Hiking time: About 1.5 hours

Seasons/schedule: Year-round; sunrise to sunset

Fees and permits: None

Trail contact: US Forest Service, Mount Shasta Ranger Station, 204 West Alma St., Mount

Shasta, CA 96067; (530) 926-4511; www.fs.usda.gov/main/stnf

Canine compatibility: Leashed dogs permitted.

Trail surface: Dirt

Land status: Shasta-Trinity National Forest

Nearest town: Mount Shasta City

Other trail users: None

Map to consult: USGS City of Mount Shasta CA

Water availability: None

Amenities available: None

Cell service: None

Trail conditions: This trail is narrow and remote.

Finding the trailhead: From I-5 in the city of Mount Shasta, take the Central Mount Shasta exit and head west on Hatchery Lane for 0.3 mile. Turn left onto Old Stage Road and go 0.2 mile to the Y junction with W A Barr Road. Go right on W A Barr Road for 2.2 miles, over the Box Canyon Dam on Lake Siskiyou, to the junction with Castle Lake Road. Turn left onto Castle Lake Road and drive 0.1 mile to the intersection with Ney Springs Road. Stay left onto Ney Springs Road, a graded gravel road, and drive 1.3 miles to a clearing at the junction with a forest road that climbs right (the Faery Falls Trailhead; about 0.3 mile beyond the Cantara-Ney Springs Wildlife Area sign). Park in the clearing. If you round a sharp bend, cross Ney Springs Creek, and reach a gate, you've gone too far. Trailhead GPS: N41 15.949' / W122 19.453'

The Hike

The setting at the trailhead doesn't promise much: a walk in a dark woodland with no views of Mount Shasta or the surrounding peaks of the Shasta-Trinity mountains. But two intriguing destinations, the ruins of the Ney Springs Resort and Faery Falls, lie not far up the forest road.

Faery Falls is tucked in a narrow gorge and screened from the sun by a heavy evergreen canopy. The waterfall descends in two tiers, the first shorter, and the second fanning across the bulk of the dark rock face before landing in a shallow pool. Cascades spill down the watercourse below the falls, also inviting exploration. The moss-obscured ruins of the late-nineteenth-century resort, which grew up around mineral springs purported to have health benefits, lie downstream of the cascades, where the creek mellows.

The route follows a nice forest road for most of the distance (the road is passable by high-clearance vehicles to a barricade not far from the falls, but makes for a nice walk). Side trails break left off the roadway to the creek side—the well-traveled path that diverges just above the trailhead leads to a line of camp/picnic sites with fire pits. The main route climbs to the barricade: There is parking here for folks with hardier cars who want a shorter hike. A nice camping/picnic spot is on the right.

Beyond the barricade the route narrows and steepens. Look down and left, toward the creek, to the ruins of the Ney Springs Resort; a short side trip on social paths allows exploration of the streamside site. Given the narrowness, steepness, and wild-ness of the canyon, it's hard to imagine the place once hosted a hotel and other amenities, but the overgrown, moss-draped foundations are obvious once they're identified, testament to John Ney's vision.

Not far above the disintegrating resort, a second unsigned social path departs to the left, dropping to cascades on the creek. The pitch of the roadway steepens sharply before the next unmarked trail breaks left, leading to the waterfall proper. Head down

Faery Falls tumbles down Ney Springs Creek above the ruins of a resort.

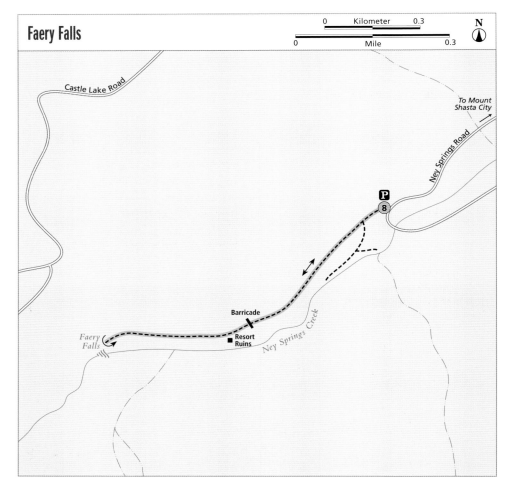

the narrow path to its end and pull up a perch on the canyon wall to view the falls. There's no easy way to the base of the falls, but you can scramble around at will. Return as you came.

Miles and Directions

0.0 Start on the dirt forest road that breaks right and uphill from parking in the clearing.

0.2 Pass a well-worn use trail that breaks left to creek-side camp/picnic sites. Stay right on the forest road.

0.5 Pass a barricade. Use social trails that break left, toward the creek, to explore the ruins of the Ney Springs resort.

0.7 A social path leads right to a series of cataracts on Ney Springs Creek.

0.9 As the forest road steepens, take the clear path that breaks left toward the waterfall.

1.0 Reach Faery Falls. Retrace your steps.

2.0 Arrive back at the trailhead.

9 Canyon Creek Falls

Follow a popular trail into the Trinity Alps Wilderness to the lowest of a series of waterfalls on Canyon Creek.

Height: About 100 feet
Beauty rating: ★★★★★
Start: Canyon Creek trailhead
Distance: 8.3 miles out and back
Difficulty: Strenuous
Hiking time: About 5 hours
Seasons/schedule: Year-round; sunrise to sunset
Fees and permits: None
Trail contact: US Forest Service, Shasta-Trinity National Forest, Weaverville Ranger Station, 360 Main St., PO Box 1190, Weaverville, CA 96093; (530) 623-2121; www.fs.usda.gov/recarea/stnf/recarea/?recid=6521. Portions of the wilderness area also fall under the purview of the Klamath National Forest and the Six Rivers National Forest.

Canine compatibility: Dogs allowed. Leashes are not required, but owners should have their pets under voice control.
Trail surface: Dirt, stone steps
Land status: Trinity Alps Wilderness
Nearest town: Weaverville
Other trail users: Equestrians
Map to consult: USGS Mount Hilton CA
Water availability: None, but you can drink from streams provided you filter the water.
Amenities available: Restrooms, trash cans, and information signboards
Cell service: None
Trail conditions: The trail is narrow, popular, well maintained, and remote. The 2021 River Complex Fire affected trail access in the Trinity Wilderness, so check with rangers before your hike.

Finding the trailhead: From Weaverville head west on CA 299 for 8 miles to Junction City. Take Canyon Creek Road to the right, before crossing the bridge. Follow Canyon Creek Road north for 13 scenic miles to the road's end at the Canyon Creek trailhead and parking area. Trailhead GPS: N40 53.234' / W123 01.447'

The Hike

Reading about the falls along Canyon Creek in the Trinity Alps, it becomes clear that proper names are an issue. The spectacular waterfall visible from the trail as you climb out of the woods nearly 4 miles from the trailhead appears to be widely regarded as "the" Canyon Creek Falls, with the cascades in the gorge above labeled Lower Canyon Creek Falls, Middle Canyon Creek Falls, and Upper Canyon Creek Falls. This day hike takes you up to view the lowest falls; the remainder are better explored as part of an overnight trip. Wilderness camping is popular in the Canyon Creek Lakes basin.

The hike to the lower falls follows one of the most well-used trails in the Trinity Alps. Though the bulk of the trail passes under cover of trees—oaks down low; pines and firs above—the naked ridges and peaks of the high Alps come into view now and again, craggy and pocked with snow, sometimes bleeding ephemeral falls down

Canyon Creek Falls is the first in a series of cataracts in this spectacular Trinity Alps drainage.

narrow folds on their stony slopes. The path breaks out of the woods near the turn-around point, ascending switchbacks on bare rock with views opening up and across the Canyon Creek drainage to the falls. The creek is jettisoned out of a tree-trimmed chute, starkly white against the dark greens and grays that surround it, then the water plummets out of sight.

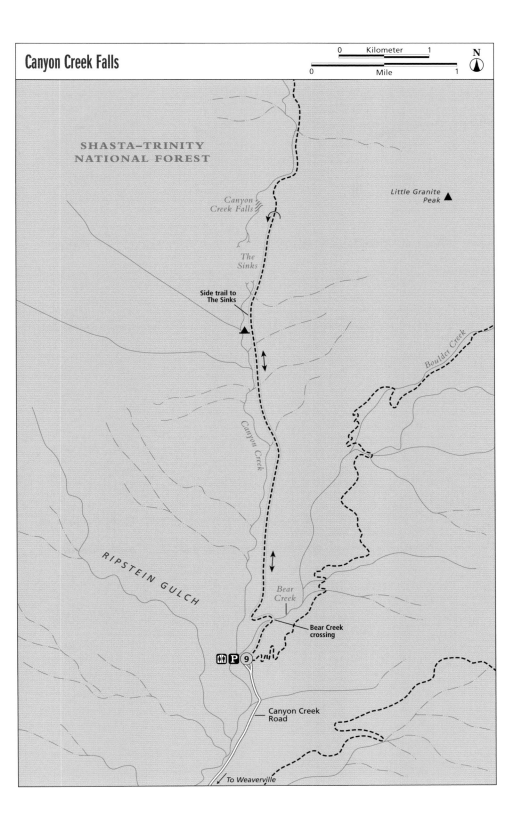

Canyon Creek Falls

0 Kilometer 1

0 Mile 1

N

SHASTA–TRINITY
NATIONAL FOREST

Little Granite
Peak ▲

Canyon
Creek Falls

The
Sinks

Side trail to
The Sinks ▲

Boulder Creek

Canyon Creek

RIPSTEIN GULCH

Bear
Creek

Bear Creek
crossing

P 9

Canyon Creek
Road

To Weaverville

Begin by climbing from the parking lot to the junction of the Bear Creek and Canyon Creek Trails, and stay left along the Canyon Creek route. The trail drops into a steep ravine and across Bear Creek, which can be a bit gnarly when the flow is high. The path then climbs over a low, forested ridge into the Canyon Creek drainage and begins a long, easy climb through mixed woods.

Not much breaks the monotony of the first few miles: a stand of madrones glowing red amid the various shades of green; brief openings in the canopy that allow you to play peekaboo with crag and creek views. Round a couple of switchbacks up a scrubby slope, then drop into a campsite, with views across the valley to the stony lower reaches of the Mount Hilton massif. An ephemeral fall courses down the far slope in season. The trail to the Sinks, where the creek may pool in a rockslide or sink below it, depending on water levels, breaks off to the left not far beyond the camp. Stay right on the Canyon Creek Trail.

The views get better and better as you climb, the trail eventually leaving the forest to switchback up exposed slopes on the east side of the creek. Ephemeral falls may flitter down the steep slopes that hem in the west side of the valley, but when the whitewater plunge of Canyon Creek Falls comes into view, its superiority is clear. The best views of the waterfall are from the traverses and switchbacks at this point.

The turnaround for a comfortable day hike is another half mile or so up the trail from the switchback views. Cross a seasonal stream and climb to a trail sign that points to the right—the Middle and Upper Canyon Creek Falls lie upstream, as does the lovely Canyon Lake basin, a popular backpacking destination located 7 miles from the trailhead. From the sign, return as you came.

Miles and Directions

0.0 Start by climbing to the junction of the Bear Creek Trail and Canyon Creek Trails. Go left on the Canyon Creek Trail.

0.4 Ford Bear Creek.

2.6 Round a pair of switchbacks on a scrub-covered slope.

3.1 Reach a campsite alongside the creek. The trail skirts the camp to the right.

3.3 At the junction with the trail to the Sinks, stay right on the Canyon Creek Trail.

3.8 The trail leaves the woods behind, climbing switchbacks of bare stone. Canyon Creek Falls comes into view; the best view you'll have of the biggest plunge.

4.1 Cross a streamlet. The trail sign is the turnaround; if you bear right, following the arrow, the trail continues to cataracts on Canyon Creek above. Retrace your steps.

8.3 Arrive back at the trailhead.

10 Whiskeytown Falls

Four waterfalls decorate the fire-scarred Whiskeytown National Recreation Area: Brandy Creek, Crystal Creek, Boulder Creek, and Whiskeytown. Each has its own charm; each is worth a visit not only for the falling water, but also to experience recovery of wildlands after wildfire.

Height: Varying from 10 to 20 feet for Brandy Creek Falls; about 50 feet for Crystal Creek Falls; about 220 feet for Whiskeytown Falls; about 80 feet for Boulder Creek Falls

Beauty rating: ★★★★

Start: Brandy Creek Falls Trailhead off Brandy Creek Road; Crystal Creek Falls Trailhead off Crystal Creek Road; Mill Creek Trailhead off Crystal Creek Road for Whiskeytown Falls; Boulder Creek Falls Trailhead off Mill Creek Road

Distance: 3.0 miles out and back for Brandy Creek Falls; 0.6 mile out and back for Crystal Creek Falls; 2.2 miles out and back for Boulder Creek Falls; 3.4 miles out and back for Whiskeytown Falls

Difficulty: Moderate for Brandy Creek Falls and Boulder Creek Falls; easy for Crystal Creek Falls; strenuous for Whiskeytown Falls

Hiking time: About 2 hours for Brandy Creek Falls; less than an hour for Crystal Creek Falls; about 2 hours for Boulder Creek Falls; about 3 hours for Whiskeytown Falls

Seasons/schedule: Year-round; sunrise to sunset. Summer can be impossibly hot; trails may be slick or icy in winter.

Fees and permits: An entrance fee is charged; pay at the Whiskeytown National Recreation Area visitor center.

Trail contact: Whiskeytown National Recreation Area, 14412 Kennedy Memorial Dr., PO Box 188, Whiskeytown, CA 96095; (530) 242-3400 or (530) 246-1225; www.nps.gov/whis/planyourvisit/waterfalls-of-whiskeytown.htm

Canine compatibility: Leashed dogs permitted.

Trail surface: Dirt singletrack and doubletrack for all falls; some crushed granite pathway, pavement, steps, and bridges along the way

Land status: Whiskeytown National Recreation Area

Nearest town: Redding

Other trail users: Mountain bikers, equestrians

Maps to consult: USGS Igo CA; trail guides and maps available on the Whiskeytown National Recreation Area website

Water availability: None

Amenities available: Restrooms and information signboard

Cell service: Bring a charged cell phone on the trail with you; service is likely to be OK.

Trail conditions: About 97 percent of the park burned in the 2018 Carr Fire. Trail conditions vary; and while three of the falls were open as of fall 2022, the trail to Brandy Creek Falls was still being repaired. Hazards in the burn scar include slides, falling trees, and hidden stump holes. Check with rangers before heading out on your hike. The trail to Crystal Creek Falls is accessible.

Finding the trailhead: From Redding follow CA 299 west for 8.2 miles to the junction with John F. Kennedy Memorial Drive, signed for the Whiskeytown National Recreation Area. Turn left onto Kennedy Memorial Drive; the visitor center is on the right (pay the fee here).

Brandy Creek Falls: From the visitor center, continue on Kennedy Memorial Drive for 1.3 miles to a sharp right turn heading across the dam on South Shore Drive. Continue to the junction with Brandy Creek Road, a total of 3.1 miles from the visitor center. Turn left onto Brandy Creek Road and follow the winding dirt road for 1.4 miles to the signed junction to Sheep Camp. Stay straight on Brandy Creek Road. At the junction at 2.2 miles, stay left toward the Brandy Creek Falls trailhead. The parking area and trailhead are at the end of the road, 3.2 miles from the junction with South Shore Drive. Trailhead GPS: N40 35.816' / W122 36.017'

Crystal Creek Falls: From the visitor center, return to CA 299 and drive 8.5 miles to the junction with Crystal Creek Road. Turn left onto Crystal Creek Road and go 2 miles to the open rocky area on the left. Turn left and follow the access road to the paved parking lot and picnic area. Trailhead GPS: N40 38.964' / W122 40.080'

Whiskeytown Falls: From the visitor center, return to CA 299 and drive 8.5 miles to the junction with Crystal Creek Road. Turn left onto Crystal Creek Road and drive 3.5 miles to the Mill Creek trailhead and parking area on the left. Trailhead GPS: N40 38.292' / W122 40.577'

Boulder Creek Falls: From the visitor center, return to CA 299 and drive 7 miles west to Carr Powerhouse Road. Turn left onto Carr Powerhouse Road and go 0.5 mile to Mill Creek Road. Follow the steep, winding, gravel Mill Creek Road for 1.3 miles to the trailhead parking area. Trailhead GPS: N40 38.240 / W122 38.189

The Hikes

Back before the Carr Fire rampaged through Whiskeytown National Recreation Area in 2018, hikers could tick off the four cascades in the park as part of the Whiskeytown Waterfall Challenge. Recovery from the wildfire is ongoing (and will be for a long time), but since the burn, trails to all but one of the waterfalls have reopened to hikers. Routes to hikes to the four falls are covered in nutshells in this entry, but be sure to check with rangers before setting out to ensure the route you've chosen (or all four) is safe for travel.

Brandy Creek Falls descends in low-angled stairsteps, the waterway fanning over slabs and weaving through boulder-choked channels. Before the burn, the path wandered over footbridges and tangles of tree roots to the falls overlooks; the complexity of the walking and the different faces of the falls made for an enlivening end-of-trail experience after an otherwise straightforward, meditative climb through a dense woodland that no longer exists. There is one trail junction, with the Rich Gulch Trail, as you approach the falls. The lower falls include a 15-foot tumble into a dark pool with a cataract below, which heralds the start of a sequence of cascades. Continue up the trail to the upper falls, a long, broken slide of whitewater, with another series of short falls spilling from pool to pool above. The surrounding rocks offer places to sit and enjoy the show. Return as you came.

Crystal Creek Falls are relatively new to the landscape, a lovely little addition to a massive construct of water diversion and storage facilities known as the Central Valley Project. The project, built to control flooding and provide water for agriculture in the Great Valley, consists of reservoirs and canals that stretch from the alpine

Brandy Creek Falls descends in tiers through a narrow canyon.

watersheds surrounding Redding to the thirsty agricultural lowlands surrounding Bakersfield, more than 400 miles to the south.

The dams that impound water in the Whiskeytown, Shasta, and Trinity reservoirs are the most obvious man-made structures on the landscape, with the lakes behind them the grandest "natural" features. Crystal Creek Falls, created when Crystal Creek was diverted to make room for a bypass structure, is tiny by comparison, but it's mighty as a scenic waypoint within the Whiskeytown National Recreation Area.

The barren landscape on the approach to the Crystal Creek picnic area is another remnant of the water diversion project: The tailings from excavation of an 11-mile-long tunnel that runs from Lewiston Lake to Whiskeytown Lake were deposited here (an estimated 250,000 cubic yards of granite). If the main parking lot is full, a walk on the pale crushed rock leads to the trailhead.

The trail proper is a wide, paved, wheelchair-friendly lane that winds alongside a meadow and then curls into the mouth of a wooded canyon, with Crystal Creek flowing below and to the left. Pass a picnic site and the falls open before you, covering the sloping face of a short cliff. The bypass building is to the right. A spread of sun-splashed slabs opposite the falls is a great viewing platform; a narrow path (not wheelchair accessible) leads down onto the rocks. Return as you came.

Brandy Creek Falls

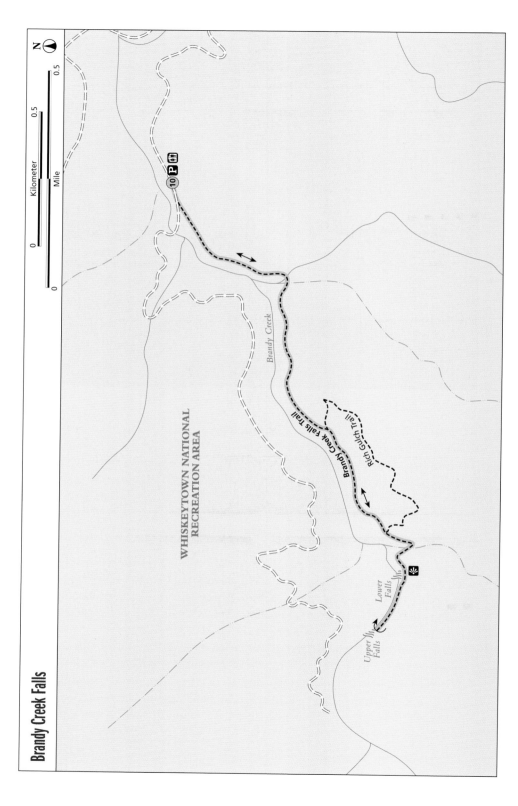

WHISKEYTOWN NATIONAL
RECREATION AREA

Brandy Creek

Brandy Creek Falls Trail

Rich Gulch Trail

Lower Falls

Upper Falls

Kilometer

Mile

0   0.5

0   0.5

N

Crystal Creek Falls is man-made and wheelchair accessible.

An unforgivingly steep track leads to **Whiskeytown Falls.** You may assume the nonstop climbing was what screened this waterfall from common knowledge for more than forty years, but not so, according to park literature. Loggers working in the rugged forest when the land was in private hands undoubtedly knew of the falls, as did rangers in the 1960s, when it was preserved as a national recreation area. But the desire of early park managers to protect the area from overuse prevented its

A stiff climb up an old logging road leads to Whiskeytown Falls.

development and resulted in the falls being "forgotten" until 2004, when a pair of park service employees—a biologist and a geologist—studied a map, ventured into the backcountry, and rediscovered them.

The trail follows a logging road used in the 1950s by the Northern California Logging Company, which harvested Douglas fir, ponderosa pine, and incense cedar from the steep slopes. The hike begins with a fairly steep descent on a crushed stone

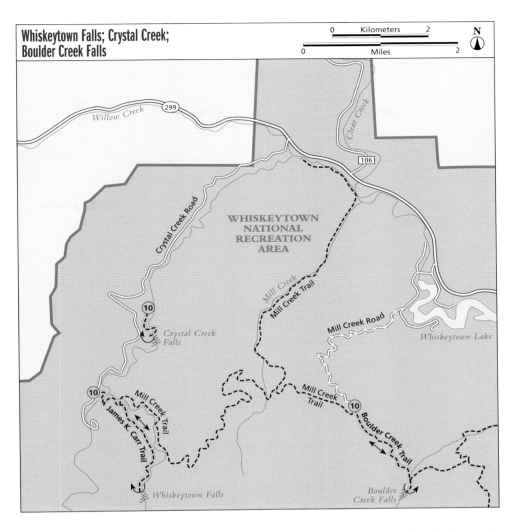

0   Kilometers   2

0   Miles   2

N

Willow Creek

299

Clear Creek

106

Crystal Creek Road

WHISKEYTOWN
NATIONAL
RECREATION
AREA

Mill Creek Trail

Mill Creek Road

Whiskeytown Lake

10

Crystal Creek
Falls

10

Mill Creek Trail

James K. Carr Trail

Mill Creek
Trail

10

Boulder Creek Trail

Whiskeytown Falls

Boulder
Creek Falls

path into the bottomlands surrounding the west fork of Crystal Creek. Cross the creek and settle into a comfortable gear for the climb. There is a brief respite as the trail rounds the bend to the junction with the Mill Creek Trail, but beyond the junction the climbing is persistent, with sections that will wind even the fittest.

Spurs break left and right as the trail ascends Steep Ravine and then tops out (briefly) at Wintu View, which overlooks the steep ridges of Whiskeytown's backcountry. The route is flat for a stretch and then meets up with the creek. Pass the trail camp (bikers and equestrians must leave their steeds here and continue on foot); at this point the path becomes a singletrack and traces the creek into a box canyon. Cross a footbridge, climb a set of stone stairs, and you've arrived at the base of the secret falls. You can see about 70 feet of whitewater from the base, which features viewing platforms sculpted into the rock, as well as the waterfall's trail register. Use

WATERFALLS AND WILDFIRES

On July 23, 2018, the wheel of a travel trailer blew apart near the Carr Powerhouse in Whiskeytown National Recreation Area outside Redding, sparking the massive Carr Fire. The region, sucked dry by years of drought, was broiling in a heat wave. Within a couple of days, the fire had jumped its containment lines and was exhibiting what experts call "extreme fire behavior," including spawning a monstrous, deadly fire whirl, or tornado, that destroyed a neighborhood in Redding and claimed the lives of several residents. Over the next month, before its containment on August 30, the Carr Fire torched 229,651 acres, including 97 percent of the land within the Whiskeytown NRA.

On July 13, 2021, a power line in the Feather River Canyon—the same canyon where the deadly Camp Fire, which destroyed the town of Paradise, began—sparked the Dixie Fire, which would torch nearly a million acres before being doused by an atmospheric river in late October. Nearly 70 percent of Lassen Volcanic National Park burned in that megafire.

The Dolan Fire, the Wine Country fire siege, the Caldor Fire, the CZU Lightning Complex fire—these names and more will crop up in this guide. Wildfires and waterfalls are linked in Northern California in these days of human-caused climate change, for better or worse.

It's easy to see the worst. Entire landscapes—evergreen forests, coastal chaparral, oak woodlands—have been incinerated in these blazes, creating challenging conditions for all the living beings who call them home or walk in their watersheds. It's tough for walkers in the woods, or walkers seeking waterfalls, to see how fire remodels what they are familiar with and what they love.

But it's becoming easier to see the better these days, as humans learn more about the role wildfire plays in the health of the ecosystems that sustain them, physically and spiritually. Fire has a role in wild places that we must come to understand, embrace, and learn to live with.

the stone steps protected with a rail to climb to a pair of viewpoints above, dubbed the Photographer's Ledge and the Artist's Ledge. Return as you came.

The trail to **Boulder Creek Falls** opened in April 2022, nearly four years after the Carr Fire blew through. The overstory that once shaded the old logging road has been mostly stripped by the flames, leaving the understory free to regenerate and ponderosa pines, which reseed after fire, to punch skyward from the ashes. Closer to the creek and falls, brilliant orange tiger lily, Solomon seal, and chain fern are reclaiming the territory.

Rehabilitation of the trail included clearing fallen and dead standing hazard trees; the park notes it removed "massive amounts" of debris from the base of the falls in

I know firsthand how challenging coming to terms with the sudden and all-consuming change wrought by wildfire can be. To bring it home to waterfalls, one of the favorites in my backyard remains off-limits five years after the Wine Country blazes of 2017. The Nuns Fire not only burned the Audubon Canyon Ranch's visitor center and trail infrastructure, it also burned the Stuart Creek watershed, home to newts, cougars, Steller's jays, hawks, and more. Recovery is slow, diligent, colorful, and fiercely protected by land managers who are not only studying how habitats recover after wildfire, but are also dedicated to ensuring the human touch is light while recovery takes place.

In Lassen, access to Mill Creek Falls and Kings Creek Falls is being rebuilt. In Whiskeytown National Recreation Area, in Limekiln State Park, in Plumas National Forest and Eldorado National Forest, infrastructure is being repaired. But real resilience is about more than making sure footbridges are in place and overlooks are rebuilt. Real resilience is in the footsteps of the hikers who traverse burn scars once they're safe, and who are able to see not only destruction in those places, but also rebirth. Look down: The wildflowers are blooming. Listen: The woodpeckers are thriving. Look up: Where the canopy once created only shadow, now light bathes the forest floor, allowing seedlings to reach for the sun and start the journey toward being giants, like the standing dead that shelter them.

Witnessing the better can be a lot to ask, especially for people like me who have intimate knowledge of how wildfire traumatizes communities—both human and wild. But once you spot the better, you can find it everywhere, even on your favorite trail to your favorite waterfall in your favorite burned park.

March 2022. Swaths of the track run through high-intensity burn zones, where the fire was most destructive, but in other places you'll encounter the mosaic, where the flames were less intense and green trees mingle with the snags. The route, given its width, is easy and straightforward to follow, though you will have to ford Boulder Creek before making the final approach to the 81-foot-high cascade.

You can also reach Boulder Creek Falls via a longer, more strenuous trail beginning on South Shore Drive. This 5.5-mile out-and-back route features about 1,000 feet of elevation gain, as compared to 150 feet following the old Mill Creek logging road.

Miles and Directions

Brandy Creek Falls

0.0 Start by climbing an old logging road.

1.1 At the junction with the Rich Gulch Trail, stay right on the signed Brandy Creek Falls Trail.

1.3 Reach the lower falls.

1.5 Reach the upper falls. Explore and relax, then retrace your steps.

3.0 Arrive back at the trailhead.

Crystal Creek Falls

0.0 Start on the paved path.

0.3 Pass the picnic site and take the side path down to view the falls. Return as you came.

0.6 Arrive back at the trailhead.

Whiskeytown Falls

0.0 Start by passing the restrooms and dropping into the West Fork Crystal Creek drainage.

0.3 Cross the creek on a footbridge. The climbing begins.

0.5 At the junction with the Mill Creek Trail, stay right on the James K. Carr Trail to Whiskeytown Falls.

0.7 Pass the first of a number of benches placed alongside the steep, eroded logging road. The benches are roughly 0.2 mile apart.

1.3 Reach Wintu View.

1.4 Pass the picnic sites and benches at the mouth of the narrowing box canyon; a bit farther along, cross a footbridge.

1.7 Reach the base of the falls. Use the steps to climb to viewing platforms above. Retrace your steps.

3.4 Arrive back at the trailhead.

Boulder Creek Falls

0.0 Start by following the old logging road toward Boulder Creek.

1.0 Ford Boulder Creek.

1.1 Arrive at Boulder Creek Falls. Take it in, then retrace your steps.

2.2 Arrive back at the trailhead.

11 Hedge Creek Falls

The trail to the waterfall on Hedge Creek showcases both the backside and the front side of the cascade.

Height: About 30 feet
Beauty rating: ★ ★ ★ ★
Start: Trailhead in Hedge Creek Park
Distance: 0.8 mile out and back
Difficulty: Easy
Hiking time: Less than 1 hour
Seasons/schedule: Year-round; sunrise to sunset
Fees and permits: None
Trail contact: City of Dunsmuir, 5915 Dunsmuir Ave., Dunsmuir, CA 96025; (530) 235-4822; www.ci.dunsmuir.ca.us. Dunsmuir Chamber of Commerce & Visitors Center, 5915 Dunsmuir Ave., PO Box 122, Dunsmuir, CA 96025; (530) 235-2177; www.dunsmuir.com/hikes-waterfalls.
Canine compatibility: Leashed dogs permitted.
Trail surface: Dirt
Land status: City park
Nearest town: Dunsmuir
Other trail users: None
Map to consult: USGS Dunsmuir CA; no map is needed
Water availability: Water is available.
Amenities available: Picnic facilities and trash cans
Cell service: Service is available.
Trail conditions: The trail is well maintained.

Finding the trailhead: From northbound I-5 in Dunsmuir (toward the north end of town), take the Siskiyou Avenue exit. Go left, under the freeway, and then immediately right onto the frontage road (Mott Road). The parking area is a pullout on the corner; the park is across the street. Trailhead GPS: N41 14.179' / W122 16.178'

The Hike

Mossbrae Falls may be Dunsmuir's forbidden, enigmatic star, but Hedge Creek Falls has what it takes to be a scene stealer. The clincher: passing through the alcove that opens behind the fall. Between the brevity and ease of the trail, the pass-around (a perfect place to repeat the tale told on the Dunsmuir Chamber of Commerce website that outlaw Black Bart used the "cave" as a hideout), and the overlook of the Sacramento River at trail's end, Hedge Creek Falls is a great hike for families with children.

The trail begins in Hedge Creek Park, with picnic sites and great views of the narrow Dunsmuir valley and Mount Shasta towering above. Pass through the picnic area to the signed trail above the creek. Three switchbacks drop easily and quickly to Hedge Creek and the falls, with the noise of the nearby highway overcome by the noise of falling water as you descend. Follow the path behind the 15-foot free-falling portion of the plume, hunching below the overhanging basalt.

From the falls the trail continues downstream alongside Hedge Creek, which forms cataracts as it completes its run into the Sacramento River. The turnaround at

A pass-through alcove is tucked behind Hedge Creek Falls.

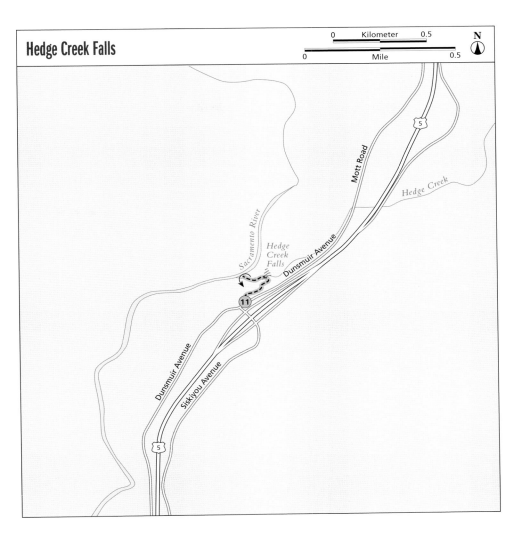

trail's end is a wooden platform overlooking the mighty Sacramento, with the Union Pacific rail line on the opposite bank. Take in the sights, then return as you came.

Miles and Directions

0.0 Start in Hedge Creek Park, heading down the switchbacks into the drainage.

0.2 Reach the falls and follow the path through the alcove.

0.4 Reach the overlook of the Sacramento River. Retrace your steps.

0.8 Arrive back at the trailhead.

12 Potem Falls

This elegant, secluded, horsetail waterfall graces a canyon embossed with mosses and ferns.

Height: 70 feet

Beauty rating: ★ ★ ★ ★ ★

Start: Trailhead at a parking pullout along FR 27

Distance: 0.8 mile out and back

Difficulty: Easy

Hiking time: Less than 1 hour

Seasons/schedule: Year-round; sunrise to sunset

Fees and permits: None

Trail contact: Shasta-Trinity National Forest Headquarters, 3644 Avtech Pkwy., Redding, CA 96002; (530) 226-2500; www.fs.usda.gov/recarea/stnf/recarea/?recid=6470

Canine compatibility: Leashed dogs permitted.

Trail surface: Dirt

Land status: Shasta-Trinity National Forest

Nearest town: Montgomery Creek

Other trail users: None

Map to consult: USGS Devils Rock CA

Water availability: None

Amenities available: None. Parking is limited alongside FR 27.

Cell service: Maybe, but don't count on it.

Trail conditions: The trail is short, narrow, and remote.

Finding the trailhead: From Redding follow CA 299 east for 30 miles to the junction with Fenders Ferry Road. Turn left onto Fenders Ferry Road and continue for 3.5 miles to FR 27, a good gravel road. Continue on FR 27/Fenders Ferry Road, staying left at 8.1 miles to stay on the forest road. Continue across the narrow bridge overlooking the dam on the Pit River (Pit Seven Reservoir), at this point a thickening arm leading into Shasta Lake. Climb up the other side of the canyon to the unmarked parking pullout on the left side of the dirt road at the 9.5-mile mark. Trailhead GPS: N40 50.332' / W122 01.620'

The Hike

The setting of Potem Falls is almost tropical. When the rains come, swelling the mosses and waking the ferns, brushstrokes of every shade of green stripe the ravine enveloping the classic waterfall. A fabulous pool wells at the base of the long, unbroken whitewater spill. Swimming on a rainy winter's day may be out of the question, but come warm days in spring and early summer, the cool, deep water invites.

The upside-down hike to the base of the falls, while moderately steep, is short. Three sweeping, easy switchbacks mitigate the incline; the waterfall comes into view at the second switchback. The last switchback deposits you near Potem Creek, which forms low-key cataracts as it rolls down the ravine. The turnaround point is poolside. Return as you came.

Even in a rainstorm, Potem Falls has a tropical flair. ▶

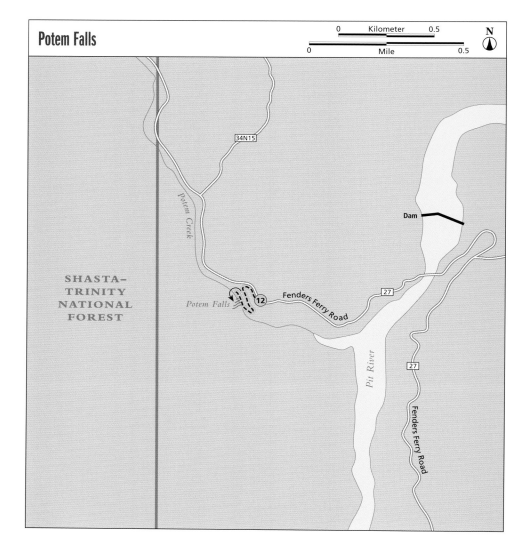

Potem Falls

Kilometer 0 — 0.5
Mile 0 — 0.5

N

34N15

Potem Creek

Dam

SHASTA–
TRINITY
NATIONAL
FOREST

Potem Falls

12

Fenders Ferry Road

27

Pit River

27

Fenders Ferry Road

Miles and Directions

0.0 Start on the narrow trail that departs from the parking pullout alongside FR 27.

0.1 Drop around the first of three sweeping switchbacks.

0.4 Reach the base of Potem Falls. Retrace your steps.

0.8 Arrive back at the trailhead.

Honorable Mentions

Mossbrae Falls

Dubbed by Jefferson Public Radio the "Forbidden Falls of Dunsmuir," fabled Mossbrae Falls remain off-limits to hikers. The reason? The falls can only be reached by trespassing on the Union Pacific Railroad right-of-way, posing an immediate danger to hikers who might be on or near the tracks when a train passes through, or via private property, which the landowner reportedly defends vigorously. While the danger and potential hostility doesn't deter all hikers from venturing to the falls, I won't guide you there. There is no parking at the "trailhead," and No Trespassing signs festoon the tracks.

The city of Dunsmuir, a local trail group, and the Union Pacific have been working for years to provide safe access to the spring-fed falls, which are 50 feet high and 150 feet across and spectacular. The hope is to link Hedge Creek Falls with Mossbrae Falls via a public trail, but exactly when that might happen is unclear. Meantime, the famous Forbidden Falls of Dunsmuir remain just that: forbidden.

Lower Burstarse Falls

You can check two boxes on the bucket list for this hike: one for reaching this secluded 40-foot seasonal waterfall and the second for completing a short section of the storied Pacific Crest Trail. The round-trip hike, which winds through the Castle Crags Wilderness outside Castle Crags State Park, totals 5.2 miles out and back and is strenuous.

A rigorous hike below the Castle Crags leads to Lower Burstarse Falls.

A stretch of the Pacific Crest Trail leads to Lower Burstarse Falls.

The falls are ephemeral, so timing is everything. The setting is surreal on misty days after the rainy season starts (but before the snow flies), with the mosses blooming fluorescent green, the Castle Crags feathered in clouds a paler shade of gray, and the falls beginning to show their vigor. Otherwise this is a springtime trek, with the window opening after the snow melts and closing when the sun parches the landscape, dries up the destination, and transforms the first stretch, up the Dog Trail, into a slog. And a word of warning: After heavy rains the ford of Burstarse Creek may be impassable. But if that's the case, the cascades make a nice destination as well.

Sweetbrier Falls

This short tumble is a nice little tag as you tick off the waterfall hikes in the Dunsmuir/ Mount Shasta area. The waterfall is 20 feet tall and not far removed from civilization, just off I-80, near the railroad tracks, and yards from the nearest neighborhood cabin in the eponymous village of Sweetbrier. The trailhead is on a bend in Falls Avenue. Walk about 25 yards down an unsigned riverside trail, past a handmade bench outfitted with sawblade plants, to reach the spill, which drops into the swift, deep-green Sacramento River as it speeds through the Dunsmuir canyon.

A short neighborhood path leads to Sweetbrier Falls.

Lion Slide Falls

A short, unmaintained path weaves through willow and oak alongside Hatchet Creek to Lion Slide Falls, a 25-foot-high block waterfall that feeds a popular local swimming hole. The fall, as broad as it is high, splits into two sheets around a huge fallen tree that tips from cliff top into the pool. Like Mossbrae Falls, Lion Slide is on private land, and despite its popularity, overuse and abuse has led the landowner to forbid access. With any luck, the falls will open again, but in the meantime there are plenty of falls on public land to visit.

Pictured in 2014, Lion Slide Falls, located on private land, has since closed to public access.

Lassen Country and Butte County

Lassen Peak is the fulcrum around which two of these waterfall trails revolve, with a pair of significant outliers at Burney Falls and along Deer Creek. The region, which encompasses Lassen Volcanic National Park, is rural and spectacular, even in the wake of the massive 2021 Dixie Fire. Major towns include Burney, Chester, and Mineral; plan on long, lovely drives to get from trailhead to trailhead.

The forks of the Feather River, flowing down out of the northern Sierra Nevada south of Lassen Country, sport some of the prettiest waterfalls in the state. Chico and Oroville, neighbors on the flatlands, offer all the amenities, while just upstream in the foothills, things get considerably wilder. CA 70 links Oroville to Quincy via the North Fork Feather River, and the Oroville-Quincy Highway/CA 162 links the two towns via a scenic drive around Lake Oroville, the hub of recreation in the area.

The Cascades above Kings Creek Falls (hike 15).

13 Burney Falls

An entire rock face spills water at Burney Falls, with the creek pouring over the top and seepage from an underground reservoir seething through cracks in the volcanic matrix.

Height: 129 feet
Beauty rating: ★★★★★
Start: Burney Falls trailhead
Distance: 1.3-mile loop
Difficulty: Easy
Hiking time: About 1 hour
Seasons/schedule: Year-round; 8 a.m. to sunset
Fees and permits: An entrance fee is charged.
Trail contact: McArthur–Burney Falls Memorial State Park, 24898 CA 89, Burney, CA 96013; (530) 335-2777; www.parks.ca.gov
Canine compatibility: No dogs allowed on the Burney Falls Trail.
Trail surface: Dirt, pavement, staircases, bridges
Land status: McArthur–Burney Falls Memorial State Park

Nearest town: Burney
Other trail users: None
Maps to consult: USGS Burney Falls CA; map in the park brochure; available online
Water availability: Water is available in the visitor center.
Amenities available: Restrooms, visitor center, gift shop and store, picnic areas, campground, fishing, and boating. The visitor center and store are open from 11 a.m. to 4 p.m. Wed to Sun.
Cell service: Marginal
Trail conditions: The trail is well maintained and popular. If you're part of a hiking group, be courteous to other trail users by walking single file. The park will close once parking capacity is reached. Do not park alongside CA 89; you can be cited and your vehicle can be towed.

Finding the trailhead: From the junction of CA 89 and CA 299 about 4 miles northeast of the town of Burney, continue north on CA 89 for 5.7 miles to the signed entrance to McArthur–Burney Falls Memorial State Park. Continue on the park road for 0.1 mile, past the entrance station, to the trailhead parking area. Trailhead GPS: N41 00.789' / W121 39.039'

The Hike

Burney Falls never fails. The massive spill—more than 100 million gallons per day—is perennial: Whatever snow falls in winter feeds both the creek and spring-fed reservoir that fuel Burney, whether it is enough to bury nearby Lassen Peak in 40-foot drifts or the feeble quantities California sees in a drought season. The falls are the centerpiece of a premier park and recreational area in the southernmost reaches of the Cascade Range. Lake Britton, opening just downstream, and the recreational opportunities of the Pit River add to the region's allure.

Before setting off on the easy day hike that tours the falls, take in the views from the overlook at the trailhead. There's the proper spill—that of Burney Creek tumbling over the 129-foot wall—but the wall also weeps with streams of white flowing

Burney Falls is fed by both Burney Creek and an underground reservoir.

down over basalt and moss to fill the 22-foot-deep, blue-green pool at the waterfall's base. Interpretive signs describe how the falls have migrated about 1 mile upstream over the course of 3 million years, every drop of water eroding the volcanic base away.

The trail, built by the Civilian Conservation Corps, is a breeze, descending easily via a stone staircase, a switchback, and long traverses to the base of the falls. Several spots along the route invite walkers to pause and enjoy the sight, with the spot at the base of the initial downhill arguably the best.

Headed downstream, information signs offer advice to the angler, who can find rainbow, brook, and brown trout in the clear waters above and below the falls. The trail courses between the creek and talus slopes to Rainbow Bridge, which offers safe passage across the creek. On the far side, head left and uphill on an easy traverse, passing through thick woodland toward the top of the falls.

Two switchbacks and easy staircases later, arrive at the top of the falls, and then continue upstream alongside the creek. Cross back to the east side via the Fisherman's Bridge, passing benches bearing plaques inscribed with inspirational quotes, and then loop back downstream. The falls aren't an obvious presence at this point; if you were headed downstream without a scout, you'd have no clue of the spectacular drop not far ahead. The route, now paved, winds up through open woodland back to the overlook and trailhead.

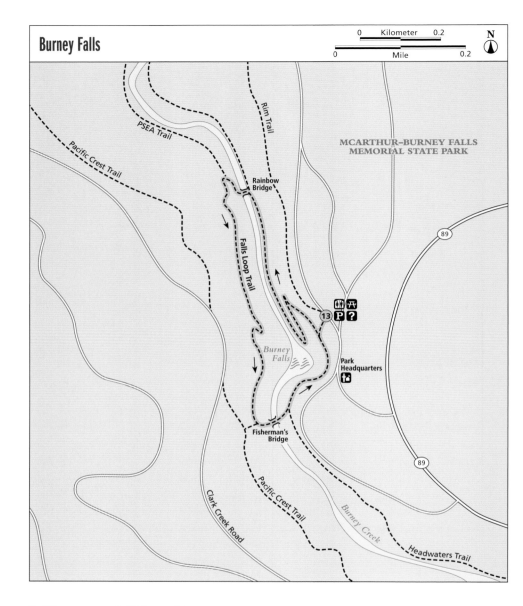

Miles and Directions

0.0 Start at the trailhead near the overlook on the Falls Trail, which descends a rock staircase.

0.3 Round a switchback near the base of the falls. Take the Falls Loop Trail to the right, headed downstream alongside Burney Creek.

0.6 Reach Rainbow Bridge. Turn left, cross the bridge, and turn left again, heading upstream and uphill on the Falls Loop Trail.

0.9 Pass the first switchback, with a falls view. Two more switchbacks and a pair of short staircases lead to the top of the falls.

The Falls Loop Trail offers a number of views of massive Burney Falls.

1.1 Pass the junction with a connector to the Pacific Crest Trail, and then go left across the Fisherman's Bridge. After crossing, stay on the paved path that heads back toward the developed areas of the park. The Headwaters Trail continues upstream.

1.2 Reach the parking lots and overlooks surrounding the trailhead. Stay left on the signed gravel path.

1.3 Arrive back at the trailhead.

Options: More than 5 miles of trails are available for exploration in beautiful McArthur–Burney Falls Memorial State Park. Continue downstream from the falls on the Burney Creek Trail to reach Lake Britton. The Headwaters Pool is a mile upstream from the falls via the Headwaters Trail.

14 Mill Creek Falls

Follow a roller-coaster trail to an overlook of Mill Creek Falls, a ribbon fall at the confluence of East Sulphur Creek and Bumpass Creek.

Height: 72 feet

Beauty rating: ★★★★

Start: Kohm Yah-mah-nee Visitor Center

Distance: 3.5 miles out and back

Difficulty: Moderate

Hiking time: About 2 hours

Seasons/schedule: Open year-round; best in summer and early fall

Fees and permits: A park entrance fee is levied.

Trail contact: Lassen Volcanic National Park, PO Box 100, Mineral, CA 96063; (530) 595-4480; www.nps.gov/lavo

Canine compatibility: No dogs permitted.

Trail surface: Dirt singletrack

Land status: Lassen Volcanic National Park

Nearest town: Mineral, with limited amenities

Other trail users: None

Maps to consult: USGS Lassen Peak CA; Lassen Volcanic National Park map

Water availability: Water is available in the visitor center and in the Southwest Walk-In Campground.

Amenities available: Restrooms at the Southwest Walk-In Campground; restrooms, information, food, and other amenities in the Kohm Yah-mah-nee Visitor Center

Cell service: Marginal; don't count on it.

Trail conditions: The Mill Creek Trail was heavily impacted by the 2021 Dixie Fire. Check with rangers about potential hazards, such as fallen trees, and be prepared to turn around if conditions warrant.

Finding the trailhead: The signed trailhead is located just inside the park's Southwest Entrance, between the Southwest Walk-In Campground and Kohm Yah-mah-nee Visitor Center's amphitheater. Trailhead GPS: N40 26.231' / W121 31.974'

The Hike

Mill Creek Falls is a narrow whitewater plunge at the confluence of East Sulphur Creek and Bumpass Creek. Spray from the 72-foot fall darkens the cream-and-gold-colored cliff over which it cascades, and the narrow gorge downstream resonates with its splendid roar.

The trail leading to the waterfall was heavily impacted by the 2021 Dixie Fire and associated Morgan Fire, ignited by lightning on Morgan Summit just outside the national park boundary while Dixie was burning, as well as by firefighting efforts within the park itself. While the falls can still be viewed from a shady overlook on the Mill Creek Falls Trail and you can reach the top of the spill via the steep track descending the scorched slopes of Mount Conard, the bridges that once spanned both Bumpass Creek and East Sulphur Creek just above the falls were destroyed. The park plans to rebuild the bridges, but they weren't in place as of fall 2022.

East Sulphur Creek and Bumpass Creek collide to form Mill Creek Falls.

The trail begins by dropping down stairs behind the Kohm Yah-mah-nee Visitor Center and the Southwest Walk-In Campground. Switchback down through burned pines and firs to cross West Sulphur Creek, which meets with East Sulphur Creek downstream to form Mill Creek. Climb up onto the hillside on the north side of the drainage and traverse southward across a sunny slope that hosts brilliant blooms of mule's ear, which survived Dixie's advance.

The trail dips into burned forest as it bends east, then northeast, into the East Sulphur Creek drainage. Like a ride on a roller coaster, the route bucks in and out of gullies as it follows the contours of the East Sulphur ravine, but the trend is generally upward.

Rock-hop across a side stream at the 1-mile mark, and then begin a relatively stiff climb, followed by a short, rather steep descent, to the overlook of Mill Creek Falls. From this shady viewpoint you can enjoy the waterfall as it rockets down terraces into

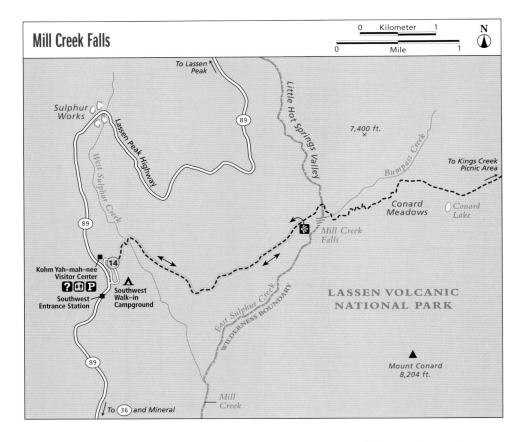

Mill Creek Falls

the shadowy creek bed below, with the rock on either side of the cascade streaked orange with mineral deposits and green with moss. Settle on the perch to enjoy a snack before returning as you came.

Miles and Directions

0.0 Start at the signed Mill Creek Falls trailhead.

0.3 Cross West Sulphur Creek.

0.5 Enter the East Sulphur Creek drainage.

1.0 Rock-hop across a side stream.

1.75 Arrive at the Mill Creek Falls overlook.

3.5 Arrive back at the trailhead.

15 Kings Creek Falls

After tumbling down a steepening gorge, Kings Creek streaks over a vertical cliff and plummets into a hidden creek bed.

Height: 70 feet

Beauty rating: ★★★★★

Start: Kings Creek trailhead off the Lassen Park Highway

Distance: 2.8-mile lollipop

Difficulty: Moderate

Hiking time: About 2 hours

Seasons/schedule: Late spring, summer, and fall (when CA 89 is open); sunrise to sunset

Fees and permits: A park entry fee is charged.

Trail contact: Lassen Volcanic National Park, PO Box 100, Mineral, CA 96063; (530) 595-4480; www.nps.gov/lavo

Canine compatibility: No dogs allowed.

Trail surface: Dirt, stone stairs

Land status: Lassen Volcanic National Park

Nearest towns: Mineral, with limited amenities; Chester

Other trail users: None

Maps to consult: USGS Reading Peak CA; Lassen Volcanic National Park map

Water availability: None

Amenities available: Parking pullouts on either side of the Lassen National Park Highway; information signboards and trash cans

Cell service: None

Trail conditions: The trail is well maintained. The Cascade Trail is one-way uphill.

Finding the trailhead: The Kings Creek Falls trailhead is located on the Lassen Park Highway/CA 89, about 15.5 miles from the Manzanita Lake entrance station and 12.5 miles from the Southwest Entrance Station. It is on the southeast side of the road. Trailhead GPS: N40 27.635' / W121 27.564'

The Hike

The premier waterfall in this spectacular, off-the-beaten-path national park, Kings Creek Falls is a cooling interlude amid a fury of volcanism. Lassen Peak looms overhead and out of sight, but down in the fire-scarred gorge, it's flowing water, not pyroclastic flows, that invigorates the senses.

Like much of Lassen Volcanic National Park, the Kings Creek drainage was heavily impacted by the massive Dixie Fire. A hike to the falls begins with a pleasant meander along the edge of the Lower Meadow, with Kings Creek winding through, amid a mosaic of the burn, with some members of the red fir forest still standing and others torched. At the trail fork near the east edge of the meadow, go left (northeast) on the trail to Kings Creek Falls; the right (southeast) trail leads to Sifford Lake.

The burn intensified near the junction where the Horse Trail departs from the Cascade Trail at the next sign. This ends the stick of the lollipop: Bear left on the Horse Trail; the one-way Cascade Trail is the return route.

Kings Creek Falls is the premier waterfall in Lassen Volcanic National Park.

Kings Creek Falls

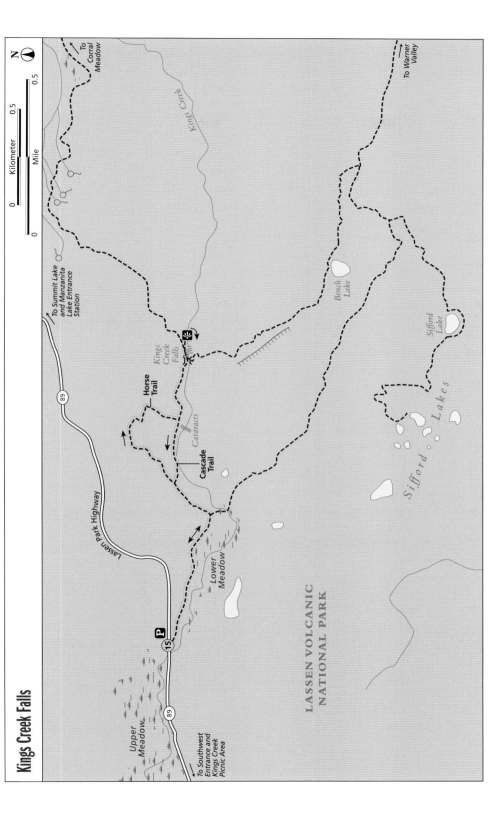

To Corral Meadow

Kings Creek

To Summit Lake and Manzanita Lake Entrance Station

Kings Creek Falls

Horse Trail

Cataracts

Cascade Trail

89

Lassen Park Highway

P

15

Lower Meadow

Upper Meadow

89

To Southwest Entrance and Kings Creek Picnic Area

LASSEN VOLCANIC NATIONAL PARK

Bench Lake

Sifford Lake

Sifford Lakes

To Warner Valley

N

0   0.5   Kilometer

0   0.5   Mile

The Horse Trail climbs to an open area offering views of the Kings Creek drainage and down toward Warner Valley, a vista point even more jaw-dropping given the expansive views it offers of the fire mosaic. A fairly steep, rocky, switchbacking descent leads back streamside, to the junction with the base of the Cascade Trail.

Turn left onto the well-worn path leading to the falls. Stay left again at the junction with the trail leading up to Bench Lake, Sifford Lake, and points beyond.

The creek drops over the falls about 100 yards downstream from the junction. The trail forks before the falls, with the right (lower and streamside) path leading to the overlook, which was in the process of being rebuilt in fall 2022. From this perch you can observe the splintered white veil spun by the 70-foot drop of Kings Creek. If you've got billy-goat skills, you can follow steep, rocky social paths to the base of the falls.

To return, retrace your steps to the junction at the bottom of the Horse Trail and stay right on the Cascade Trail. The narrowing path quickly tucks into a rock-walled ravine. Kings Creek churns to whitewater as it's funneled through the gorge, and a steep, artful staircase leads up alongside the froth, with wildflower rock gardens blooming where they find root holds. The climb is broken with landings where you can catch your breath and take in the spectacle.

At the top of the cataract, the trail hitches back to the Horse Trail. From this point, retrace your steps past the Lower Meadow to the trailhead.

Miles and Directions

0.0 Start at the Kings Creek Falls trailhead.

0.5 Reach the trail intersection in the Lower Meadow and go left on the signed path for Kings Creek Falls.

0.7 At the junction with the top of the one-way Cascade Trail, go left on the Horse Trail.

1.25 The Horse Trail meets the Kings Creek Falls Trail at the base of the Cascade Trail. Go left, tracing the creek downstream.

1.4 Pass the signed trail to Sifford and Bench Lakes. Stay left toward Kings Creek Falls.

1.5 Reach the falls overlook. Take in the spill, then retrace your steps to the junction with the Cascade Trail.

1.75 At the junction stay left on the Cascade Trail, climbing stone steps alongside the cataract.

2.1 Reach the top of the staircase at the junction with the Horse Trail. Stay left to retrace your steps to the trailhead.

2.8 Arrive back at the trailhead.

16 Upper and Lower Deer Creek Falls

An inviting apron of volcanic rock surrounds Deer Creek's upper falls, while a more secluded trail leads down alongside the creek to the tiered lower falls.

Height: 18 feet (upper falls); lower falls are a series of 10- to 30-foot drops.

Beauty rating: ★ ★ ★ ★

Start: The lower falls trailhead is on the west side of the metal truss bridge spanning Deer Creek.

Distance: 0.1 mile out and back for Upper Deer Creek Falls; 4.0 miles out and back for Lower Deer Creek Falls

Difficulty: Easy for Upper Deer Creek Falls; moderate for Lower Deer Creek Falls

Hiking time: Less than 1 hour for Upper Deer Creek Falls; about 3 hours for Lower Deer Creek Falls

Seasons/schedule: Year-round; 6 a.m. to 10 p.m.

Fees and permits: None

Trail contact: Lassen National Forest, Almanor Ranger District, 900 CA 36 / PO Box 767, Chester, CA 96020; (530) 258-2141; www.fs .usda.gov/lassen

Canine compatibility: Leashed dogs permitted.

Trail surface: Dirt

Land status: Lassen National Forest

Nearest towns: Chester; Chico

Other trail users: None

Map to consult: USGS Onion Butte CA

Water availability: Plenty in the creek, but be sure to filter if you don't bring your own.

Amenities available: None. Potato Patch Campground, with restrooms, water, and camping facilities, is about 1.5 miles southeast of the upper falls on CA 36.

Cell service: None

Trail conditions: The upper falls, given the easy access, may be crowded on warm summer days. The lower falls trail is also popular.

Finding the trailhead: From the junction of CA 36 and CA 32, about 14 miles west of Chester and about 16 miles east of Mineral, head southeast on CA 32. Follow the scenic highway for about 10.8 miles to a signed pullout on the left (east) side of the road to view the upper falls. Continue 1.4 miles on CA 32 (12.2 miles total from the junction) to a metal truss bridge crossing Deer Creek for the Lower Falls Trailhead. There is limited parking in a paved pullout with an information signboard alongside the highway on the east side. The trailhead is on the west side; there's a small sign near the northern bridge abutment. Trailhead GPS: Upper falls: N40 12.107' / W121 30.837'; lower falls N40 10.411' / W121 33.319'

The Hikes

Deer Creek's upper falls aren't more than a 5-minute walk from CA 32, but the cascade, the creek that pools above and below, and the surrounding spread of sun-warmed rock invite a long stay. The falls themselves are a punchbowl: The creek is funneled into a narrow chute and then plunges into the deep pool below. Deer Creek is a year-round stream, so even with some of the flow diverted into the adjacent fish ladder, the falls should be noisy and vigorous.

Deer Creek begins its punchbowl plunge at the upper falls.

Lower Deer Creek Falls

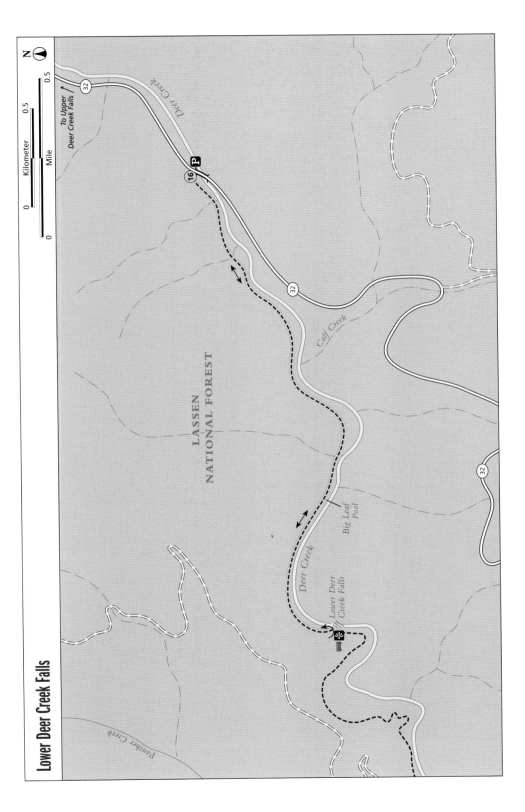

Deer Creek

To Upper
Deer Creek Falls

Calf Creek

LASSEN
NATIONAL FOREST

Big Leaf
Pool

Deer Creek

Lower Deer
Creek Falls

Panther Creek

N

Kilometer
0   0.5   0.5

Mile
0   0.5

Big Leaf Pool offers a great rest stop along the trail to Lower Deer Creek Falls.

Lower Deer Creek dives into a pool amid dark volcanic rock.

The trail is short, leading down from the edge of the roadway for about 25 yards to a Y junction. Go left onto the aprons of volcanic rock that surround the creek and falls; you can walk right up to the brink of the drop and look down into the bowl. Head right to an overlook with a picture-perfect view of the falls. Either stop, bordered by forest but open to the sun, with access to the creek, its fishing opportunities, and its swimming holes, is an excellent choice for a picnic lunch or an afternoon's rest. Retrace your steps to the parking area.

Reaching the lower falls involves a peaceful wander downstream alongside Deer Creek. Cupped in a rocky bend and accessible only by scrambling down a steep hillside, the falls present an elusive destination, though one that's been admired by many, as the memorial bench tucked in the woods above attests. The creek, its falls, and its steep-walled canyon offer solace and solitude if you are lucky enough to take the hike on a quiet day.

To start, a short staircase leads up from the highway bridge spanning Deer Creek, passing an information signboard describing the salmon and steelhead that spawn in the stream. The creek, like many in Lassen country, is popular with anglers. Head down the dirt track into a mingled forest of oak woodland and the waterside riparian zone, manzanita tangling with maple. Moss, puffed up and green when wet, coats the surfaces of the volcanic rocks that occasionally loom over the path. Road noise occasionally drifts down the canyon, but mostly what you'll hear is the creek rolling in its bed.

A series of side streams intersects the trail; these are mostly dry by late season but can require rock-hopping or wading after rains, and a couple flow year-round. The route is mostly shaded, and the rock formations, whether bordering the trail or hunkering above on the steep walls of the canyon, add drama.

Big Leaf Pool, with a fire pit and creek access, is a little more than halfway along the route. Below the pool the creek widens and deepens and then spills as a brief cataract into yet another deep, green pool. Beyond, the trail continues to roller-coaster through the woodland, never steep but mostly descending.

Eventually the path breaks out of the woods into a narrow curve of the canyon, with the start of the falls tumbling through slate-gray rocks below. The walking gets more serious at this point, with the singletrack climbing up into and through a gully before ducking back under the canopy. Views of the falls are plentiful along this final stretch, which leads to a bench commemorating the preservation of the stream and falls by the Western Rivers Conservancy in 2012. This is the turnaround point, though you can scramble down the steep hillside, flows permitting, to the stream, where a pebbly beach may be exposed and you can get closer views of the falls and the neighboring fish ladder/tunnel. Just beware the poison oak.

After your explorations, retrace your steps to the trailhead.

Miles and Directions

Lower Deer Creek Falls

0.0 Start by crossing the highway to the bridge abutment. Climb a short staircase to an information signboard and go left, into the woods.

0.3 Cross the fourth in a series of side streams.

0.5 Pass an alcove hollowed in a huge boulder on the right.

1.1 Cross a more substantial side stream.

1.3 Pass the fire pit and lovely stand of maples at Big Leaf Pool.

1.8 Reach an open section overlooking the start of the falls.

2.0 Reach the turnaround point above the fish ladder. Retrace your steps.

4.0 Arrive back at the trailhead.

17 Feather Falls

Excellent trails lead to a spectacular overlook of Feather Falls and the Middle Fork Feather River canyon.

Height: 640 feet

Beauty rating: ★ ★ ★ ★ ★

Start: Trailhead in the Feather Falls parking lot

Distance: 8.8-mile lollipop and spur

Difficulty: Strenuous

Hiking time: About 5 hours

Seasons/schedule: Year-round; sunrise to sunset

Fees and permits: None

Trail contact: Plumas National Forest, Feather River Ranger District, 875 Mitchell Ave., Oroville, CA 95965; (530) 534-6500; www.fs .usda.gov/plumas

Canine compatibility: Leashed dogs permitted.

Trail surface: Dirt singletrack

Land status: Plumas National Forest

Nearest town: Oroville

Other trail users: None

Maps to consult: USGS Forbestown CA and Brush Creek CA; US Forest Service map and brochure available online at www.fs.usda.gov/Internet/FSE_DOCUMENTS/fsm9_034836.pdf

Water availability: None

Amenities available: Restrooms, trash cans, campsites, and information signboard

Cell service: Marginal; don't rely on it

Trail conditions: This fine singletrack route lies in the burn zone of the 2020 North Complex Fire and was expected to be closed into 2024. Check with rangers before your visit.

Finding the trailhead: From CA 70 in Oroville, take the Oro-Quincy Highway/CA 162 exit and head west for 6.2 miles to Forbestown Road. Turn right onto Forbestown Road and go 6 miles to Lumpkin Road (signs at junctions for Feather Falls point the way). Turn left onto Lumpkin Road and go 10.7 miles to the signed Feather Falls Road/FR 21N35Y. Turn left and follow the paved access road for 1.6 miles to the large paved parking lot. Trailhead GPS: N39 36.858' / W121 16.001'

The Hike

Before the North Complex Fire burned through the area in 2020, hiking to Feather Falls was outstanding—the hike to the waterfall remains one of my favorites from research for the first edition of this guide. I was unable to redo the hike this time around due to the post-fire trail closure, and the aerial imagery was sobering. The evergreen forest that was so calming and provided wonderful shade is mostly obliterated, though green things —shrubs, seedling evergreens, wildflowers—are also visible from the air. So are parts of the trail, which bodes well for its rehabilitation.

While the forest of mixed evergreens—oaks, pines, firs, and the occasional incense cedar and madrone—that made the trail a pleasure in warm weather will take decades to regenerate, the route's good bones remain: the rock promontory upon which the overlook was and will be again; the fine grading of the Upper Trail; the challenging pitches and views to Bald Rock Dome from the Lower Trail. Feather Falls, a mighty horsetail plunging more than 600 feet down a vertical rock face, endures, as does

Feather Falls tumbles more than 600 feet into the Fall River canyon.

the Middle Fork Feather River canyon, steep-walled, remote, and ringing with the thunder of the river and falls.

While you may find minor alterations to the route from what's described here, land managers generally don't reroute trails even after disasters. Like the bones of the paths themselves, I'll provides the bones of a trail description, knowing time and experience will flesh things out.

Two trails lead to the falls overlook. The Lower Trail, at 3.5 miles, is steeper and shorter. The Upper Trail, at 4.5 miles, is longer but perfectly graded, taking the edge off an elevation change of just more than 1,200 feet. This route makes a loop of both trails, with short sticks at both ends where the trails unite, but many hikers travel out and back on the Upper Trail, adding a gentle mile to the round-trip distance.

Begin by heading down the path to the junction. To make the loop, go left on the signed Lower Trail. Circular depressions—bedrock mortars used by the Maidu Indians to prepare acorns for consumption—may be visible along this section of the route.

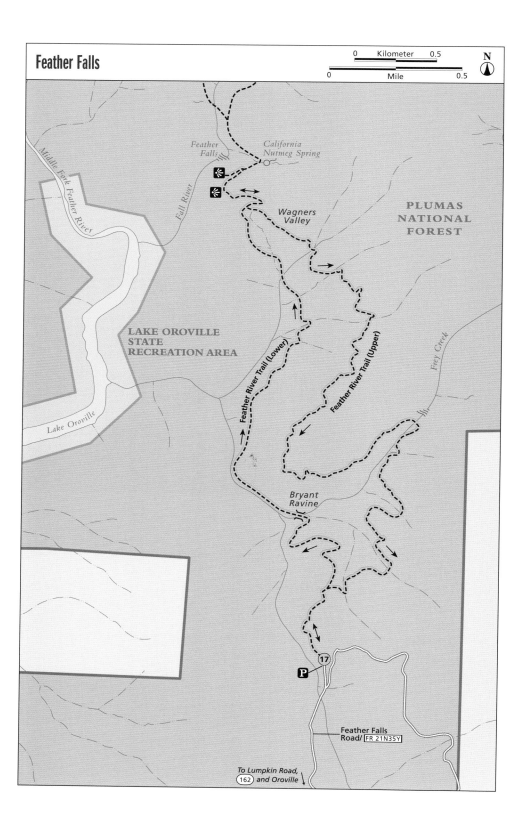

Feather Falls

0 _____ Kilometer _____ 0.5

0 _____ Mile _____ 0.5

N

Feather Falls

California Nutmeg Spring

Middle Fork Feather River

Fall River

PLUMAS NATIONAL FOREST

Wagners Valley

LAKE OROVILLE STATE RECREATION AREA

Feather River Trail (Lower)

Feather River Trail (Upper)

Frey Creek

Lake Oroville

Bryant Ravine

17

P

Feather Falls Road/ FR 21N35Y

To Lumpkin Road, (162) and Oroville

The steepening trail rounds a pair of switchbacks as it nears and crosses Frey Creek. Less than a mile beyond the creek, Bald Rock Dome comes into view, a significant feature on the landscape for the Maidu. Drop through a couple of ravines fed by seasonal streams supporting riparian plants, and then climb to the trail junction. Your knees may have noticed the grade on the downhill; your lungs will notice it on this stretch.

At the junction of the Lower Trail, the Upper Trail, and the trail to the overlook, stay left on the ascending trail. The uphill pitch ends at a viewpoint looking down into the Middle Fork Feather River canyon. The route descends to the overlook promontory. The bones of the trail leading to swimming holes upstream of the waterfall break away from the main route above the promontory. Whether this will be restored is unknown; if you choose to explore upstream, use extreme caution as there are slippery rocks and other hazards.

Feather Falls, the sixth highest in the continental United States, is one of the main attractions in the 15,000-acre designated scenic area. The waterfall is actually on Fall River, which flows into the Middle Fork Feather River just downstream from the plunge. The waterfall is Yosemite-impressive, sprawling across the reddish-blond rock face and perpetually powered by the river's flow. Take it in, then retrace your steps to the junction of the Lower and Upper Trails.

To close the loop—and take the easy way up—stay left on the Upper Trail. The route climbs nearly imperceptibly at first, though moderately steeper pitches spice up the climb at intervals. The trail winds in and out of innumerable gullies, some with seasonal streams, most just curves in the mountainside. The crossing of Frey Creek is a highlight, with a 30-foot slide fall on the uphill side. More sweeping curves lie between the creek and the junction with the Lower Trail above. The junction is at 8.5 miles; retrace your steps from here to the trailhead.

Miles and Directions

0.0 Start by heading down the main Feather Falls trail.

0.3 At the junction go left onto the Lower Trail.

1.0 Round the first switchback.

1.3 Cross Frey Creek.

1.7 Pass the Bald Rock Dome viewpoint.

2.6 Begin to climb.

3.3 The Upper and Lower Trails meet at a junction. Stay left and uphill on the merged trail.

3.7 Stay left on the trail to the overlook promontory.

3.8 Arrive at the overlook. Retrace your steps to the junction of the Upper and Lower Trails.

4.3 At the junction go left on the Upper Trail.

7.0 Reach Frey Creek and its slide waterfall.

8.5 Close the loop at the junction with the Lower Trail. Stay left on the main path to the trailhead.

8.8 Arrive back at the trailhead.

18 Hollow Falls

Walk across the top of a flat-topped mountain to waterfalls that cut through broken basalt.

Height: 100 feet (Hollow Falls)
Beauty rating: ★★★★★
Start: North Table Mountain Ecological Reserve trailhead
Distance: 2.5 miles out and back (more if you visit more waterfalls in the reserve)
Difficulty: Moderate
Hiking time: About 1.5 hours
Seasons/schedule: Year-round; sunrise to sunset. Spring is best for wildflowers.
Fees and permits: A California Department of Fish and Wildlife Land pass is required and can be purchased online.
Trail contact: California Department of Fish and Wildlife, (916) 358-2900 or (916) 358-2869; https://wildlife.ca.gov/Lands/Places-to-Visit/North-Table-Mountain-ER. The Chico Hiking Association also provides information on the hike—visit chicohiking.org to learn more.
Canine compatibility: Dogs must be leashed.

Trail surface: Dirt singletrack
Land status: North Table Mountain Ecological Reserve
Nearest town: Oroville
Other trail users: None
Map to consult: USGS Oroville CA
Water availability: None
Amenities available: Information signboard. Please respect property boundaries and close cattle gates as directed.
Cell service: Mostly good; sketchy at the base of the falls
Trail conditions: The formal trail is not maintained by the land manager but is good, rocky, and may be muddy after rain. Sturdy shoes are recommended, as the basalt may shred less-hardy footwear. The cross-country trails leading to other waterfalls in the reserve may cross private property.

Finding the trailhead: From CA 70 in Oroville heading south, take the Nelson Avenue/Grand Avenue exit (exit 48). Go east on Nelson Avenue for 0.7 mile to Table Mountain Boulevard. Cross Table Mountain Boulevard onto Cherokee Road, and follow Cherokee Road northeast for 6.2 miles to the North Table Mountain Ecological Reserve parking area and trailhead on the left. From CA 70 heading north, take exit 48 and go east on Grand Avenue for about 1 mile. Turn left onto Table Mountain Boulevard and go about 0.1 mile to Cherokee Road. Turn right onto Cherokee Road and proceed to the trailhead. Trailhead GPS: N39 35.750' / W121 32.499'

The Hike

The basalt foundation of North Table Mountain Ecological Reserve gives rise to a remarkable landscape, one that boasts profuse springtime wildflower blooms, vernal pools supporting unique plant species, and seasonal waterfalls that tumble down broken-rock ravines. A number of waterfalls flow on the reserve property when conditions are right—this route leads to one of the best.

Hollow Falls streams over the broken basalt cliffs of North Table Mountain. ▶

Hollow Falls (North Table Mountain Waterfalls)

0   Kilometer   0.4

0   Mile   0.4

N

NORTH TABLE
MOUNTAIN ECOLOGICAL
RESERVE

Hollow Falls

18

P

Cherokee Road

To 70

   The trail to Hollow Falls wanders across the top of North Table Mountain, and in winter and early spring, the trek is breathtaking. The Central Valley opens below, with the shadowy coast ranges defining the western horizon. To the south the rugged Sutter Buttes punch the sky. If fog or haze has settled onto the valley floor, a carpet of white streaks across the blues and greens and browns of the viewscape—and the palette gets more brilliant when the wildflowers bloom. Foothills poppy, Indian paintbrush, bitterroot, meadowfoam, sky lupine, and monkeyflower, among others, paint the rolling landscape yellow, purple, blue, red, and white, beginning as early as February and typically peaking in April. Waterfalls may be the destination, but getting there is sublime.

   The formal trail to Hollow Falls is relatively new, but it follows a route beaten into the rangeland by the hikers who've come before. Avoid informal paths to the other waterfalls on the reserve, as they may cross private land. Reserve boundaries are shown on the Chico Hiking Association map for reference.

   You may also encounter grazing cattle on the reserve. They will mostly stay out of your way, but you should maintain a distance of 300 feet if possible to keep everybody safe and comfortable. Both cow pies and broken basalt help define the track. The reasons for avoiding the former are obvious; to deal with the latter, follow the path of rock that's been crushed a little flatter by footfall, reducing the potential for ankle twisting.

The route begins in the parking lot and wanders out into the fields, where hikers may splinter off to enjoy whatever wildflowers are in bloom. Drop down to a seasonal stream with a crossing near a spreading oak, then continue downstream past a cascade where salamanders and newts congregate to make new salamanders and newts in late winter.

The route continues down the steepening hillside, skirting the top of the waterfall. Switchbacks lead down through oaks to the stream below. Once on flat ground along the creek in Beatson Hollow, walk upstream to the dark pool that catches the 100-foot-high whitewater cascade. Depending on water levels—rainfall helps, and the falls in the preserve are also fed by water that pools in the basalt interior of the mountain—Hollow Falls may feather out to wash the face of the hollow or splinter into two flows that diverge as they descend. On a hot day the pool invites a dip. Return as you came.

Miles and Directions

0.0 Start by passing through the stile. Pick up the beaten path that follows the stream downhill to the west.

0.5 Cross the stream at the oak.

0.7 Reach the top of the falls and follow the most obvious path down into Beatson Hollow.

1.25 Reach the pool at the base of Hollow Falls. Return as you came.

2.5 Arrive back at the trailhead.

Options: Hikers can link up to ten waterfalls, depending on rainfall, by traveling cross-country to their chosen destination(s). Visit www.chicohiking.org/ValleyFoot hill/Many-Waterfalls.htm for details.

Honorable Mentions

Pit River Falls

While in this region, you can also check out the Pit River Falls, which can be viewed from an overlook about 15.3 miles east of the junction of CA 89 and CA 299 on CA 299 (west of Fall River Mills; GPS: N40 59.544' / W121 28.464'). With no easily accessible designated trail or trailhead, the most direct route to the falls is a cross-country trek through scrub.

Bluff Falls

This 40-foot ephemeral waterfall spills over a broken bluff above CA 89 near Lassen Volcanic National Park's southwest entrance. Reaching the base of the falls is more bushwhack than hike: The spill originates in a willow thicket on the bluff top and ends in a talus field, with another willow thicket stretched between the talus and the roadside, presenting a formidable barrier to a direct assault on the base of the falls. Most visitors view the pretty spill from alongside the roadway. Look for a pullout before you reach the park boundary, about 3.6 miles up from the junction of CA 89 and CA 36; the bluff is on the unburned side of the road.

Bluff Falls topples over a cliff just outside the boundaries of Lassen Volcanic National Park.

Hat Creek Falls tumbles alongside the trail to Paradise Meadow in Lassen Volcanic National Park.

Hat Creek Falls

A shaded walk alongside a series of cascades capped by a tiered 20-foot waterfall leads to Paradise Meadow in Lassen Volcanic National Park. The falls are not the destination of this 3.2-mile out-and-back excursion, but they are a nice stop, at about the 1-mile mark, on the way up to one of the prettiest destinations in the park. The trailhead is on the CA 89/Lassen Park Highway 9 miles from the Manzanita Lake entrance station and 19 miles from the southwest entrance.

Battle Creek Falls

Spilling over a bouldery ledge nearly two stories high, Battle Creek Falls fills a small pool in the South Fork Battle Creek near the Battle Creek Campground. The 16-foot waterfall can be seen from the neighboring forest road and is reached via several short social trails. The stream flows year-round, with the fall cascading down separate channels as water levels drop later in summer and autumn. The pool and creek are a cool destination for campers and locals on hot summer days.

To reach the trailhead from Mineral, southwest of Lassen Volcanic National Park, follow CA 36 west for about 1.6 miles to the junction with the Viola-Mineral Road. Turn right onto the Viola-Mineral Road and then immediately left onto FR 104A. Follow FR 104A for 0.7 mile to a parking pullout on the left.

Battle Creek Falls spills into a pool just outside the small town of Mineral.

Chambers Creek Falls

The waterfall itself, about 200 feet high and rumbling down a secluded canyon in 20- to 30-foot tiers, is lovely, but the Dixie Fire did a number on the trail to Chambers Creek Falls. The blaze destroyed the bridge that offered the best viewpoint for the cascade, but even with the bridge in place, the hike wasn't particularly inviting.

The trail consists primarily of an unrelenting, sun-exposed, 2-mile uphill slog (gaining 1,600 feet), partly under high-voltage power lines, which are now infamous in the Feather River canyon for sparking both the disastrous Camp Fire in 2018 and the Dixie Fire in 2021 (the cause of the Storrie Fire, which also scorched the trail and surrounding acreage, has been attributed to the nearby railroad running alongside the Feather River). Now, with fire hazards and the bridge out, I'd only recommend this hike for the hardiest, more waterfall-obsessed hikers—at least until the terrain has recovered and trail infrastructure has been rebuilt.

It's also a bit of a slog to get there, though the fire scars make for dynamic scenery in the Feather River canyon. From Oroville follow CA 70 for about 40 miles toward Quincy. The trailhead is about 1.3 miles beyond a bridge that swings the highway to the north side of the North Fork Feather River.

North Sierra and Lake Tahoe

The wonders of the northern Sierra Nevada, which are mellower and greener than the High Sierra to the south, include the sprawling Lakes District and the Sierra Buttes. Watersheds originating in these forested highlands feed the powerful Yuba and Feather Rivers, which in turn flow into the mighty Sacramento. Graeagle, a quaint resort community, is the biggest little town in this part of the high country, with historic Sierra City and Downieville downslope to the west along scenic CA 49.

Travel south through the Range of Light and you reach Lake Tahoe, the blue gem of the Sierra Nevada and a hikers' wonderland. Trails to waterfalls around the lake and in the surrounding high country range from short, easy treks along streams and through meadows to challenging, long-distance treks among the stony peaks of Desolation Wilderness. Major towns around the lakeshore include Tahoe City and South Lake Tahoe. The bulk of the waterfall hikes in the region are on the South Shore, near Emerald Bay, with a few lying outside the Tahoe basin to the south, including a great waterfall destination near the historic hamlet of Markleeville.

Emerald Bay and southern Lake Tahoe (hike 24).

19 Little Jamison Falls

Hike through the remnants of a historic mine to a secluded waterfall and lake.

Height: About 45 feet

Beauty rating: ★ ★ ★ ★

Start: Trailhead at the Jamison Mine day-use area

Distance: 3.0 miles out and back

Difficulty: Moderate

Hiking time: About 2 hours

Seasons/schedule: Year-round; sunrise to sunset. Winter snow and cold may preclude a comfortable hike.

Fees and permits: An entrance fee is charged.

Trail contact: Plumas-Eureka State Park, 310 Johnsville Rd., Blairsden, CA 96103; (530) 836-2380; www.parks.ca.gov. Plumas-Eureka State Park Association, PO Box 1148, Graeagle, CA 96103; www.plumas-eureka.org.

Canine compatibility: No dogs allowed on trails; leashed dogs allowed on fire roads.

Trail surface: Dirt singletrack, stone steps

Land status: Plumas National Forest

Nearest town: Graeagle

Other trail users: None

Maps to consult: USGS Gold Lake CA; Plumas-Eureka State Park map available at the visitor center and online

Water availability: None at the trailhead; water available at the visitor center

Amenities available: Information signboard with map; picnic sites

Cell service: None

Trail conditions: Well-maintained singletrack

Finding the trailhead: From Graeagle, go left on CR A14 for about 4.5 miles to a left turn onto the gravel road signed for the Jamison Creek/Mine day-use area. Travel the gravel road for 1.2 miles to the parking area near the mine buildings. Trailhead GPS: N39 44.532' / W120 42.085'

The Hike

History meets the mountain on the trail to Little Jamison Falls. An old service road links the remnants of a gold rush–era mining complex in Plumas-Eureka State Park to a relatively remote, lovely waterfall and a peaceful lake in the shadow of Mount Washington.

The trail begins by winding through the remnants of the Jamison Mine complex, curling around a tin-walled shack and overlooking foundations and pits (leave no trace, and take no souvenirs). After a brief, easy, traversing ascent above the mine complex, the route becomes more challenging, climbing stone steps, some of them with substantial, thigh-building rises. The steps come in flights of three to six (or so) and negotiate a pair of switchbacks. The elevation gain isn't extreme, but the stairs may present a challenge both on the way up (for the lungs) and on the way down (for the knees).

The route breaks out of the woods near the 1-mile mark, with views opening up to the Jamison Creek valley. Eureka Peak, where gold was discovered back in the mid-1800s, rises across the valley to the north.

Little Jamison Falls plunges down a cliff opposite an overlook.

MINING LEGACY IN THE NORTH SIERRA

Hallmarks of California's gold rush are preserved in the Plumas-Eureka State Park museum and on the surrounding grounds, including an assay office, an adit (entry to a mine), a blacksmith shop, and a stamp mill. The site was a working mine for nearly a century, from the mid-1800s until World War II, and gold worth millions of dollars was dug from the surrounding mountains in that time. Visitors can tour the preserved mine structures and the museum year-round (hours are limited outside the summer months); the park also hosts living history days, with docents reenacting life in an old-time mining town.

The story here is one of several captured in state parks scattered about the region. At Malakoff Diggins State Historic Park, west and downhill from Graeagle, the remnants of a hydraulic mine, where ore was washed from the mountainside using water cannons, offer fine hiking and more information about the pros and cons of the gold rush era. Empire Mine State Historic Park in Grass Valley offers not only insights into how deep California's mining legacy dives into the Sierra Nevada, but also into the opulent culture enjoyed by the few successful mining barons. And down south, at Marshall Gold Discovery State Historic Park outside Placerville, you can see where it all began, including the tailrace of Sutter's sawmill; pan for nuggets in the South Fork American River; and hike a lovely trail that overlooks the historic site.

Unlike these other historic parks, however, Plumas-Eureka, on the National Register of Historic Places, has another claim to fame. The park is also recognized as the site of the first ski competition in the Western Hemisphere. According to park literature, skiers in the 1860s hitched themselves to 12-foot-long Nordic boards and screamed downhill at speeds of up to 80 miles per hour, and the mine's tramways likely served as makeshift ski lifts. Skiers mining the slopes for fresh powder also has a long history in California's mountains.

At the junction with the trail to Smith Lake, stay right on the signed trail to Grass Lake. The route flattens, crosses a seasonal stream, and passes the park boundary before reaching the junction with the spur trail to Little Jamison Falls. A short hop over open terrain drops to the falls overlook, where several evergreens shade a rock outcropping that makes a nice viewing platform. The falls cascade down a brushy cliff across the ravine, streaming down and out of sight into the Jamison Creek gorge.

From the falls it's a short, easy walk up to Grass Lake at 1.5 miles. Hike back to the falls trail junction and turn right, heading gently uphill through willow and aspen sculpted by winter snows. As its name implies, Grass Lake is surrounded by meadow, with the long, gray-and-green slopes and ridges of Mount Washington forming the northern rampart of the valley. This is the turnaround; return as you came.

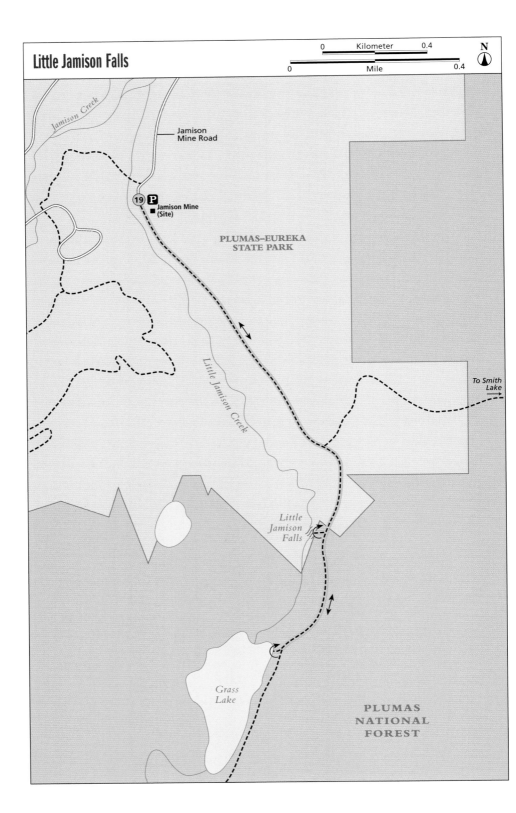

Little Jamison Falls

0   Kilometer   0.4
0   Mile   0.4

N

Jamison Creek

Jamison
Mine Road

19 P
Jamison Mine
(Site)

PLUMAS–EUREKA
STATE PARK

Little Jamison Creek

To Smith
Lake

Little
Jamison
Falls

Grass
Lake

PLUMAS
NATIONAL
FOREST

Miles and Directions

0.0 Start by passing the gate onto the Grass Lake Trail.

0.3 Reach the first staircase.

0.6 Round a pair of switchbacks.

0.9 At the junction with the trail to Smith Lake, stay right toward Grass Lake.

1.0 Pass the park boundary and enter Plumas National Forest.

1.1 Turn right onto the Little Jamison Falls trail. The falls are about 50 yards ahead.

1.2 Return to the signed junction and turn right to continue to Grass Lake.

1.5 Reach the shores of Grass Lake. Retrace your steps.

3.0 Arrive back at the trailhead.

20 Frazier Falls

An easy, paved path leads through groves of mixed conifers and rock gardens to stunning Frazier Falls.

Height: 178 feet
Beauty rating: ★★★★★
Start: Trailhead in the Frazier Falls picnic area
Distance: 1.0 mile out and back
Difficulty: Easy
Hiking time: Less than 1 hour
Seasons/schedule: Year-round; sunrise to sunset. Winter snow and cold may preclude a comfortable hike.
Fees and permits: A seasonal fee is charged.
Trail contact: Plumas National Forest, Beckwourth Ranger District, 23 Mohawk Rd., PO Box 7, Blairsden, CA 96103; (530) 836-2575; www.fs.usda.gov/recarea/plumas/recreation/recarea/?recid=82706&actid=50

Canine compatibility: Leashed dogs permitted.
Trail surface: Pavement, wooden bridges
Land status: Plumas National Forest
Nearest town: Graeagle
Other trail users: None
Maps to consult: USGS Gold Lake CA; www.fs.usda.gov/Internet/FSE_DOCUMENTS/fseprd706813.pdf
Water availability: None
Amenities available: Restrooms and a handful of picnic sites
Cell service: None
Trail conditions: The trail pavement may be a little bumpy, but the route is accessible.

Finding the trailhead: From Graeagle, follow CA 89 south for about 1 mile to a right turn onto the Gold Lake Highway/FR 24, serving Gold Lake and the Lakes Basin Recreation Area. Climb for 1.6 miles to the signed left turn onto Frazier Falls Road (CR 501). Follow narrow, winding, scenic Frazier Falls Road for 4 miles to the Frazier Falls picnic area. You can also reach the trailhead from the other end of Frazier Falls Road, located 8.3 miles up the Gold Lake Highway opposite the access road to Gold Lake. Trailhead GPS: N39 42.494' / W120 38.766'

The Hike

Frazier Creek drops about 2,000 feet from Gold Lake, high in the Lakes Basin Recreation Area, to the Feather River near Graeagle, and about 200 feet of that drop is a dramatic waterfall. The trail leading to the Frazier Falls overlook gives no hint of the chasm ahead, or the cleft in the mountainside that the creek flies through as a flume of whitewater.

The stairstep backbone of the falls is only apparent when the water flow is lower, in late season. But it's there, carved by the same glacial forces that sculpted the rest of this spectacular stretch of the northern Sierra.

The trail leading to the falls overlook is short and straightforward, with a number of benches lining the route. From the trailhead on scenic Frazier Falls Road, a paved path winds through fragrant evergreen forest and gardens of rolling granite and mountain manzanita to a bridge crossing Frazier Creek. A short distance beyond,

Not yet swollen by snowmelt, Frazier Falls displays its stairstep underpinning.

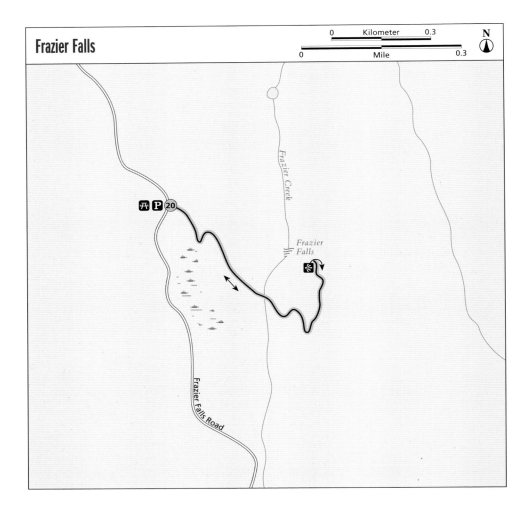

Frazier Falls

the path curls northward and descends to a series of overlooks outfitted with low protective fencing. Interpretive signs describe the forces that sculpted the unexpected landscape. Take in the amazing views, then return as you came.

Miles and Directions

0.0 From the trailhead in the picnic area, follow the paved path into the woods.

0.3 Cross the bridge spanning Frazier Creek.

0.5 Reach the falls overlook. Retrace your steps.

1.0 Arrive back at the trailhead.

21 Hawley Falls

A series of pool-to-pool cascades tumble through a canyon upstream from Gray Eagle Lodge.

Height: 30 feet, with smaller cascades below
Beauty rating: ★ ★ ★
Start: The Long Lake Trailhead near Gray Eagle Lodge
Distance: 2.5 miles out and back
Difficulty: Easy
Hiking time: About 2 hours
Seasons/schedule: Year-round; sunrise to sunset. Winter snow and cold may preclude a comfortable hike.
Fees and permits: A seasonal fee is charged.
Trail contact: Plumas National Forest, Beckwourth Ranger District, 23 Mohawk Rd., PO Box 7, Blairsden, CA 96103; (530) 836-2575; www.fs.usda.gov/recarea/plumas/recarea/?recid=71116

Canine compatibility: Leashed dogs permitted.
Trail surface: Dirt singletrack
Land status: Plumas National Forest
Nearest town: Graeagle
Other trail users: None
Maps to consult: USGS Gold Lake CA; online map for Long Lake Trail at www.fs.usda.gov/Internet/FSE_DOCUMENTS/fseprd710553.pdf
Water availability: None
Amenities available: Restrooms and information signboards
Cell service: None
Trail conditions: The route is singletrack and remote. These falls are also known as Halsey Falls.

Finding the trailhead: From Graeagle, follow CA 89 south for about 1 mile to a right turn onto the Gold Lake Highway/FR 24, serving Gold Lake and the Lakes Basin Recreation Area. Follow the Gold Lake Highway for about 5 miles to the signed junction with the access road to Gray Eagle Lodge. Turn right onto the Gray Eagle Lodge Road and go 0.5 mile to a right turn onto the Gray Eagle Creek/Smith Lake trailhead access road. Go 0.1 mile on the gravel road to the Smith Lake and Long Lake trailheads, located behind the restroom. Trailhead GPS: N39 43.553' / W120 39.828'

The Hike

Gray Eagle Lodge is a major draw in this part of the Lakes Basin Recreation Area, but you don't have to stay at the lodge to hike the easy, forested trail that follows Gray Eagle Creek up to the lovely set of cascades deemed Hawley Falls by the forest service, but also known as Halsey Falls.

The trailhead serves several routes. Take the trail to the left, toward Long Lake; the Smith Lake Trail heads right, and the Gray Eagle Creek Trail is farther back down the trailhead road. Pass a pair of junctions near the Gray Eagle Lodge and stay right on the Long Lake Trail, first following the singletrack up and around a little knob, and then proceeding straight through the clearing.

Hawley Falls tumbles down a narrow, forested canyon upstream from Gray Eagle Lodge.

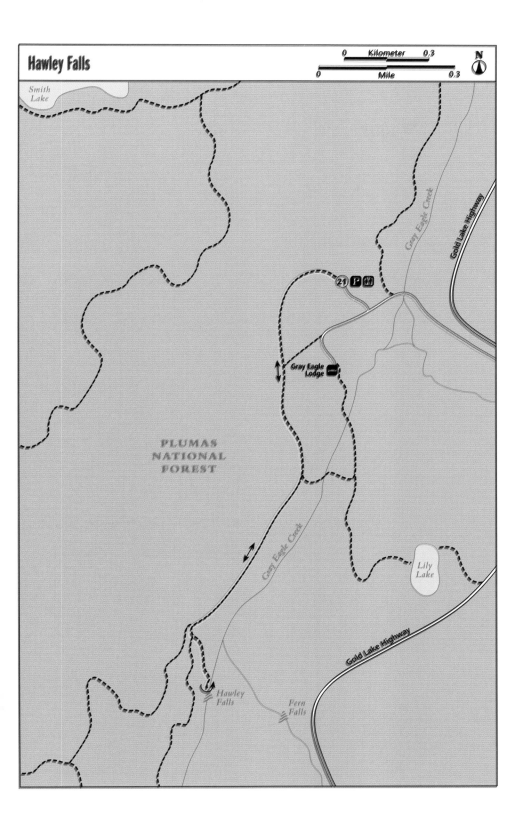

Hawley Falls

Smith Lake

Gray Eagle Creek

Gold Lake Highway

21

Gray Eagle Lodge

PLUMAS
NATIONAL
FOREST

Gray Eagle Creek

Lily Lake

Gold Lake Highway

Hawley Falls

Fern Falls

Kilometer   0.3

Mile   0.3

N

Beyond the lodge intersections the path leads through open woodlands alongside the stream, climbing almost imperceptibly. The last junction is signed; take a left toward Hawley Falls, following the narrowing path into the rocky gorge that cradles the waterway.

The falls are preceded by cataracts, with the water tumbling over a series of short drops. Climb over rocks into the narrowing canyon, where the cataracts morph into a series of falls up to about 10 feet high, which spill from pool to pool and are corralled by steep slabs on either side. A final scramble into the rock-walled gorge reveals Hawley Falls, an impressive 30-foot cascade. Find a perch on a rock and enjoy the sights, then return as you came.

Miles and Directions

0.0 Start behind the restroom on Long Lake Trail, to the left. The trail to the right leads to Smith Lake.

0.3 At the junction go right on the trail to Long Lake. The left trail leads to Gray Eagle Lodge.

0.6 At the junction stay right on the Long Lake Trail.

1.1 Rock-hop a streamlet to a junction. Go left on the path to Hawley Falls.

1.3 Scramble into the rocky gorge to view the falls. Return as you came.

2.5 Arrive back at the trailhead.

22 Loves Falls

An easy, traversing hike leads to a thunderous fall on the North Yuba River.

Height: A series of 10- to 25-foot cascades

Beauty rating: ★ ★ ★ ★

Start: Pacific Crest Trailhead on CA 49

Distance: 0.9 mile out and back

Difficulty: Easy

Hiking time: Less than 1 hour

Seasons/schedule: Year-round; sunrise to sunset

Fees and permits: None

Trail contact: Tahoe National Forest, Truckee Ranger District, 10811 Stockrest Springs Rd., Truckee, CA 96161; (530) 587-3558; www.fs.usda.gov/recarea/tahoe/recarea/?recid=80792

Canine compatibility: Leashed dogs permitted.

Trail surface: Rocky dirt singletrack, metal bridge

Land status: Tahoe National Forest

Nearest town: Sierra City

Other trail users: None

Map to consult: USGS Haypress Valley CA

Water availability: None

Amenities available: None

Cell service: None

Trail conditions: The trail is well maintained, short, and easy.

Finding the trailhead: From Sierra City follow CA 49 1 mile east to the signed Pacific Crest Trailhead. Parking for about five cars is on the left (north) side of the highway. Trailhead GPS: N39 34.602' / W120 36.762'

The Hike

Look both upstream and downstream from the bridge at Loves Falls in the spring or early summer, and the North Yuba River roars big and furious. Flush with snowmelt, it explodes through the boulders hemming in the canyon bottom, and even when summer mellows the flows, the cataracts still flash and jump.

Reaching the falls entails hiking a friendly stretch of the famous Pacific Crest Trail (PCT), which rides the ridges from the Mexican border to Canada (2,650 miles end to end). The path traverses the north side of the North Yuba River canyon, passing through stands of mixed evergreen forest, and is vaguely upside down. The only steep pitch is the final drop to the bridge spanning the Yuba, but neither legs nor lungs should be inordinately taxed.

The route begins by crossing CA 49 from the trailhead. Pick up the signed PCT on the south side of the road and turn left, heading upstream. Signs for Loves Falls and Milton Creek keep you on track as you drop into the North Yuba canyon, paralleling the highway. Pass a set of tanks on the right, and then roller-coaster along the canyon side through the woods. A flume runs between the trail and the river for a stretch.

The short descent drops you onto the narrow metal bridge crossing the river at the falls. The river is a tempest both coming and going, with cascades varying in

Looking upstream from the bridge spanning the North Yuba River at Loves Falls.

height from 10 to 25 feet upstream and downstream of the span. The noise of the falls drowns out the highway and the voices of companions. And the setting is spectacular, with close, steep canyon walls and monstrous boulders cluttering the riverbed. There's really no place other than the bridge to safely enjoy the falls, though a use trail skitters down the canyon wall to the riverside. Unless you plan on following the PCT farther south to tick off more mileage on this famous thru-route, return as you came.

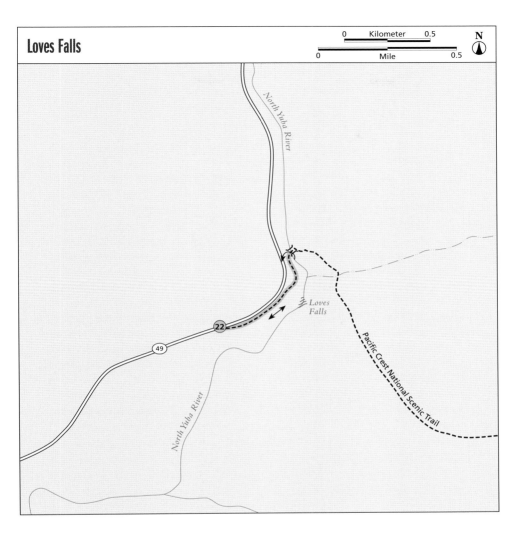

0   Kilometer   0.5

0   Mile   0.5

N

Miles and Directions

0.0   Start by crossing CA 49. Pick up the Pacific Crest Trail on the south side of the highway and go left (east).

0.1   Pass a cluster of tanks.

0.4   Round a bend in the trail. Loves Falls comes into view. Drop onto the bridge spanning the North Yuba River and check out the cataracts, then retrace your steps.

0.9   Arrive back at the trailhead.

23 Shirley Canyon Cascades

A series of cascades is an easy walk upstream from the base of the Palisades Tahoe ski resort.

Height: 15 feet, with smaller falls above and below

Beauty rating: ★★★

Start: Shirley Canyon trailhead near the Palisades Tahoe Village

Distance: 1.5 miles out and back

Difficulty: Easy

Hiking time: About 1.5 hours

Seasons/schedule: Year-round; sunrise to sunset. Winter snow and cold may preclude a comfortable hike.

Fees and permits: None

Trail contact: Palisades Tahoe, 1960 Olympic Valley Rd., PO Box 2007, Olympic Valley, CA 96146; (800) 403-0206 or (530) 452-4331; www.palisadestahoe.com. US Forest Service, Lake Tahoe Basin Management Unit, Forest Supervisor's Office, 35 College Dr., South Lake Tahoe, CA 96150; (530) 543-2600; www.fs.usda.gov/ltbmu.

Canine compatibility: Leashed dogs permitted.

Trail surface: Dirt, rock

Land status: Tahoe National Forest

Nearest towns: Palisades Tahoe Village; Tahoe City

Other trail users: None

Maps to consult: USGS Tahoe City CA, and Granite Chief CA; Lake Tahoe Basin Management Unit map; National Geographic 803 Lake Tahoe Basin trail map; Palisades Tahoe map at www.palisadestahoe.com/-/media/palisades-tahoe/pdfs/summer/2022hikingbrochure.pdf

Water availability: None at the trailhead, but plenty for sale in the adjacent village

Amenities available: An information signboard. All amenities are available in the Palisades Tahoe Village. If you can't find parking near the trailhead, plenty is available down-valley in the village.

Cell service: Good

Trail conditions: The singletrack sometimes wanders away from the guiding stream, but it's easy to follow. It also can be very busy, so walk single file if you're with a group, and be courteous to other hikers.

Finding the trailhead: From the intersection of CA 89 and CA 28 in Tahoe City, follow CA 89 northwest (toward Truckee) for 5 miles. Turn left (west) onto Olympic Valley Road and go 2.5 miles, past the huge village parking lot, to Shirley Canyon Road. Turn right onto Shirley Canyon Road and follow it for 0.4 mile to its junction with Marmot Way. The trailhead is at the junction. Trailhead GPS: N39 11.910' / W120 14.480'

The Hike

These falls tumble down a creek that used to be known by a racist and sexist term now being rightfully banished from the landscape and the lexicon. The nearby resort already has a new name—Palisades Tahoe—and the valley and the main road serving the resort are now called Olympic. Palisades Tahoe has dubbed the stream Washeshu, which it says is the Washoe word for "people," but the name change was

Waterfalls leave watermarks: White stains delineate the seasonal cascades along Washeshu Creek, which go dry in the summer season.

not formalized by the state of California and the US Geological Survey's Board of Geographic Names when this guide was being revised. That'll hopefully happen sooner rather than later.

Meantime, I'll call the creek Washeshu, with apologies if another indigenous name is chosen.

Washeshu Creek rocks and rolls in a meltwater rush in late spring and early summer, fueling small waterfalls and cascades that mist travelers on the trail that runs alongside. The falls are ephemeral even though the creek, originating in the Shirley Lake basin, flows throughout the year. Fortunately, even if you miss the whitewater show, the trail is worth exploring. Just keep in mind that the cascades are within easy walking distance of the Palisades Tahoe resort, which can be as busy in summer as it is during the ski season—and so can the path. You might also keep in mind that, after the hike, you can immerse yourself in other activities offered at the resort, where the aerial tram runs daily, offering access to High Camp's pool, skating rink, restaurant and bar, and hiking trails that skim the high ridges overlooking the Truckee River valley and the Tahoe Basin.

Shirley Canyon Cascades

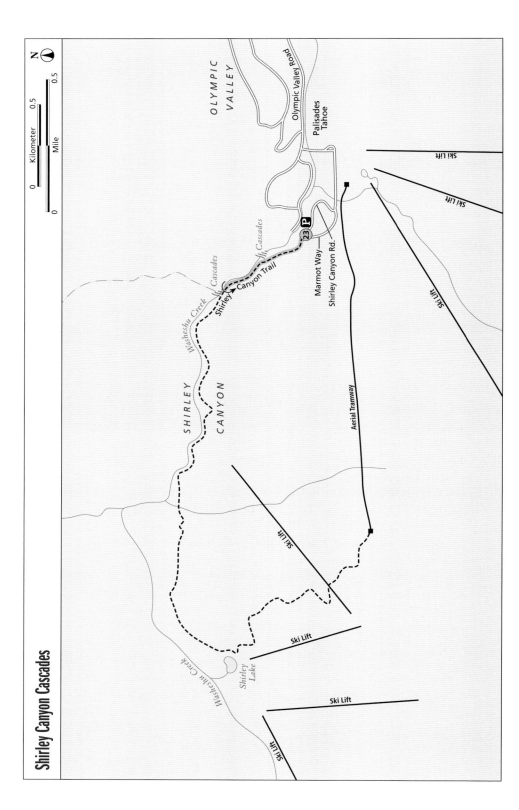

The trail up Shirley Canyon is rustic almost from the start: No wide treadways or boardwalks keep you on track. Because the rocky singletrack borders the creek, it sometimes flows with meltwater itself. Begin by passing behind the large information signboard. The trail is obvious at first but grows indistinct as it meanders up into the steep-walled canyon. Watch for brown trail signs and blue blazes on rocks, which show the way, staying on the left side of the creek. The path steadily ascends, but the real challenge is in picking the best way forward.

The first cascade/waterfall is at the 0.3-mile mark. This is the biggest plunge, with the water tumbling over a 15-foot rock lip into a jumble of granite boulders. But there is more above: Continue uphill to a second tumble, shorter and muddled by boulders but still frothy. To reach a second set of cascades, bear left through the woods on a nice, straightforward stretch of trail. Where paths diverge at about 0.75 mile, stay left and cross a granite slab (follow the blue blazes) to the second cascade view. The trail continues upward and onward, but this is the turnaround for those satisfied with a waterfall walk.

Miles and Directions

0.0 Start at the Shirley Canyon trailhead. Where the trail becomes indistinct, blue blazes mark the way.

0.2 Pass a trail marker.

0.3 Reach the first waterfall. You can turn around here or continue to a second series of cascades.

0.5 Pass a second trail marker, cross a side stream, and then stay left on a straightforward path through the woods.

0.75 Where paths diverge, stay left, cross a granite slab following blue blazes, and reach the second cascade view. Check it out, and then return as you came.

1.5 Arrive back at the trailhead.

Option: For hardier hikers, the trail continues upward to Shirley Lake and then to High Camp and a spectacular (and free) tram ride from the top of the ski resort to the base. To complete the one-way hike to the tram from the second cascade, continue uphill, following the blazes where the trail grows faint. Steep pitches are interspersed with relatively flat sections, leading up to a trail junction at 1.3 miles, where signs point to Shirley Lake. At about the 2-mile mark, you'll encounter the crux of the hike: a sloping but steep granite headwall. Climb the imposing slab on its left side, again following blazes and the occasional rock cairn. Top out and proceed through woodland to Shirley Lake and the Solitude basin (with a ski lift), which is 3.25 miles from the trailhead.

The trail to High Camp climbs a rocky slope out of the basin (follow the Solitude/High Camp trail markers) and then winds up the barren slopes to the broad roadway that links back to High Camp and the aerial tram. The views from on high are panoramic, with Lake Tahoe winking blue among the ridges. Total mileage to High Camp from the trailhead is just more than 4 miles.

24 Eagle Falls

The falls on Eagle Creek are part of a watercourse that links Lake Tahoe's lovely Emerald Bay with the Desolation Wilderness.

Height: About 40 feet

Beauty rating: ★★★★

Start: Eagle Falls trailhead off CA 89

Distance: 0.6 mile out and back

Difficulty: Easy

Hiking time: Less than an hour

Seasons/schedule: Year-round; sunrise to sunset. Winter snow and cold may preclude a comfortable hike.

Fees and permits: A parking fee is charged.

Trail contact: US Forest Service, Lake Tahoe Basin Management Unit, Forest Supervisor's Office, 35 College Dr., South Lake Tahoe, CA 96150; (530) 543-2600; www.fs.usda.gov/ltbmu

Canine compatibility: Leashed dogs permitted.

Trail surface: Dirt, granite

Land status: Tahoe National Forest; Lake Tahoe Basin Management Unit

Nearest town: South Lake Tahoe

Other trail users: None

Maps to consult: USGS Emerald Bay CA; a map on the signboard at the trailhead; Lake Tahoe Basin Management Unit Map; National Geographic 803 Lake Tahoe Basin trail map

Water availability: None at the trailhead

Amenities available: Parking, restrooms, picnic sites, trash cans, information signboard, and wilderness permit site. The parking lots at Eagle Falls and neighboring Vikingsholm are congested during the high season. Additional parking is available along the highway. Please be courteous and safe in selecting a parking space. A free day-use wilderness permit is required to hike in Desolation Wilderness and is available at the trailhead.

Cell service: Good

Trail conditions: The trail is well maintained but is very popular and very congested in the summer season.

Finding the trailhead: From the intersection of US 50 and CA 89 in South Lake Tahoe, head north on CA 89 for 10.3 miles to the signed Eagle Falls parking area on the left (south). From Tahoe City follow CA 89 south for 18 miles, past the parking area for Vikingsholm, to the Eagle Falls parking lot on the right. Trailhead GPS: N38 57.118' / W120 06.811'

The Hike

The cascade on Eagle Creek is a waypoint for most hikers as they climb to Eagle Lake. The upper falls, reached via the Eagle Lake Trail, is a lovely destination, and the setting couldn't be more spectacular. From the bridge spanning the creek below the upper falls, look east toward aptly named Emerald Bay and the vast blue expanse of Lake Tahoe. In every other direction the silver granite walls of the Desolation Wilderness tower overhead. The main plunge of Eagle Falls is on the east side of CA 89 and not accessible by formal trail, though you can follow use trails to view it from CA 89.

To reach the upper falls, pass the information signboard and begin walking up the stone staircase. (If you plan to continue past the falls into the Desolation Wilderness,

Eagle Falls; Cascade Falls

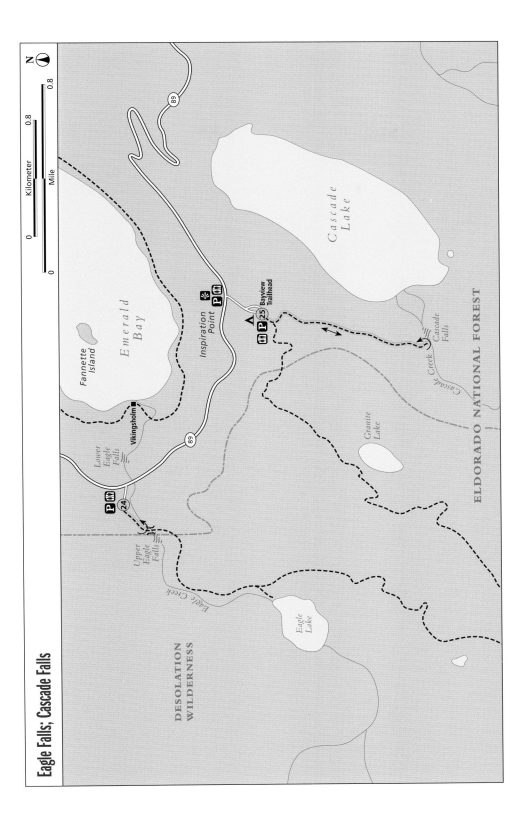

Kilometer

Mile

N

Fannette Island

Emerald Bay

Inspiration Point

Vikingsholm

Lower Eagle Falls

Upper Eagle Falls

Eagle Creek

DESOLATION WILDERNESS

Eagle Lake

Granite Lake

Bayview Trailhead

Cascade Lake

Cascade Creek

Cascade Falls

ELDORADO NATIONAL FOREST

89

24

25

Lower Eagle Falls descends toward Emerald Bay.

you must fill out a wilderness permit at the trailhead.) Stay on the signed Eagle Lake Trail where it connects with the shorter Eagle Loop. The path climbs gently at first, allowing you to enjoy views of the cascades and the pinnacles and great gray domes of the Desolation Wilderness.

Nearing the cascade, a twisting stone stairway leads up and then down to a vista point and the sturdy bridge spanning the base of the cataract. Check out the falls, which roar with snowmelt early in the season and grow gentler as summer's heat mellows the snow above. Return as you came.

Miles and Directions

0.0 Start by climbing steps to the junction of the Eagle Lake Trail and the Eagle Loop. Stay left (southwest) on the Eagle Lake Trail.

0.2 Climb granite steps past the second Eagle Loop trail junction and stay left, heading down the stone steps.

0.3 Reach the bridge below the falls. Retrace your steps.

0.6 Arrive back at the trailhead.

Option: Eagle Lake is a short climb beyond the fall, and a classic Tahoe destination. Cupped in a stark Desolation Wilderness cirque—steep, silver, and formidable—the lake is likely the easiest alpine destination on Tahoe's South Shore. The trail to the lake is varied and moderately challenging but quite short, making it well within reach of any hiker seeking an alpine experience without excess effort. From the bridge below the falls, climb another set of stairs, cross a granite slab, and traverse above the stream canyon. Stay right at the junction with the trail to the Velma Lakes, dropping to the shores of Eagle Lake. The out-and-back distance is 2.0 miles.

25 Cascade Falls

Follow a rocky path to the raucous creek that feeds Cascade Falls. The falls themselves can only be viewed from a distance, but a seat on the granite terrace at the apex presents great views of Cascade Lake and Lake Tahoe.

Height: About 200 feet

Beauty rating: ★ ★ ★ ★

Start: Trailhead in the Bayview Campground

Distance: 2.0 miles out and back

Difficulty: Moderate due to climbs and descents over rocky terrain

Hiking time: About 1.5 hours

Seasons/schedule: Year-round; sunrise to sunset. Winter snow and cold may preclude a comfortable hike.

Fees and permits: A parking fee is charged.

Trail contact: US Forest Service, Lake Tahoe Basin Management Unit, Forest Supervisor's Office, 35 College Dr., South Lake Tahoe, CA 96150; (530) 543-2600; www.fs.usda.gov/ltbmu

Canine compatibility: Leashed dogs permitted.

Trail surface: Dirt, granite

Land status: Tahoe National Forest; Lake Tahoe Basin Management Unit

Nearest town: South Lake Tahoe

Other trail users: None

Maps to consult: USGS Emerald Bay CA; Lake Tahoe Basin Management Unit Map; National Geographic 803 Lake Tahoe Basin trail map

Water availability: None at the trailhead; water available in the Bayview Campground

Amenities available: Restrooms, trash cans, an often-full parking area, and information signboards

Cell service: Good

Trail conditions: This well-maintained route is popular and often crowded.

See map on page 127.

Finding the trailhead: From the intersection of US 50 and CA 89 in South Lake Tahoe, head north on CA 89 for 9.4 miles to a left (south) turn into the Bayview Campground. Follow the campground road 0.3 mile to limited parking at the trailhead. Direct access to the trailhead may be difficult in high season; be prepared to park outside the campground in safe pullouts along the highway. Trailhead GPS: N38 56.607' / W120 06.000'

The Hike

Cascade Creek spills out of the rocky heights of the Desolation Wilderness, fueling Cascade Falls and filling secluded Cascade Lake. Both the falls and the dark, still lake are off-limits to hikers, with the falls rendered inaccessible by steep granite cliffs and the lake by private property. But above the misting waterfall, hikers can cool their heels in pools and riffles on Cascade Creek, which courses over and among smooth granite slabs before taking the plunge. A seat at trail's end on a platform of sunbaked stone affords great vistas across the Cascade Lake basin to Lake Tahoe.

To begin, walk behind the trailhead information kiosk and turn left (south) onto Cascade Trail. The trail bends around stubby trail posts in the mixed evergreen forest and then climbs a short stone stairway to an overlook of the falls, Cascade Lake, and Lake Tahoe.

129

A seat on the sunbaked slabs atop Cascade Falls offers great views down onto Emerald Bay and Lake Tahoe.

At about the 0.5-mile mark, begin a rocky downward traverse high above the northwest end of Cascade Lake. Pick your way down to, and then along, the base of a granite cliff; watch your step on the uneven trail surface. You can catch glimpses of the falls tumbling toward the lake from the traverse, but stop before you look, just to be safe.

Cross a relatively narrow ledge, and then climb granite steps and broken rock to the broad sunny slabs that cradle the creek. A lovely granite bowl opens upstream, stretching back into Desolation Wilderness. A maze of trails has been worked onto the landscape over the years, some marked by "ducks" (stacks of rocks also called cairns) and others delineated by lines of rocks. Look left and downhill for a wooden trail marker that points the way to the falls overlook. Stay low (left and north) to get closer to the falls, but don't get too close, as you don't want to take a tumble near the cliff face. Stay high (right and south) to reach stretches of the creek that permit water play and toe dipping.

The whole terrace opens on wonderful views across the southern Tahoe Basin. Take in the sights, and then return as you came.

Miles and Directions

0.0   Start behind the information signboard, turning left (south) onto the trail to Cascade Falls.

0.5   Head up the stone steps to views of Cascade Lake and Cascade Falls.

0.7   Traverse via slabs and steps at the base of a granite wall. The trail levels as you approach the creek, and the granite cirque opens uphill to the south.

1.0   Reach the creek above the falls. Enjoy the views, then return as you came.

2.0   Arrive back at the trailhead.

26 Glen Alpine Falls and Modjeska Falls

Two waterfalls, roaring with snowmelt in late spring and early summer, enliven the cobblestone road/trail that climbs to ruins of the historic Glen Alpine Springs Resort.

Height: 75 feet (Glen Alpine), 50 feet (Modjeska)

Beauty rating: ★★★★

Start: Glen Alpine trailhead

Distance: 2.2 miles out and back

Difficulty: Easy

Hiking time: About 1.5 hours

Seasons/schedule: Year-round; sunrise to sunset. Winter snow and cold may preclude a comfortable hike.

Fees and permits: A parking fee is charged. A free wilderness permit is available at the trailhead if you plan to continue into Desolation Wilderness.

Trail contact: US Forest Service, Lake Tahoe Basin Management Unit, Forest Supervisor's Office, 35 College Dr., South Lake Tahoe, CA 96150; (530) 543-2600; www.fs.usda.gov/ltbmu

Canine compatibility: Leashed dogs permitted.

Trail surface: Rocky gravel service road and singletrack

Land status: Tahoe National Forest; Lake Tahoe Basin Management Unit

Nearest town: South Lake Tahoe

Other trail users: Horse packers

Maps to consult: USGS Emerald Bay CA; Lake Tahoe Basin Management Unit Map; National Geographic 803 Lake Tahoe Basin trail map

Water availability: None

Amenities available: Restrooms, trash cans, an information signboard, a wilderness permit station at the trailhead. Parking fills quickly at the Glen Alpine trailhead, and more parking may be available in pullouts along the access road. Fallen Leaf Lake Road is one lane and busy in summer. Travel slowly and be courteous by stopping in wide spots to let oncoming traffic pass safely.

Cell service: Marginal to none

Trail conditions: The trail is wide, well maintained, and busy in the summer season. Be courteous, and if you're hiking with a group, stay right and single file to allow oncoming hikers to pass.

Finding the trailhead: From the intersection of US 50 and CA 89 in South Lake Tahoe, take CA 89 north for 3 miles to Fallen Leaf Lake Road. Turn left (west) on Fallen Leaf Lake Road and go 5 miles, past the lodge and marina, to a fork. Go left (west) on FR 1216, following the sign for Lily Lake. The trailhead parking area is 0.6 mile ahead, across the bridge. Trailhead GPS: N38 52.627' / W120 04.836'

The Hike

Glen Alpine Creek drops over two falls in the final leg of its descent from the Desolation Wilderness to Fallen Leaf Lake, and depending on the quantity of snowmelt and the timing of your visit, the falls can be furious. But the hiking is not: The route follows a wide, moderately graded, gravel-and-cobblestone road that offers access to private cabins, the remnants of the Glen Alpine Springs Resort, and the wilderness.

The remnants of Glen Alpine Springs Resort, including the soda spring, lie upstream from the two trailside waterfalls.

This route takes you to the resort, as it's not that far above the second fall (Modjeska) and adds yet another attraction to a fine day hike.

The trail is relatively straightforward. At the outset the treadway is paved in ankle-twisting cobbles, but the grade isn't steep. Early in the summer season or during heavy snow years, however, the track may be half submerged in flowing snowmelt, foretelling the abundance of water in the roadside falls. Gates and trail signs keep you on route at forks in the road, though the signs are inconspicuous and mounted above eye level on tree trunks. Parcels of private land line the trail, with rugged driveways leading to small cabins.

Glen Alpine Falls and Modjeska Falls

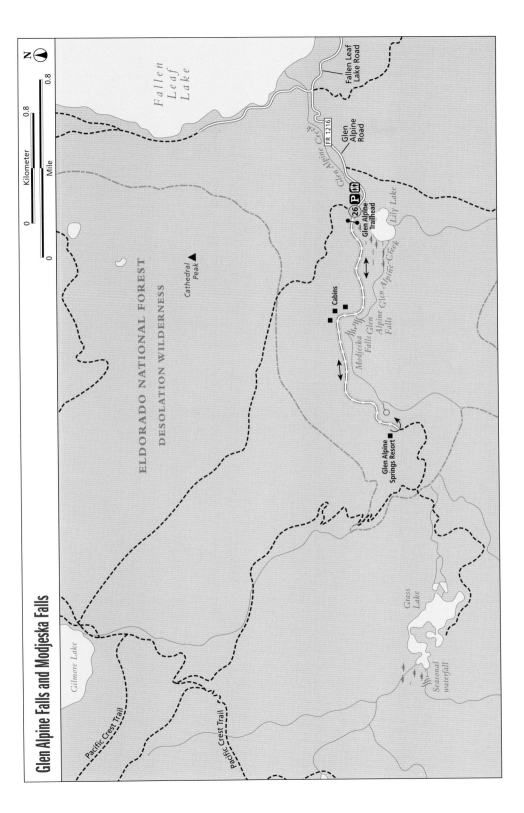

Glen Alpine Falls is the first along the route. It's broad and impressive when brimming, hiding the broken cliff behind in a curtain of white. Modjeska Falls, reportedly named for an actress who frequented the Glen Alpine Springs Resort, tumbles not far above, but being smaller and narrower it doesn't garner the awe that its downstream neighbor does. You can turn around here, but hiking beyond the falls is well worth the time and minimal effort.

Continuing up, ramble through a lovely mixed evergreen forest with a lush understory of wild berries and flowers. Just beyond the old barn, a sign directs you to the right and into the remains of the Glen Alpine Springs Resort, established in 1878. Paths wind through the remnants of the once-thriving enterprise, interpretive signs describe the history of the resort, which operated into the 1960s, and a map directs you to different structures that were part of the complex, including the soda spring itself, still burbling and popping. Nathan Gilmore, prospector and cofounder of the Sierra Club, established the resort, Lake Tahoe's first upscale getaway; other Gilmore landholdings in the area eventually became part of the Desolation Wilderness, designated in 1969. The threat of development led to Glen Alpine's designation as a Federal Historic District in the 1970s.

After exploring the site, return as you came.

Miles and Directions

0.0 Start by passing the green gate and heading up the gravel-and-cobblestone roadway.

0.3 Cross a stream (dry in late season) and pass a gate and trail sign.

0.4 Reach Glen Alpine Falls, on the left side of the roadway. At the junction with a private access road, stay right, following the "Trails" sign.

0.5 Reach Modjeska Falls, also on the left side of the roadway. At the next junction stay left, again following the "Trails" sign.

1.1 Pass the old barn and enter the Glen Alpine Springs Resort. Explore the site, then return as you came.

2.2 Arrive back at the trailhead.

Option: To reach a seasonal waterfall at Grass Lake, continue into the Desolation Wilderness, which begins at a granite staircase at the far end of the Glen Alpine Springs Resort. The route is lovely, traversing alternating groves of ponderosa pine and open granite shelves, with views across the valley onto the Keith Dome ridgeline. At the trail fork just beyond the Desolation Wilderness sign at 1.5 miles, go left (west) to Grass Lake. Three creek crossings follow—they're of varying difficulty depending on water flow and your tolerance for crossing logs and rock-hopping. Beyond the last creek crossing, a series of short granite-and-timber staircases leads up the short ramparts of granite below the lake. Travel a final stretch through a brushy gully to reach Grass Lake at 2.4 miles. Contained by low, rolling expanses of granite and clusters of fir, pine, and brush, a spectacular waterfall spills off a red rock cliff to the west in season. Beyond and above the lake and falls, the walls of the glacial basin rise skyward. The total round-trip distance is 5.0 miles.

27 Horsetail Falls

This path follows Pyramid Creek up toward the giant spill of whitewater pouring from the heights of the Desolation Wilderness above Twin Bridges, skimming a lovely cataract along the way.

Height: 791 feet

Beauty rating: ★★★★

Start: Pyramid Creek Trailhead near Echo Summit

Distance: 2.5-mile lollipop and spur

Difficulty: Moderate due to route finding

Hiking time: About 2 hours

Seasons/schedule: Year-round; sunrise to sunset. Winter snow and cold may preclude a comfortable hike.

Fees and permits: A parking fee is charged.

Trail contact: Eldorado National Forest, Forest Supervisor's Office, 100 Forni Rd., Placerville, CA 95667; (530) 303-2412 or (530) 622-5061; www.fs.usda.gov/main/eldorado/home

Canine compatibility: Leashed dogs permitted.

Trail surface: Dirt, granite

Land status: Eldorado National Forest

Nearest town: Strawberry

Other trail users: None

Map to consult: USGS Echo Lake CA

Water availability: Water is available at the trailhead.

Amenities available: Restrooms, parking lot, trash cans, an information signboard with map, and picnic tables at the trailhead. Visitors planning to enter the Desolation Wilderness must fill out a free wilderness permit.

Cell service: Possible, but don't count on it.

Trail conditions: The trail lies within the burn scar of the 2021 Caldor Fire. Proceed with care, watching for hazard trees and hidden stump holes. Trailhead parking may be difficult in summer; arriving early or later in the day will optimize your chance of finding space.

Finding the trailhead: From the Y junction of US 50 and CA 89 in South Lake Tahoe, head west on US 50 for 15.3 miles, over Echo Summit, to the Pyramid Creek Trail parking area on the right. Trailhead GPS: N38 48.698' / W120 07.420'

The Hike

Though visible from US 50 as you descend a switchback from Echo Summit to Twin Bridges—in fact, a traffic stopper in peak season—Horsetail Falls is relatively remote. No established trail leads directly to the base or to the summit, which is high in the Desolation Wilderness. But the trail along Pyramid Creek offers great views of the waterfall, and the creek rocks with excitement when flush with meltwater.

Pyramid Creek charges Horsetail Falls and the cascades below year-round, fed by outflows from alpine lakes high in the wilderness, including Avalanche Lake, Pitt Lake, Ropi Lake, and Lake of the Woods. Only the top few tiers of the falls can be seen from the trail; cross-country travel (and the appropriate advanced route-finding skill set) is required to reach those heights. But granite slopes and terraces below the falls present classic Sierran hiking terrain, spiced by the fact that the trail can be

A rock cairn marks the Pyramid Creek Trail; Horsetail Falls plummets from the cliff top in the distance.

difficult to follow in places. Artfully constructed rock cairns litter the slabs above the lower cataract, linking lengths of crushed stone treadway. The intent is to keep hikers on track, but the route the cairns demark is meandering. No worries: Keep the creek on your right, head up-valley toward the falls, and you won't get lost.

Recovery from the Caldor Fire may complicate matters, though the inflammable granite ramparts of the wilderness were instrumental in slowing its progress. As in other fire scars, you may encounter hazardous conditions and route finding may change—and improve—as time passes. Check with rangers about trail conditions before your hike.

Begin in the woods, hiking past a modest platform of granite overlooking a small splash of whitewater, and then climb to a trail junction at the base of a steep granite slab. Noise from the highway follows you up the trail, but once you ascend the slab and walk farther north into the woods, all but the loudest engine sounds fade away. Trend right as you climb the slab, angling toward the creek, to intersect the trail at a junction on top.

Continue by following the path of crushed stone threading through the slabs. You can see the top tiers of Horsetail Falls as you navigate this flat section. The wilderness boundary is a tenth of a mile beyond, but you won't find a wilderness permit station here—only the end of the trail proper, petering out on the banks of Pyramid Creek. This is the turnaround point, though if you are prepared to go cross-country and water levels permit, you can ford the creek and carry on. The base of Horsetail Falls is about a half mile farther. Otherwise, retrace your steps to the trail junction and turn left, heading down along the creek corridor.

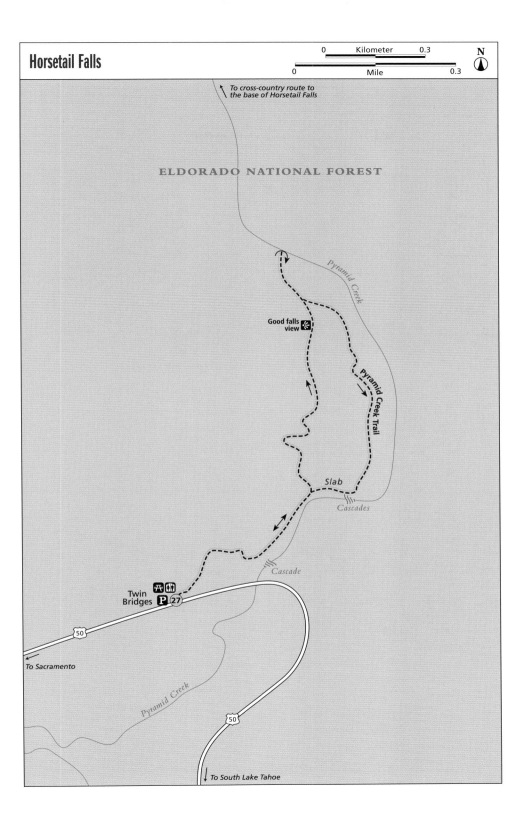

Horsetail Falls

0 | Kilometer | 0.3

0 | Mile | 0.3

N

To cross-country route to
the base of Horsetail Falls

ELDORADO NATIONAL FOREST

Pyramid Creek

Good falls
view

Pyramid Creek Trail

Slab

Cascades

Cascade

Twin
Bridges 27

50

To Sacramento

Pyramid Creek

50

To South Lake Tahoe

Pyramid Creek cascades down a slab at trailside.

Cairns dot the slabs above the creek drainage, leading down to the Pyramid Creek cataract. An excellent destination in and of itself, the cataract races down a low–angle slab, jumping or sliding depending on the flow. It can be enjoyed from perches on the neighboring granite shelves. From the cataract head down to the right, following the easiest route to the trail junction at the base of the slab. From the junction retrace your steps to the trailhead.

Miles and Directions

0.0 Start at the trailhead behind the restroom.

0.2 Pass a slab overlooking a small cascade.

0.5 Reach the base of a steep granite slab. Stay left toward the wilderness boundary, and then angle right and pick your way up the slab. The Pyramid Creek Trail (the return route) breaks to the far right.

1.1 At the trail junction, stay left (straight). The right-hand path along Pyramid Creek is the return route.

1.3 Arrive at Pyramid Creek, the end of the formal trail and the turnaround point. Retrace your steps from here to the Pyramid Creek Trail junction.

1.5 At the Pyramid Creek Trail junction, go left.

2.0 Reach the cataract. Continue down the granite to the first junction at the base of the steep slab. Retrace your steps from here.

2.5 Arrive back at the trailhead.

28 Bassi Falls

A short hike leads to a welcoming expanse of sunny slabs below the stairstep drop of Bassi Falls.

Height: About 110 feet

Beauty rating: ★★★★

Start: Trailhead on Upper Bassi Road

Distance: 1.2 miles out and back

Difficulty: Easy

Hiking time: About 1.5 hours

Seasons/schedule: Year-round; sunrise to sunset. Winter snow and cold may preclude a comfortable hike.

Fees and permits: None

Trail contact: Eldorado National Forest, Forest Supervisor's Office, 100 Forni Rd., Placerville,

CA 95667; (530) 622-5061; www.fs.usda .gov/main/eldorado/home

Canine compatibility: Leashed dogs permitted.

Trail surface: Dirt, granite

Land status: Eldorado National Forest

Nearest town: Strawberry

Other trail users: Cyclists, equestrians

Map to consult: USGS Loon Lake CA

Water availability: None

Amenities available: None

Cell service: None

Trail conditions: This trail is rough and remote.

Finding the trailhead: From Placerville drive about 21 miles east on US 50 to the Ice House Road turnoff, which is right before a bridge sweeping over the South Fork American River. Turn left onto Ice House Road and drive 16.1 miles, across the Silver Creek bridge, to the junction with the access road to Big Silver Group Camp on the left and Bassi Road on the right. Turn right onto Bassi Road. Go 0.2 mile to a left turn onto Upper Bassi Road/FR 12N32A, which is signed "Bassi Falls Access." This road is best navigated with a high-clearance vehicle, though passenger cars can make it to the trailhead, which is 1.5 miles up the dirt track. If the road is too slick or bumpy to drive, you can walk the dirt track to the trailhead. Parking is limited at the trailhead and in pullouts; do not block the narrow roadway. Trailhead GPS (Upper Bassi Road access): N38 52.960' / W120 21.520'

The Hike

Located on the Bassi Fork of Big Silver Creek, Bassi Falls spills into a channel on a rolling terrace of granite open to the sun and sky. The surrounding ridges are shaded with ponderosa pine and incense cedar, which also hide the reservoirs—Ice House and Union Valley—that draw visitors to this remote locale on the western slope of the Sierra Nevada. A scattering of cedar and pine also finds purchase on the rocky borders of the waterfall, which arcs down a broken cliff face before disappearing into the boulders at its base.

The hike is mostly upside down and relatively easy, rolling first through a parklike woodland of evergreens and scattered alder. Where the woods end and the slabs begin, the roar of the falls overtakes the whisper of wind through the treetops. Stay left on the slabs, following the sound and rock cairns marking the way. A dike of paler granite runs down toward the creek, evoking a massive, almost ruler-straight concrete foundation.

Broad slabs spread below Bassi Falls and alongside the mellowing creek.

The top of the falls is visible from the upper slabs and is lost to view as you near the base. Depending on the time of year, water may puddle in depressions on the slabs

or flow briskly through depressions seeking to rejoin the creek. But mostly the slabs are open and sun-warmed, inviting exploration and relaxation.

Return as you came. It's mostly uphill, and route finding across the slabs may get tricky. Follow the cairns, and when in doubt, look right.

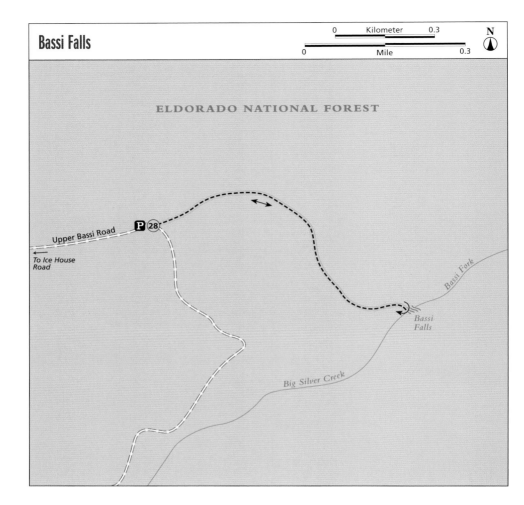

Miles and Directions

0.0 Begin by climbing a few steps from the parking area onto the trail and into the woods.

0.3 The woods open onto the granite slabs.

0.6 Reach the base of the falls near the Big Silver Creek channel. Check it all out, then retrace your steps.

1.2 Arrive back at the trailhead.

Option: If the parking area at the trailhead is full, or if you don't want to take on the bumpy dirt access road in a passenger vehicle, you can walk from additional parking areas located near the start of the Bassi Falls access road. A hike on the road, mostly in the woods and gently ascending to the trailhead, will add about 3 miles round-trip.

29 Hot Springs Creek Falls

An easy walk through the woods ends with a mildly challenging scramble to waterfall overlooks. Not to be missed: the park's hot springs pool and its unbeatable views.

Height: 50 feet
Beauty rating: ★★★★★
Start: Burnside Lake Trailhead at the end of the campground road
Distance: 3.5 miles out and back
Difficulty: Easy
Hiking time: About 2 hours
Seasons/schedule: Year-round; sunrise to sunset. Winter snow and cold may preclude a comfortable hike.
Fees and permits: An entrance fee is charged.
Trail contact: Grover Hot Springs State Park, PO Box 188, Markleeville, CA 96120; (530) 694-2248 (park office), (530) 694-2249 (hot springs pool); www.parks.ca.gov
Canine compatibility: Leashed dogs permitted.
Trail surface: Dirt

Land status: Grover Hot Springs State Park; Toiyabe National Forest
Nearest town: Markleeville
Other trail users: Cyclists
Maps to consult: USGS Markleeville CA; park map available online or in park brochure
Water availability: Water is available in the park.
Amenities available: There's only a parking lot at the trailhead, but restrooms, information, trash cans, and camping facilities can be found in Grover Hot Springs State Park.
Cell service: Maybe, but don't count on it.
Trail conditions: The Tamarack Fire burned through the park in 2021. While the Burnside Lake (waterfall) Trail has been resurfaced, watch for hazards such as fallen trees and hidden stump holes, and check with rangers about trail conditions before your hike.

Finding the trailhead: From the Y junction of CA 89 and US 50 in South Lake Tahoe, follow US 50 west for 4.5 miles to the junction with CA 89 in Meyers. Turn left onto CA 89 and drive 10.9 miles to where CA 89 and CA 88 meet. Turn left onto CA 89/88 and drive 5.7 miles to Woodford. Turn right onto CA 89 and continue 6.3 miles to Markleeville. Turn right onto Hot Springs Road and continue to Grover Hot Springs State Park. Parking is available in the day-use area near the campground entrance station; this is best for off-season access. In season follow the campground road to its end in the trailhead parking area. Trailhead GPS (entrance station): N38 41.722' / W119 50.227'

The Hike

Before the Tamarack Fire blew through in early summer 2021, this out-of-the-way hike led through quintessential Sierran woodland bordering a classic mountain meadow to a waterfall that flowed year-round. Conditions have changed, but recovery in the burn scar is underway, and thankfully the iconic meadow and the rejuvenating hot spring pools survived the blaze. Given its remoteness, Grover Hot Springs hasn't been a top destination on the bucket lists of hikers, but even after the fire, it should be.

Mineral-infused hot spring water pools adjacent to the broad meadow at Grover Hot Springs.

The park has a relatively typical western mountain history. First came the Washoe, who hunted and gathered in the lovely alpine valley in the summer months. Historians believe explorer John Frémont traveled through on one of his treks through the Sierra Nevada. Then came emigrant homesteaders, including John Hawkins, who, according to park literature, used the hot springs water to fortify a bath on his ranch,

It may slow to a trickle at season's end, but Hot Springs Creek Falls runs year-round.

and later Alvin Grover, who built the hot springs pool on the site, as well as a hotel in the nearby high-country village of Markleeville.

The water feeding the hot springs—snowmelt filtered down through fractures in the earth to a hot spot, and then regurgitated at a scalding 148°F—seeps from the slopes above the pools and burbles from a font on the edge of the meadow. Fortified

Hot Springs Creek Falls

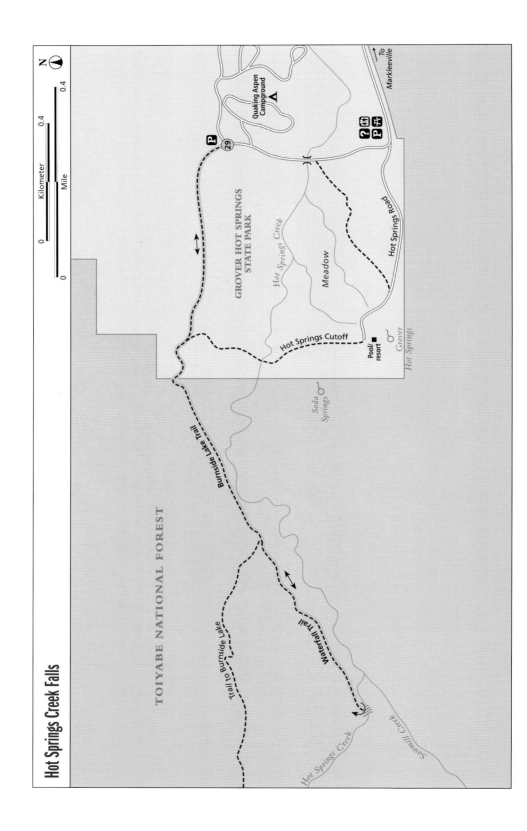

N

Kilometer

0   0.4   0.4

Mile

0   0.4

TOIYABE NATIONAL FOREST

Burnside Lake Trail

Trail to Burnside Lake

Waterfall Trail

Hot Springs Creek

Sawmill Creek

GROVER HOT SPRINGS
STATE PARK

Hot Springs Creek

Meadow

Quaking Aspen
Campground

P

29

Hot Springs Cutoff

Pool/
resort

Soda
Springs

Grover
Hot Springs

Hot Springs Road

To
Markleeville

with sodium and a plethora of other minerals, but mostly lacking sulfur (responsible for the off-putting rotten-egg smell of many hot springs), the water is tempered and funneled into a soaking pool maintained at between 102° and 104°F. Aaahhh. A lap pool heated by hot springs water via a heat exchanger is also available.

The Burnside Lake Trail, for the most part, is wide enough for hikers to walk two abreast upon a flat, meandering walk-and-talk path that offers views onto the wide Hot Springs meadow to the left. The trail was rehabilitated in 2022, so route finding should be easy, though falling trees and other fire-related hazards may persist for years. Several trail junctions serve as landmarks and options, but the main route heads straight into the narrowing canyon where the waterfall flows.

At the 1-mile mark, alongside Hot Springs Creek, take a left onto the narrower Waterfall Trail, which rolls through gullies as it heads upstream. Rocky ridges that burned in the Tamarack Fire frame the sky on three sides. The well-defined trail ends in a jumble of rocks and slabs below the falls, becoming a web of footpaths that leads through boulders to the falls themselves. It's a minor route-finding challenge and, depending on how you proceed, may demand some hands-on scrambling. But all routes lead to the falls, which in high water spill down a rock face more than 100 feet across, and in low water (or drought) trickle down the stairsteps in slender splashes. Platforms on the rocks and below the trees offer great vantage points. Retrace your steps to the trailhead.

Miles and Directions

0.0   Start on the wide, obvious path heading left from the trailhead parking area.

0.25 At the first trail Y, stay left, following the Burnside Lake/Waterfall Trail.

0.4   Pass a trail marker and cross a side stream.

0.5   At the signed trail junction, stay straight on the trail to Burnside Lake. The left turn is the Hot Springs Cutoff.

0.9   The trail swings alongside Hot Springs Creek.

1.0   At the junction with the Waterfall Trail, go left. A right turn leads to Burnside Lake.

1.5   Start the scramble up and around rock faces to reach the falls overlook.

1.75 Reach the falls. Retrace your steps.

3.5   Arrive back at the trailhead.

Option: Honestly, I'd say this is more mandatory than an option. Granted, the hot springs pools may be crowded in high season, but the setting couldn't be more lovely, and a good soak after a good hike—well, let's just call that bliss. The hike isn't so long that you can't tote a suit and towel in your pack, and branching off from the waterfall route to the hot springs pool leads across a meadow that glows with color: green in spring, white in winter, golden in fall. To reach the pools from the Waterfall Trail (on the return), head right on the Hot Springs Cutoff. Cross the bridge over the creek at the midpoint and then climb gently to the pool parking area. A fee is charged, but it's well worth the price. Return to the trailhead via Hot Springs Road. Total mileage for this lollipop is about 3.7 miles.

Honorable Mentions

Fern Falls

This cascade is not a destination in and of itself, but the short hike to Fern Falls is easy to check off while exploring other waterfalls in the Lakes Basin Recreation Area. The 35-foot spill is more of a cataract—a series of small drops on a stream not far off the Gold Lake Highway. The short walk to the cascade is pleasant, the setting is pretty, and the rock outcroppings beside the creek are particularly inviting when bathed in sunshine. Reaching the cascade is straightforward. From the parking area drop into the woods and cross the footbridge. The trail arcs right and downstream on the far side. Follow the winding path alongside the cataracts to where it peters out at the rim of the Gray Eagle Creek drainage. The large paved pullout and signed trailhead is about 6 miles up the Gold Lake Highway from Graeagle.

Sunny slabs border Fern Falls in the Lakes Basin Recreation Area.

Webber Falls

A hike and scramble lead to this out-of-the-way, two-tiered fall on the Little Truckee River north of Lake Tahoe. At the falls the angler-friendly Little Truckee puts on a fierce face, bunching up in a narrowing canyon and then diving over broken basalt cliffs in a narrow gorge. The first plunge is shorter—maybe 25 feet—and the second plunge is about 50 feet high.

To reach the falls from Truckee, follow CA 89 north for about 14.5 miles to the signed junction for Jackson Meadows Road/Bear Valley Road. Turn left onto Jackson Meadows Road (also labeled FR 07) and then sharply left again to stay on FR 07. Follow the graded gravel forest road for 6.6 miles, past the junction with the signed dirt road to Lake of the Woods, to a small pullout on the left. From the pullout, pass the boulders blocking vehicle access to the unused dirt road and follow the road around a switchback. Cross a clearing and head down to the canyon's edge; use the sound of the waterfall as your guide. You'll see the falls as soon as you clear the woods. Pick one of the social trails that drops toward the river, and take care on the descent as the footing is loose and the slope steeply pitched.

The Little Truckee River gets a little tricky at Webber Falls.

Big Springs Falls is a roadside attraction along CA 49 in the north Sierra.

Big Springs Falls

The massive pullout on the north side of CA 49 about 1.5 miles south of Bassetts Station and the Gold Lake Highway junction would be an eye-catcher in itself, but the waterfall that sprawls across the mountainside is what pulls people off the highway. Big Springs Falls, with its dedication plaque and ease of access, is a magnet for pictures and for those seeking a break as they descend out of the Sierra into the foothills toward Downieville. The source is in the private Big Springs Gardens.

Sapped by drought, Bridal Veil Falls dribbles down a rock face off US 50.

Bridal Veil Falls

This waterfall, located on US 50 between South Lake Tahoe and Placerville, is easy to check off before or after visits to its nearest neighbors, Bassi Falls and Horsetail Falls. A bit more than 80 feet high, the falls are a burst of white and wet in the otherwise deep green of the South Fork American River canyon. They make a nice stop along the historic highway, which originated as part of an emigrant trail during the California gold rush and also served as part of the Pony Express route. To reach the pullout from Placerville, drive east on US 50 for about 18 miles; the Bridal Veil picnic area is located 0.4 mile to the east.

Gold Country

California's path to statehood began in the foothills of the Sierra Nevada in 1848 with the discovery of gold west of Sacramento. Nearly every waterfall trail in this region has gold rush history, whether it follows a former flume or connects two former mining boomtowns. Auburn anchors the area, with significant satellites in Nevada City, Grass Valley, and Colfax. The main east–west thoroughfares are I–80 and US 50, with CA 49 and CA 20 serving as significant (and scenic) secondary roads.

The trail to Bear River Falls leads through a foothills woodland bright with color in autumn.

30 Shingle Falls

A pleasant loop through rolling woodlands in the foothills east of Marysville ends at a waterfall and swimming hole on Dry Creek.

Height: 70 feet

Beauty rating: ★★★★

Start: The trailhead at the old stone bridge in the Spenceville Wildlife Area

Distance: 5.2-mile lollipop

Difficulty: Moderate

Hiking time: About 3 hours

Seasons/schedule: Year-round, sunrise to sunset

Fees and permits: None

Trail contact: Spenceville Wildlife Area, California Department of Fish and Wildlife, 945 Oro Dam Blvd. West, Oroville, CA 95965; (530) 538-2236; www.wildlife.ca.gov/Lands/Places-to-Visit/Spenceville-WA

Canine compatibility: Leashed dogs permitted.

Trail surface: Dirt service road and singletrack

Land status: Spenceville Wildlife Area

Nearest towns: Yuba City; Marysville

Other trail users: Cyclists, equestrians, hunters in season

Maps to consult: USGS Camp Far West CA, and Wolf CA; online at www.wildlife.ca.gov/Lands/Places-to-Visit/Spenceville-WA

Water availability: None

Amenities available: None

Cell service: None

Trail conditions: The route is well maintained and remote. Hunting is allowed in the Spenceville Wildlife Area from Sept 1 to Jan 31, and the wildlife area is closed to all users except special turkey permit holders during the first 9 days of the spring turkey season. The spring turkey season opens on the last Saturday in March. If hiking in hunting season, be sure to wear bright colors, such as blaze orange.

Finding the trailhead: From Sacramento head north on I-5 to CA 99. Continue north on CA 99 for about 12 miles to CA 70. Make a slight right onto northbound CA 70 toward Marysville. Travel another 22 miles to the Feather River Road exit off CA 70. Go right (east) on Feather River Road to the first intersection and then right again onto North Beale Road. Travel 0.2 mile to a signalized arterial and go left to continue on North Beale Road. Go another 0.8 mile on North Beale to Hammonton-Smartville Road. Go left on Hammonton-Smartville Road, staying right at the signalized Y intersection with Simpson Lane, which leads to downtown Marysville. Drive for about 15 miles to the intersection with Chuck Yeager Road. Go right on Chuck Yeager Road for about 4 miles to Waldo Road. Go left on Waldo Road, a graded dirt road, for nearly 2 miles, across the single-lane bridge, to Waldo Junction and the intersection with Spenceville Road. Go left on Spenceville Road, traveling about 2.3 miles to the parking area on the left, past the camping area and near the road's end. The trailhead is at the yellow gate at the old stone bridge. Trailhead GPS: N39 06.824' / W121 16.245'

The Hike

I've gone with calling this Shingle Falls, deferring to the US Geological Survey, but this waterfall is identified as Fairy Falls on trail signs and as Beale Falls or Dry Creek Falls in some printed and online guides. Being "also known as" may create some

Shingle Falls finishes by plunging into a punchbowl.

confusion, but no matter the name, the falls are a stunning destination, a stairstep spill into a punchbowl that runs year-round, though fullest in spring when swollen with snowmelt or after rainstorms. The second drop is the longest, a 50-foot plunge into a dark pool. The inkwell gives the impression of bottomlessness, which makes it as mysterious as the falls are invigorating.

A linkage of well-maintained wildlife-area service roads, perfect in width and grade for family or group outings, and an engaging singletrack lead to the falls. A web of social paths connects the main trail to the overlook at the top of the falls and to the creek below the spill, where a swimming hole awaits. These smaller trails may be challenging in steepness and footing, especially for little ones, but standing at the overlook and watching the whitewater dive into the inkwell is ample reward for the effort.

The trail begins at the site of the Spenceville mine, crossing the stone bridge over Dry Creek and heading right at the fence line on the dirt roadway. Cross two smaller bridges, then follow the road up into the hills, avoiding a pair of side trails that diverge in the first half mile. Beyond these junctions the route is straightforward and marked with signs for the falls, leaving little chance to stray.

After a long, gentle climb, with scattered oaks offering dollops of shade, the trail hooks sharply right at a gate (a sign may point the way, though signs may be missing due to vandalism). Pass a second gate and then climb through a sloping meadow, with views stretching down into the Dry Creek drainage and north across rolling pasture-land into the foothills.

A cattle guard spans the road at the hilltop. You have a choice here: You can follow either the trail to the right or the road beyond the cattle guard to the left. Both meet within sight at the edge of the woods. At the second trail junction, you have another choice: The described route heads up on singletrack into the oaks and returns via the roadway to the right. The road may be signed for Upper Falls and the trail for Fairy Falls, but the falls are one and the same. The trail climbing into the woodland is described, but following the road out and back is a great option too.

The singletrack is mildly challenging, with occasional downed trees forcing hikers onto social trails that bypass the obstacles. It dips through several drainages and then traverses a grassy hillside before hitching up with the dirt roadway. Go left on the road paralleling Dry Creek, now rollicking in its rock-bottomed bed through a

A RECLAMATION SUCCESS STORY

For more than fifty years, copper and other mineral resources were removed from the Spenceville mine. The site was also used during World War II for military training, including bombing and strafing. After the mine/training site became part of the Spenceville Wildlife Area in the late 1960s, the California Department of Fish and Wildlife (DFW) and the California Department of Conservation (DOC) worked to reclaim the land so that its residual toxicity would not pose significant danger to the fish populations in Dry Creek or threaten the well-being of other critters in the area, including humans. The result is what you see today: Essentially nothing remains of the mine except stone bridges that aid stream crossings at the Shingle Falls trailhead, a chain-link fence, and low-key signage noting closed areas. The mitigation was so successful that the DOC earned the Governor's Environmental and Economic Leadership Award for its work.

As with other wildlife areas under the purview of the DFW, hunting and fishing are permitted in the area, as is grazing. The terrain is ideal for both. Rolling hills support a healthy blue oak–gray pine woodland, home to deer and other game. Open meadows provide ample forage for cattle. The grasslands are mostly cropped close, but where they aren't (and even after they've been grazed), wildflowers bloom in profusion. Encompassing almost 12,000 acres, the wildlife area offers plenty of space for all users to enjoy.

Shingle Falls

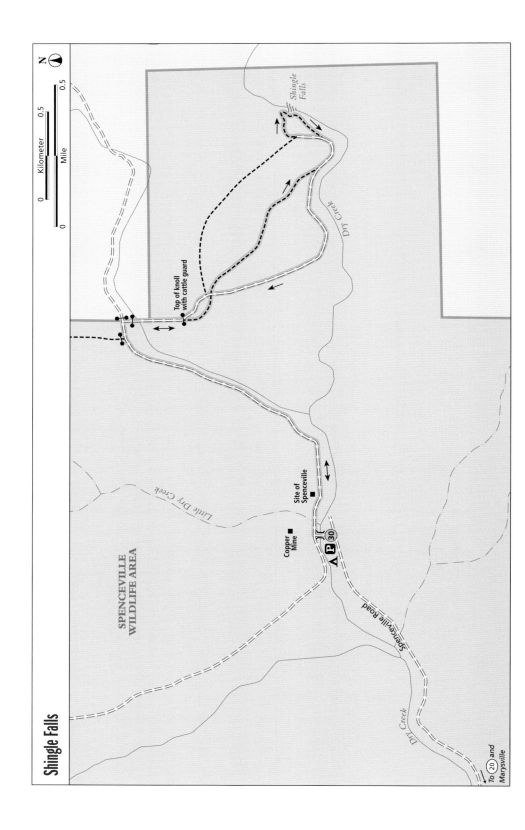

SPENCEVILLE
WILDLIFE AREA

Little Dry Creek

Copper
Mine

Site of
Spenceville

Dry Creek

Top of knoll
with cattle guard

Dry Creek

Shingle
Falls

Spenceville Road

To 20 and
Marysville

N

0   0.5   Kilometer   0.5

0   Mile

riparian corridor thick with brambles, poison oak, and maples that fire yellow and orange in late fall.

After passing a streamside clearing, the roadway hitches uphill. A use trail breaks right just before a gate, offering access to a large swimming hole fed by two short falls, each no higher than 3 feet.

A web of steep and winding use trails climbs the hillside between the swimming hole and Shingle Falls proper. The paths merge onto a narrow track running alongside rickety fencing that separates hikers from the 100-foot drop into the steep-walled chasm below the falls. Take care to stay well away from the edges. Though a long jump into the dark chocolate waters of the inkwell may look inviting to an adventurous soul, it's better to approach from below and simply observe from above.

To vary the return, stick to the road on the way back to the trailhead. Stay left where the trail meets the singletrack path you descended and make a gentle climb back to the upper trail junction and then to the cattle guard on the hilltop. From there, retrace your steps to the trailhead.

Miles and Directions

0.0 Start by crossing the stone bridge with the gate. On the far side of the bridge, turn right and follow the dirt roadway over two smaller bridges.

0.1 Pass a singletrack trail behind a gate on the left. Stay right on the gravel road.

0.5 At the unsigned junction, stay left on the roadway. The right-hand path drops into a blackberry hedge.

1.2 At the first gate, go right. Pass a second gate and head up through the meadow.

1.5 Reach a cattle guard and go right on the trail. You can also follow the roadway down to the next trail junction.

1.7 At the five-way junction, a trail sign may indicate that Fairy Falls is 1 mile ahead via a singletrack path and that Upper Falls is 0.9 mile distant via the roadway. Take the singletrack trail.

2.2 The trail ends on the dirt road. Go left on the broad track.

2.4 Take the well-worn use trail that breaks right, toward the creek, just before a gate. This leads down to the swimming hole.

2.6 Wander up social trails to the falls overlook. Check out the falls and punchbowl. To return, retrace your steps to the junction with the singletrack you descended on. Stay left on the gravel roadway, working up to the cattle guard on the hilltop. From here retrace your steps.

5.2 Arrive back at the trailhead.

31 Rush Creek Falls

The fabulous, accessible trail that led to the wooden flume/bridge overlooking Rush Creek Falls was damaged by wildfire in 2020, but plans are afoot to rebuild.

Height: About 100 feet

Beauty rating: ★ ★ ★ ★ ★

Start: The Independence Trailhead above the South Yuba River

Distance: 2.2 miles out and back

Difficulty: Easy

Hiking time: About 2 hours

Seasons/schedule: Year-round; sunrise to sunset

Fees and permits: None

Trail contact: South Yuba River State Park, 17660 Pleasant Valley Rd., Penn Valley, CA 95946; (530) 432-2546; www.parks.ca.gov

Canine compatibility: Leashed dogs permitted.

Trail surface: Dirt singletrack, stairs

Land status: South Yuba River State Park

Nearest towns: Nevada City and Grass Valley

Other trail users: None

Maps to consult: USGS Nevada City CA; map in park brochure available online

Water availability: None

Amenities available: Restrooms, trash cans, and information signboard

Cell service: Marginal; don't count on it.

Trail conditions: As of fall 2022 the trail remained closed due to damage from wildfire. Check with rangers at nearby Empire Mines State Historic Park to get the latest on trail status.

Finding the trailhead: From CA 20 in Nevada City, take the CA 49 exit. Go north on CA 49 for 7 miles, dropping into the South Yuba River drainage. The parking area is a pullout on the right side of the highway, signed for the Independence Trail. If you reach the bridge spanning the river, you've gone too far. Trailhead GPS: N39 17.493' / W121 05.842'

The Hike

This was once a remarkable, well-maintained, accessible trail—and it will be again. But two years after the 2020 Jones Fire destroyed much of the infrastructure along the portion of the trail that led to Rush Creek Falls, including the historic flume that overlooked the 100-foot cascade, the trail remained closed. The Bear Yuba Land Trust, along with California State Parks, plans to rebuild and rehabilitate the trail. Learn more about the effort by visiting the land trust site at www.bylt.org/rebuild-independence-trail.

Before the fire the flumes incorporated into the Independence Trail West in the South Yuba River Canyon were part of a system of hundreds of miles of wooden or earthen channels built in the late 1800s and early 1900s to move water from rivers and streams to mining and logging camps in the Sierra Nevada. The declines of the channels were typically gentle so flows could be controlled, and paths ran alongside so that miners and loggers could maintain the flumes and, in the case of those built to help transport lumber, clear logjams. Long fallen into disuse, these relics serve as crumbling reminders of California's gold rush boom times.

The historic flume that once spanned the top of Rush Creek Falls was destroyed by fire in 2020.

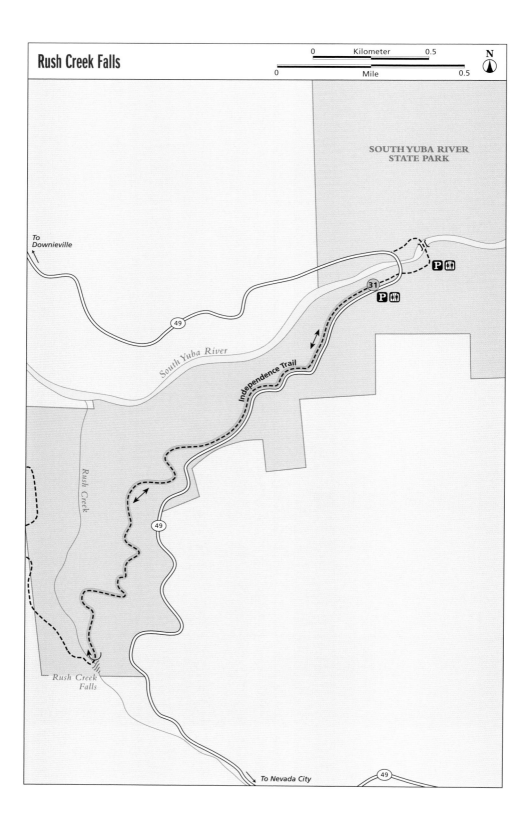

Rush Creek Falls

0   Kilometer   0.5

0   Mile   0.5

N

SOUTH YUBA RIVER
STATE PARK

To
Downieville

49

South Yuba River

Independence Trail

31

P

P

Rush Creek

49

Rush Creek
Falls

To Nevada City

49

But they also serve as the foundations for recreational trails. The stretch of the Independence Trail between CA 49 and Rush Creek Falls was a former mining ditch that funneled water out of the South Yuba River for use in hydraulic mining operations. It was transformed into a first-class trail by any standard, but was even more impressive for the fact that it was accessible, outfitted with ramps, benches, and railings thoughtfully constructed not only for ease of use but also so that they blended seamlessly into the surrounding oak woodland.

As with other trails in fire zones, this one will likely follow the same path once it's rehabilitated, but in this case the historic flumes can't be restored. The trail begins at the uphill end of the stone retaining wall in the parking pullout on CA 49. It passes under the highway through a low-ceilinged tunnel and then winds along the mountainside above the South Yuba. The route was two-tiered, with a wider path below (in the bed of the ditch) and a narrower path riding the low berm on the canyon side; the two were connected in a few places by footpaths and short wooden staircases. Footbridges and ramps eased passage when needed, and a number of overlooks and benches were installed.

The main attraction for waterfall seekers was the flume curling through the Rush Creek drainage, suspended on the hillside by a string of wooden support beams, with the waterfall flowing part of the span. On the west side of the creek, a switchbacking ramp offered access to picnic sites at the head of the waterfall. As for the fall itself, water cascades in tiers for more than 100 feet before being lost to sight in the overgrown gorge below. Views open north and west of the ridges of the western slope of the river canyon and down toward the South Yuba itself.

Miles and Directions

0.0 Start at the uphill end of the retaining wall in the parking area, and go right on the Independence Trail, passing through the tunnel.

0.2 Pass the junction with the Jones Bar Trail, which departs to the right. Stay left on the Independence Trail.

1.1 Reach the site of the curving flume spanning Rush Creek Falls that was destroyed by fire. The falls are the turnaround point. Retrace your steps.

2.2 Arrive back at the trailhead.

Options: Continue down CA 49 for 0.5 mile to the South Yuba River bridge. A large parking area/trailhead is on the south side of the bridge, outfitted with restrooms, trash cans, and information signboards. A short walk down to the river leads to the South Yuba's historic rainbow arch bridge, built in the 1920s. The lovely structure now serves as a pedestrian bridge; the vehicular bridge just downstream, built in 1993, mimics the design. Picnic sites are available, as is the Hoyt's Crossing Trail, which climbs upstream on the north side of the river. But the highlight is the river: Stand on the bridge and watch the South Yuba crash through the huge boulders in its bed, green and white and furiously playful.

32 Little Humbug Creek Falls

Malakoff Diggins State Historic Park offers provocative evidence of the damage wrought by hydraulic mining in the Sierra Nevada, while the falls on Little Humbug Creek display the power of natural hydraulics.

Height: About 150 feet
Beauty rating: ★★★★★
Start: The Humbug Trailhead
Distance: 3.2 miles out and back
Difficulty: Moderate
Hiking time: About 2 hours
Seasons/schedule: Year-round; sunrise to sunset
Fees and permits: An entrance fee is charged.
Trail contact: Malakoff Diggins State Historic Park, 23579 N. Bloomfield Rd., Nevada City, CA 95959; (530) 265-2740; www.parks.ca.gov. Sierra Gold Parks Foundation; www.sierragold-parksfoundation.org.
Canine compatibility: Leashed dogs permitted.
Trail surface: Dirt service road and singletrack

Land status: Malakoff Diggins State Historic Park
Nearest towns: North Bloomfield (small); Nevada City and Grass Valley
Other trail users: None
Maps to consult: USGS North Bloomfield CA; park map available at the museum/visitor center and online
Water availability: Water is available in North Bloomfield.
Amenities available: None at the trailhead. A museum, restrooms, trash cans, and picnic facilities are in North Bloomfield.
Cell service: None
Trail conditions: This route is well maintained and remote.

Finding the trailhead: From Nevada City, follow CA 49 north from its junction with CA 20, toward Downieville, for 10.5 miles. Turn right onto Tyler-Foote Crossing Road, marked with a Malakoff Diggins State Historic Park sign. Follow the paved road for 15 miles; the name will change to Cruzon Grade and then to Backbone. When the double yellow line ends, turn right onto Derbec Road and proceed about 1 mile to North Bloomfield Road. Turn right onto North Bloomfield Road and drive 1.5 miles, past the Chute Hill Campground, to historic North Bloomfield and park headquarters. The Humbug Trailhead is about 1.5 miles farther along North Bloomfield Road.

Alternatively, weather permitting, you can get to the trailhead using graded gravel roads. From the junction of CA 20 and CA 49, head north on CA 49 for 0.3 mile to North Bloomfield Road. Go right onto North Bloomfield Road, and at the T-junction go right again, staying on North Bloomfield Road toward South Yuba River State Park. Stay on North Bloomfield Road for 8.1 winding miles, to the bottom of the river canyon at Edwards Crossing, across the bridge, and then up to a junction. Stay right again on North Bloomfield Road and continue to a second signed junction, again staying right on North Bloomfield Road to Malakoff Diggins State Historic Park. Continue for 2.5 miles to the park boundary. The Humbug Creek parking area is 3.3 miles from the last junction. This route may be closed in winter due to snow. Trailhead GPS: N39 21.920' / W120 55.409'

Runoff from the diggings uphill color the water ▶
that pools at Little Humbug Creek Falls.

The Hike

Malakoff Diggins State Historic Park lies well off the beaten path but is worth the travel time and effort. It preserves a swath of gorgeous foothills country, a secluded waterfall, and the remnants of some remarkable gold rush history.

The centerpiece of the park is the diggings. The cliffs of the mining pit, the legacy of a massive hydraulic mining operation that thrived in the late 1800s, are a colorful exclamation point in the midst of the heavy greens of the surrounding pines and firs, orange fading to peach fading to cream from top to bottom. A path leads through the pit, which is slowly being reclaimed by evergreens. Other paths explore historic North Bloomfield, the company town that grew up around the mining operation.

Little Humbug Creek Falls, reached via a long downhill run through shady ravines, is a hydraulic exclamation point of an entirely different kind. Here the relentless passage of water over time has created a natural feature. Its power reinforced annually by snowmelt, Humbug Creek begins its fall by plunging from pool to pool and then is shot as if from a flume down a relatively low-angled cliff. The force of the water

THE LEGACY OF HYDRAULIC MINING

In the mid-1800s, after gold was discovered in the foothills surrounding Nevada City, miners flooded into the region, some building a camp/town called Humbug (later North Bloomfield). When the placer gold, easily panned from rivers and creeks, played out, enterprising argonauts turned to more radical methods, carving a pit and cliff into the mountainside using a powerful, destructive new mining technique: They trained water cannons on the mountainside, blasting ore and everything else into the diggings, and making a nice profit in the process.

But hydraulic mining had a huge environmental downside, creating massive tailings piles and thousands of cubic feet of debris, some of which continued downstream into the Humbug Creek drainage, then down into the South Yuba River, then into the Sacramento River, and on into San Francisco Bay. Accumulations of silt hampered navigation in the bay and surrounding rivers and led to the flooding of towns in the lowlands. After Marysville was devastated by flood in 1875, a lawsuit was filed against the North Bloomfield Gravel Mining Company, which operated at Malakoff Diggins. Judge Lorenzo Sawyer handed down an injunction against hydraulic mining in that case, essentially rendering the practice unprofitable. The Sawyer legislation led to the shuttering of operations of the North Bloomfield Gravel Mining Company.

The history is horrific by modern ecological standards, but in the wake of the massive mining operations at the site, a provocative and strangely beautiful landscape has emerged. Nature is reclaiming the diggings slowly but surely, and the message is powerful. What humankind creates is impermanent—wilderness will always win.

has sculpted the rock face and etched a thin channel that partially hides the flow. A platform about midway down the steep hillside next to the fall offers a safe viewpoint, with cables protecting the steep, rocky path above and below.

The Humbug Trail begins by crossing a tributary of Humbug Creek via a footbridge and then curling alongside the stream through a dark, dense woodland of second-growth pines. The needle-coated, moderately graded trail passes several mining pits as it drops, one bleeding an unnaturally vivid orange runoff.

Negotiate several steep descents (and ascents) through ravines, crossing the feeder streams by rock-hopping or wading, and then the route merges with an unmaintained roadway. Continue downhill on the walk-and-talk track. At the base of the decline, pass a big pit on the left, cross a streamlet, and continue on the hikers-only path. The trail becomes a winding singletrack beyond, rounding switchbacks and descending steeply over rocky terrain to the waterfall and its overlook. Check out the fall, with its slots and pools, and then return as you came.

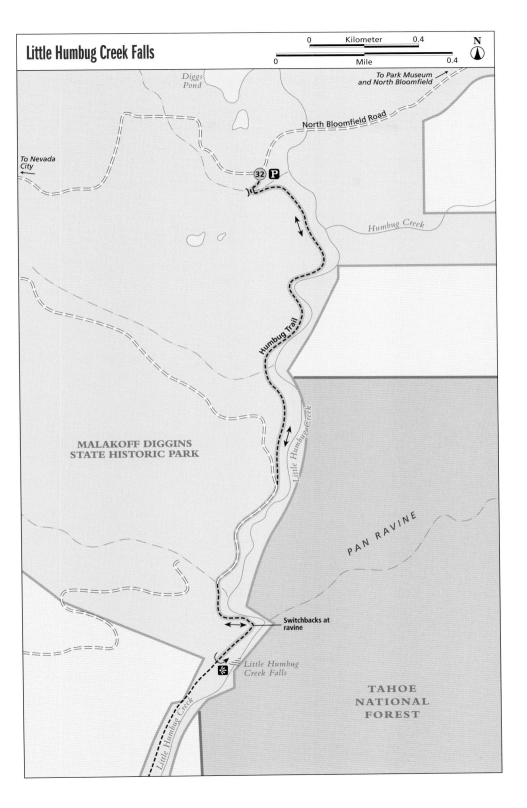

Little Humbug Creek Falls

0 Kilometer 0.4

0 Mile 0.4

N

Diggs Pond

To Park Museum and North Bloomfield

North Bloomfield Road

To Nevada City

32 P

Humbug Creek

Humbug Trail

Little Humbug Creek

MALAKOFF DIGGINS STATE HISTORIC PARK

PAN RAVINE

Switchbacks at ravine

Little Humbug Creek Falls

Little Humbug Creek

TAHOE NATIONAL FOREST

Miles and Directions

0.0 Start by dropping across a bridge spanning a tributary of Humbug Creek. The trail curves downstream.

0.4 Pass an old pit filled with water stained an unnatural shade of orange.

0.7 Roller-coaster through a ravine, crossing a streamlet in the bottom.

1.0 Meet up with an unmaintained roadway. Continue left, heading downhill on the wide track.

1.2 At the base of the hill, cross a streamlet and continue on the hikers-only trail.

1.4 A cataract spills out of a side canyon; the trail curls sharply around a switchback, narrows, and steepens.

1.6 Reach Little Humbug Creek Falls. Descend the steep, sometimes slick trail to the platform that serves as an overlook. Retrace your steps.

3.2 Arrive back at the trailhead.

Option: The Humbug Trail continues down to the South Yuba River Trail. The round-trip distance for this strenuous upside-down hike is 5.4 miles.

33 Stevens Trail Falls

A walk in the footsteps of the forty-niners leads to a long cascade and a great overlook of the North Fork American River canyon.

Height: About 300 feet
Beauty rating: ★ ★ ★ ★
Start: Stevens Trailhead in Colfax
Distance: 3.0 miles out and back
Difficulty: Moderate
Hiking time: About 2 hours
Seasons/schedule: Year-round; sunrise to sunset. Exposed sections of the trail may be hot in summer.
Fees and permits: None
Trail contact: Bureau of Land Management, Mother Lode Field Office, 5152 Hillsdale Circle, El Dorado Hills, CA 95762; (916) 941-3101; www.blm.gov/visit/stevens-trail-trailhead
Canine compatibility: Leashed dogs permitted.

Trail surface: Dirt service road and singletrack
Land status: Bureau of Land Management
Nearest town: Colfax
Other trail users: Cyclists
Map to consult: USGS Colfax CA
Water availability: None
Amenities available: Restrooms, trash cans, and information signboards at the trailhead
Cell service: Good at the trailhead; marginal as you descend into the canyon
Trail conditions: The route is narrow and steep in sections. The parking lot may fill on weekends; if you can't find a place, park carefully along North Canyon Way.

Finding the trailhead: From I-80 westbound in Colfax, take exit 135 for Colfax/Grass Valley. Go left at the stop sign onto North Canyon Way. Follow North Canyon Way, which parallels the interstate, for 0.5 mile to the signed trailhead and parking area on the left. Trailhead GPS: N39 06.330' / W120 56.824'

The Hike

The Stevens Trail dates back to the California gold rush, built and managed as a toll road by a pair of enterprising miners, one with the surname of Stevens. The trail linked Colfax with the boomtown of Iowa Hill and was well traveled in the late 1800s. When the boom went bust, the route fell out of service—and essentially out of sight. It began its renaissance in the late 1960s when a Boy Scout from Sacramento rediscovered it. It is on the National Register of Historic Places.

The route sees a lot of traffic these days, with hikers, mountain bikers, and equestrians seeking rich vistas, fresh air, and exercise. The upside-down trek to the falls—and to the North Fork American River, if that's the goal—begins in a wash of highway noise from the interstate, which runs parallel at the start. But the noise fades as the path traverses down a slope forested in oaks, slipping across a few seasonal streams that feed a more substantial stream on the right.

The falls on Stevens Trail are best viewed from an overlook opposite Robbers Ravine.

At the base of the first descent, rock-hop across a small stream in the bed of the ravine and then bear right on the dirt road (a trail sign with an arrow may point the way). The roadway leads up into a saddle, where several dirt roadways meet. Head down and left on the singletrack that slips back into the oaks; an inconspicuous trail sign, again, may point the way.

A final descent under a shady oak canopy leads to the waterfall, which flows in tiers down the brushy cleft of Robbers Ravine. You can walk to its base or beat a path through brush and poison oak up alongside, but arguably the best place to experience the fall in all (or most) of its glory is from the substantial rock outcropping you've passed on the descent. A use trail leads out onto the layered rock of the outcropping's summit. Look north to check out the entirety of the waterfall, which begins hundreds of feet above what can be seen from the approach. Then look south and down the wooded North Fork American River canyon, hundreds of feet below, as a silver thread winds through folds of green. Return as you came.

Stevens Trail Falls

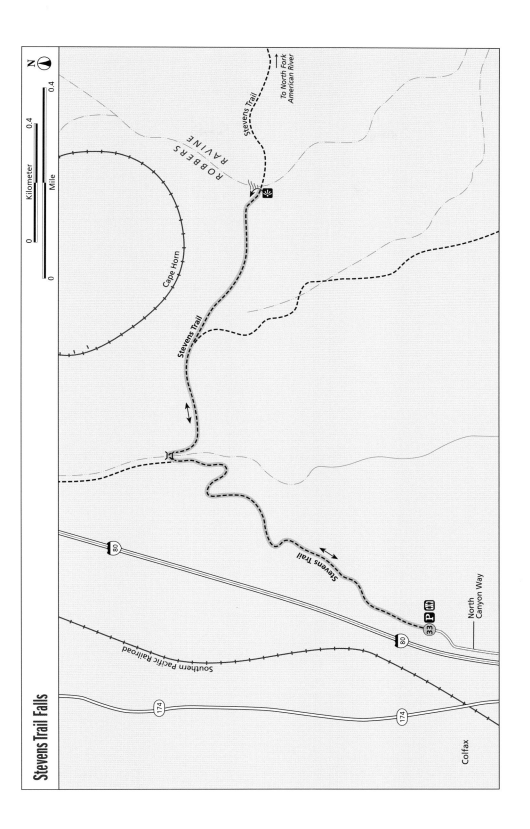

N

Kilometer
0   0.4

Mile
0   0.4

Cape Horn

ROBBERS RAVINE

Stevens Trail

Stevens Trail
To North Fork
American River

Stevens Trail

80

80

Southern Pacific Railroad

174

174

Colfax

33 P

North Canyon Way

Miles and Directions

0.0 Start on the Stevens Trail, which begins in a clearing. The path soon passes into oak wood-land, with the trees and a hillside screening the sounds of the nearby freeway.

0.8 Reach a creek crossing in the bed of a ravine. Cross either on rocks or on a narrow plank. On the far side go right, down a wide dirt road.

1.0 At the saddle where dirt roadways meet, stay left for a short distance on the road, then go left on the singletrack trail, which may have a sign.

1.3 At the Y junction, stay left on the hikers' trail. The route to the right is for cyclists.

1.5 Round a bend, and the falls come into view. Descend to the base, and then retrace your steps to a substantial rock outcropping, which offers the best waterfall views as well as views down into the North Fork American River canyon. Retrace your steps.

3.0 Arrive back at the trailhead.

Option: If time and leg power permit, you can continue downhill to the conflu-ence of the North Fork and Steep Ravine and the end of the Stevens Trail. Keep in mind that it's all uphill on the return trip. The round-trip distance is 9.0 miles, and the elevation change is about 1,200 feet. Highlights include views of Cape Horn, a radical turn in the historic Central Pacific rail line, and the remnants of gold rush–era mines, as well as the river itself.

34 Calcutta Falls

Reach these year-round falls via a rail trail that runs through the American River canyon.

Height: About 50 feet

Beauty rating: ★★★

Start: Mountain Quarries Railroad/Black Hole of Calcutta trailhead

Distance: 4.2 miles out and back

Difficulty: Easy

Hiking time: About 2.5 hours

Seasons/schedule: Year-round; sunrise to sunset

Fees and permits: None

Trail contact: Auburn State Recreation Area, 501 El Dorado St., Auburn, CA 95603-4949; (530) 885-4527; www.parks.ca.gov

Canine compatibility: Leashed dogs allowed.

Trail surface: Dirt rail trail

Land status: Auburn State Recreation Area

Nearest towns: Auburn; Cool

Other trail users: Mountain bikers, equestrians

Maps to consult: USGS Auburn CA; Auburn State Recreation Area brochure available at recreation headquarters on CA 49 and online at www.parks.ca.gov. The interpretive guide put together by the Auburn State Recreation Area Canyon Keepers is a helpful resource and is available at www.canyonkeepers.org/page5.html.

Water availability: None

Amenities available: Roadside parking; trash cans. Restrooms and information signboards are at the Stagecoach trailhead on the west side of the Old Foresthill Bridge, about 0.5 mile north of the trailhead.

Cell service: Marginal; don't bet on it.

Trail conditions: This rail trail is wide, well maintained, and relatively flat. It's also popular, so parking can be tricky. A shuttle runs from Auburn to the Confluence Area where the trailhead is located on weekends from Apr 1 to Oct 1; more information is available at www.auburn.ca.gov/585/Confluence-Route.

Finding the trailhead: From I-80 in Auburn take the CA 49 exit. Take CA 49 south through Auburn (toward Placerville), following the signs for 0.5 mile through the downtown area to where the highway plunges down into the American River canyon. CA 49 meets Old Foresthill Road at the base of the hill at 2.5 miles. Turn right (southeast), cross the bridge, and park alongside the road. The trailhead is at the gate immediately on the southeast side of the bridge. Trailhead GPS: N38 54.894' / W121 2.404'

The Hike

The trail to Calcutta Falls, also known as the Black Hole of Calcutta Falls, rolls across the historic Mountain Quarries Railroad Bridge, also known as the No Hands Bridge, and is known variously as the Calcutta Falls Trail, the Mountain Quarries Railroad Trail, and the Western States Trail. Fortunately, there's no confusing this scenic rail trail with any other below the confluence of the Middle and North Forks of the American River: It's the only one that follows the river downstream through

The trail to Calcutta Falls follows an old railroad grade across No Hands Bridge.

this lovely stretch of canyon, and Calcutta Falls, spilling down a splintered cliff, is a singular trailside attraction.

The trail follows the bed of a historic rail line that linked a limestone quarry on the Middle Fork American River with the town of Auburn and the Southern Pacific tracks that continued down into Sacramento. The No Hands Bridge is so named, according to local trail guides, because for many years it didn't have guardrails (now it does). Once the longest bridge of its kind in the world, the scenic bridge survived the collapse of the Hell Hole Dam in 1964, as well as subsequent floods, and now provides hikers with a tangible encounter with history.

Enjoyably straightforward, the trail deviates from the original rail bed only where trestles have been removed. Concrete abutments, overgrown with shrubs, are inscribed with the dates the trestles were poured—1915 and 1921. The railroad, unable to negotiate the sharp curves in the river canyon, used the trestles to straighten the line. Swinging through these folds in the terrain poses no hardship to those on foot.

Railroads, even in the mountains, had to follow gentle grades, and the Mountain Quarries line was no exception. You'll encounter only one steep set of pitches along the route, where the trail dips into a gully washed by Calcutta Falls. The year-round cascade offers a dark, cooling respite along the track. It's not very tall, but the dark

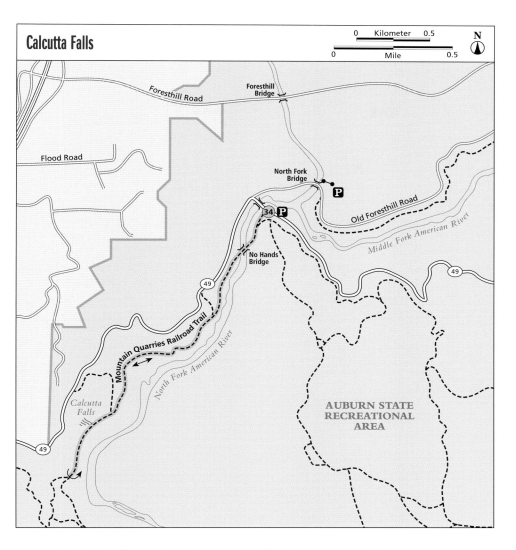

Calcutta Falls

Foresthill Road

Foresthill Bridge

Flood Road

North Fork Bridge

P

Old Foresthill Road

34 P

Middle Fork American River

No Hands Bridge

49

49

Mountain Quarries Railroad Trail

North Fork American River

Calcutta Falls

49

AUBURN STATE RECREATIONAL AREA

rock of the cliff behind is striking, and finding flowing water (other than in the river) in a landscape parched by the summer sun is refreshing.

You can turn around at the falls, but following the rail trail to its end makes for a pleasant walk and sports great views down to the river. The exposed section of trail at the base of Eagle Rock, a steep, flaking monolith with debris spilling downslope, is also striking. Side trails lead both uphill and down to the riverside, but stay straight and flat and you'll never lose your way. If there's a downside to this route, it's only that road noise from nearby CA 49 echoes in the canyon, but the scenic and historic attributes of the route mitigate the distraction. From trail's end, return as you came.

Miles and Directions

0.0 Start by passing the gate at the trailhead.

0.2 Pass the junction with the Pointed Rocks Trail (which leads up toward Cool) on the left. Go right across the No Hands (Mountain Quarries Railroad) Bridge.

0.3 Reach the west side of the No Hands Bridge and continue on the obvious rail trail. An interpretive sign at the end of the bridge offers information about its historic significance.

0.6 Pass a Western States Trail sign and a pair of side trails. Remain on the obvious rail trail.

0.8 Reach the first trestle abutment. The trail departs from the railroad grade, narrows to singletrack, and scoops through a gully.

1.0 Pass a trestle foundation dated 1915.

1.1 Reach Calcutta Falls, negotiating a steep up-and-down around the falls. You can turn around here or continue on the railroad grade, where you'll pass another Western States Trail marker.

1.3 Pass another trestle abutment. At the unmarked trail intersection, stay left on the obvious railroad grade.

1.7 Skirt Eagle Rock.

2.1 Pass a mile marker and another Western States Trail marker at the end of the railroad grade. This is the turnaround. Retrace your steps.

4.2 Arrive back at the trailhead.

OH DAM, NO!

The confluence of the North and Middle Forks of the American River occupies the bottom of a spectacular canyon long slated for submersion beneath a huge and controversial reservoir. But the proposed Auburn Dam, besieged by seismic, environmental, and economic concerns since construction began in the mid-1960s, was brought to an apparently permanent halt in late 2008 when water rights held by the US Bureau of Reclamation were revoked. If completed, the dam would have impounded the river behind a 690-foot concrete wall, and the popular trails exploring the North and Middle Forks would have been drowned. Now (hopefully) they can be enjoyed in perpetuity.

The man-made structures in the canyon near the confluence also demand attention. The green lattice arches and massive concrete support columns of the Foresthill Bridge frame the upriver stretch of the North Fork. The trail to Lake Clementine passes beneath, with the boom and clank of cars passing overhead echoing into the canyon. The high-flying bridge, reportedly the tallest in California, was built to span the reservoir that never materialized; the water would have reached as high as 22 feet below the deck once the lake was filled. More information on this bridge, and others along the route, is provided in an interpretive guide produced by the Auburn State Recreation Area Canyon Keepers.

35 Hidden Falls

A lollipop hike through Hidden Falls Regional Park leads to the headline falls, another cascade, and to an overlook of the Seven Pools.

Height: About 30 feet (Hidden Falls); 20 feet (Canyon View Falls); Seven Pools is a series of 5- to 10-foot cascades.

Beauty rating: ★★★★★

Start: Poppy Trailhead

Distance: 5.4-mile double loop to view Hidden Falls, Canyon View Falls, and the cataracts on Coon Creek

Difficulty: Moderate

Hiking time: About 3 hours

Seasons/schedule: Year-round; sunrise to sunset. Avoid hiking in the heat of a summer day—it'll suck the life out of you.

Fees and permits: An entrance/parking fee is charged. Reservations to visit the park are required on weekends and on high-use days, which include most federal, seasonal, and school holidays.

Trail contact: Placer County Parks and Open Space, 11476 C Ave., Auburn, CA 95603; (530) 886-4901; www.placer.ca .gov/6106/hidden-falls-regional-park

Canine compatibility: Leashed dogs permitted.

Trail surface: Gravel service road, dirt single-track, stone steps

Land status: Hidden Falls Regional Park

Nearest town: Auburn

Other trail users: Mountain bikers, equestrians

Maps to consult: USGS Gold Hill CA; online at www.placer.ca.gov/6106/hidden-falls-regional-park. Maps are also posted at numbered trail junctions, along with mileages.

Water availability: None; be sure to bring plenty if it is hot.

Amenities available: Parking for both cars and equestrian trailers, restrooms, trash cans, picnic sites, information signboard with park map at the trailhead

Cell service: Good to start; marginal in the canyons and backcountry

Trail conditions: The trail is popular and well maintained. The park closes when fire danger is high.

Finding the trailhead: From Sacramento head east on I-80 for about 25 miles to the exit for CA 49 to Grass Valley and Placerville in Auburn. Go north on CA 49 toward Grass Valley. Drive 2.5 miles to the junction with Atwood Road and turn left onto Atwood. Follow Atwood Road for about 1.7 miles to where it becomes Mount Vernon Road; then follow Mount Vernon Road another 0.5 mile (2.2 miles total) to a T junction with Joeger Road. Go left, continuing on Mount Vernon Road for another 2 miles to the intersection with Mears Road on the right. Turn right on Mears Road and drive 0.5 mile to Mears Place. Turn right on Mears Place and go 0.2 mile to the signed park entrance. Trailhead GPS: N38 57.516' / W121 09.830'

The Hike

Hidden Falls spills over a cliff in the ominously named Deadman Canyon, but don't let the canyon's moniker intimidate you. The trails leading to Hidden Falls, Canyon View Falls, and the cataracts that make up the Seven Pools are far from frightening,

A large observation deck overlooks Hidden Falls.

and two overlook decks offer visitors safe platforms from which to enjoy the water-falls. The platforms also serve as gathering places for park visitors and their dogs: Acquaintances are made, lunches are shared, and dogs are allowed to meet and greet each other and their humans.

The Seven Pools, by contrast, are reclusive. It would take a feat of bushwhacking through tick- and snake-infested brush to reach them from the rocky overlook on the Seven Pools Vista Trail. The cascade spills through the steep-walled Coon Creek canyon, overflowing from pool to pool in short bursts of whitewater.

The trails that link Hidden Valley Regional Park's water highlights cruise through draws, follow creeks, and traverse slopes shaded by a variety of oaks, bay laurels, man-zanita, and the occasional digger pine, with bracken fern, blackberry, toyon, poison oak, and wildflowers enlivening the understory.

The route begins by dropping away from the parking area on the Poppy Trail, a well-maintained path broad enough to allow hikers—or horses—traveling in opposite directions to pass without having to step off the track. The trail drops into Deadman Canyon via a few switchbacks and then runs alongside Deadman Creek down to a convergence of trails at a bridge spanning the waterway.

From the bridge pick up the Hidden Falls Trail, which follows the creek downstream. A hikers-only trail breaks left from the overlook trail, dropping down a short flight of stone steps. Stay right where social paths lead down to the creek through purple-flowering vinca, which competes with blackberry as ground cover among the groves of spindly oaks and other riparian flora.

Views of the creek below, flowing through rock-lined pools that form perfect swimming holes, open as the trail switchbacks. Pass a stone staircase on the right that leads down to the swimming holes before reaching the wooden deck overlooking stop no. 1 at Hidden Falls. The deck offers a great vantage of the stepped spill, which remains vigorous year-round but is most spectacular (and loudest) in spring when the creek is flush with rain and meltwater.

From the platform you can retrace your steps to the trailhead for an easy 3-mile out-and-back hike. To continue to the Canyon View Falls overlook, retrace your steps to the Hidden Falls Trail and turn left, following the singletrack down to the Canyon View Bridge, which spans the confluence of Deadman Creek and Coon Creek. Cross the bridge and make the short, steep climb to the covered viewing platform overlooking the two-tiered falls and the swimming hole upstream.

To reach the Seven Pools, backtrack across the bridge and head uphill on the North Legacy Trail, a gravel access road that climbs to the crest of the ridge. Just before topping out, jog left onto the Quail Run Trail, which breaks to the left. Quail Run meets up with the Seven Pools Loop, which in turn drops around switchbacks into the Coon Creek drainage, passing through thickets of manzanita, poison oak, and scrub oak.

Down near the creek the route parallels the stream for a distance, passing a junction with the Pond Turtle Trail (an optional route back to Deadman Canyon and then up to the trailhead). As you ascend away from the waterway, the trail is bordered by toyon; in the fall its bright-red fruits glow in the sunlight. Below, the creek tightens into cataracts.

When you arrive at the next trail junction, take the Seven Pools Vista Trail. This leads up to a rock outcropping that offers a bird's-eye view of the Seven Pools, spilling through the rocky, brush-choked canyon. The pools are all but inaccessible, with nary even a social trail ferreting down through the tangle of brush and rocks.

From the viewpoint the Vista Trail climbs back onto the ridge separating the Deadman and Coon Creek drainages. Pick up the Blue Oak Trail and descend via sweeping traverses and a switchback into Deadman Canyon. The Blue Oak Trail ends at the bridge and the junction with the Pond Turtle, Poppy, North Legacy, and Hidden Falls Trails. Climb the broad South Legacy Trail—actually a road, wide enough for horses to travel side by side and still leave plenty of room for a hiker to pass. Look for bracken fern and wild grape on the hillside above and below the

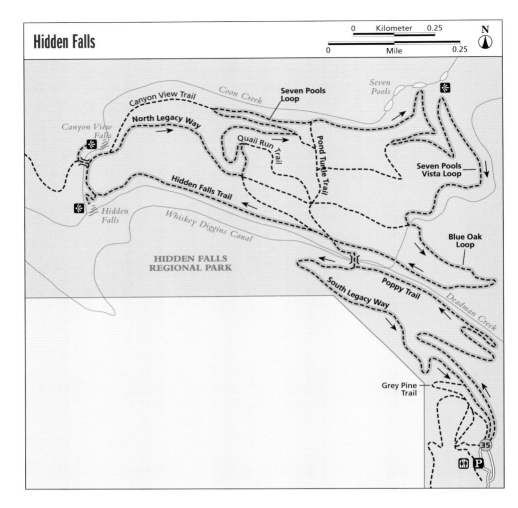

Hidden Falls

roadway as you climb; this gives way to grassland at the end of the route. Pass the junctions with the paved Hidden Gate Trail and the Poppy Trail, and then arrive back at the trailhead.

Miles and Directions

0.0 Start by passing the restrooms and information signs. Where the South Legacy Trail, paved Hidden Gate Trail, and singletrack Poppy Trail meet, take the Poppy Trail to the right.

0.1 At the trail junction, stay right on the Poppy Trail.

0.8 The Poppy Trail ends at Whiskey Diggins Bridge. Cross the bridge to the trail junction and go left on the Hidden Falls Trail.

1.3 Reach the junction with the hikers-only trail down to the falls. Go left on the Falls Trail, staying on the main route where a social trail breaks toward the creek.

1.5 Arrive at the observation deck overlooking Hidden Falls. Enjoy the views, visit a swimming hole, then retrace your steps to the beginning of the hikers-only trail.

1.7 At the junction with the Hidden Falls Trail, turn left and continue to the Canyon View Bridge.

1.8 Cross the Canyon View Bridge, then climb to the overlook of the falls. When you're ready to move on, retrace your steps over the bridge and pick up North Legacy Way, turning left and climbing toward the ridgetop.

2.3 Go left on Blue Oak Loop. Within 0.1 mile, reach the Quail Run Trail junction. Go left on Quail Run, which loops back toward the cattle gate and then arcs sharply right into the woods.

2.6 At the junction go left on the Seven Pools Loop.

3.1 At the junction with the Pond Turtle Trail, stay straight on the Seven Pools Loop.

3.5 At the trail intersection, go left on the Seven Pools Vista Trail.

3.7 Arrive at the rock outcropping overlooking the Seven Pools. Check out the views, then continue up the Seven Pools Vista Trail.

4.0 The Seven Pools Vista Trail ends on North Legacy Way. Cross the road to the Blue Oak Loop and descend via the Blue Oak into Deadman Canyon.

4.6 Reach the Whiskey Diggins Bridge and the junction with the North Legacy and Hidden Falls Trails. Go left, across the bridge, and then right on the broad South Legacy Trail.

5.4 Arrive back at the trailhead.

Honorable Mentions

Spring Creek Falls

The waterfall at the confluence of Spring Creek and the South Yuba River outside Nevada City is a 15-foot spill into a pretty pool. The friendliness of the falls and the pool depends on how much water is flowing: If the flows are high, it's best to sit on the rocky sidelines and watch, but if the flows are low, you can pick your way through the boulders down to the water. Scrambling up alongside Spring Creek is also inviting, with the creek cascading through boulders in drops several feet high into smaller pools, all shaded by oaks and madrones. The route is straightforward, heading upstream along the north side of the river from the rustic Edwards Crossing bridge. Stay straight on the obvious, if narrow and rough, traversing path; at times you may find yourself proceeding hands-on across portions of the route that have washed out. At the confluence of the South Yuba and Spring Creek, the formal trail splits into social paths. Go left to the river and waterfall.

To reach the trailhead from Nevada City, follow CA 20 east to the junction with CA 49. Head north on CA 49 for 0.3 mile to North Bloomfield Road. Go right onto North Bloomfield Road; at the T junction go right, staying on North Bloomfield Road (following the sign for South Yuba River State Park). Stay on winding North Bloomfield Road for 7.3 miles, driving to the bottom of the river canyon at Edwards Crossing. Parking is on the south side of the river and bridge.

Buckeye nuts and the Edwards Crossing highlight an early winter trek to Spring Creek Falls.

An easy interpretive loop includes an overlook of Bear River Falls.

Bear River Falls

A 1.1-mile lollipop on the interpretive Sierra Discovery Trail leads to this pretty 15-foot waterfall, and also provides lessons in native and emigrant history, including showing how settlers lowered their wagons 700 feet into the Bear River valley, the wildlife and plant life that thrives in the woods and meadows, and the hydroelectric power generated by the water that flows out of the high country. The waterfall isn't terribly big, but the setting is peaceful and the route is easy to follow. Watch for petite water ouzels, which frequent the falls.

To reach the trailhead from I-80 at Emigrant Gap, take the CA 20 exit toward Nevada City. Drive west on CA 20 for 3.5 miles to Bowman Lake Road. Turn right onto Bowman Lake Road and drive 0.4 mile to the Sierra Discovery Trail parking lot and trailhead on the left.

A thrilling drive to the bottom of the North Fork American River leads to the remote Codfish Falls trail.

Codfish Falls

The 3.2-mile out-and-back trail leading to secluded Codfish Falls begins by following the North Fork American River. In late spring and early summer—the prime waterfall viewing times—the river swells with snowmelt. When the fury dies back and the summer sun begins to bake the foothills, the route skirts pools that invite side trips to swim. That's when the 25-foot-high, year-round waterfall fades to thin streams, moistening a pocket of verdant mosses, oaks, and grasses in an otherwise parched environment.

Ponderosa Way, which dives into the American River canyon from Weimar, offers a huge hint at how out-of-bounds this stretch of trail in the Auburn State Recreation Area is. The dirt road leading to the trailhead falls steeply into the gorge, requiring a driver's full concentration and a high-clearance vehicle. The narrow trail departs from the north abutment of the Ponderosa Way bridge, which spans the north fork at the bottom of the canyon. In summer a beach spreads below the trailhead, offering access to the cooling waters of the river—the first of several such opportunities to take a break and dip your toes, if the weather and water flow permit.

Lake Clementine Spillway Falls

If a waterfall is defined as falling water, this fine, 155-foot spill out of Lake Clementine, reached via an easy out-and-back hike along the North Fork American River, definitely qualifies. What tumbles over North Fork Dam spillway can only be described as a block or sheet waterfall, in the tradition of Niagara Falls, and with the lake pooling behind and the American River flowing away down a steep-walled canyon, it's a worthy destination.

The 4.6-mile out-and-back route begins near the confluence of the north and middle forks of the American River and the junction of CA 49 and Old Foresthill Road, downhill from the town of Auburn. From the trailhead on Old Foresthill Road on the east side of the North Fork American River, follow the service road/trail under the towering Foresthill Bridge, past Clarks Hole, a popular swimming spot formed by an "underwater dam" built by placer miners more than one hundred years ago, and then climb to the paved Lake Clementine Road. A short walk down a singletrack leads to the spillway overlook.

Lake Clementine's spillway isn't a natural waterfall, but it's a great destination for a day hike nonetheless.

Devils Falls and Indian Creek Falls

The bridge at the base of Yankee Jim Road in the scenic North Fork American River canyon is the jumping-off point for two waterfall hikes, as well as a popular base for anglers and kayakers. Devils Falls is one of the most accessible waterfalls in the Auburn State Recreation Area, tumbling into Shirttail Creek near its confluence with the North Fork American River. You can drive to the base, but I recommend walking across the bridge and up the gravel road to check it out. Not only is there no parking alongside the roadway at the falls, but hiking the half mile up the gently ascending road also allows you to enjoy the cataracts on Shirttail Creek in the steep ravine to the north. The entirety of the cascade can't be seen from the track, but the 70 or so feet that are visible are impressive when the water falls in full force, fanning out across a mossy rock face.

Indian Creek Falls lies upstream from the Yankee Jim bridge. To reach it you must navigate a jumble of boulders and channels that can be impassable in springtime, when meltwater swells the watercourse. Take on the challenge as water levels permit, and be prepared to turn around if the crossing is unsafe. To reach the ford, cross the Yankee Jim bridge and head left, dropping onto the staircase to the riverside and then upstream to the creek. And then? Well, good luck.

To reach the Yankee Jim bridge from westbound I-80 in Colfax, take the Canyon Way exit. Go right onto Canyon Way and drive 0.7 mile to the Yankee Jim Road intersection. Turn left onto the narrow, unpaved, winding Yankee Jim Road and go 4.5 miles to the rustic bridge spanning the river. There are small parking areas on either side of the bridge, but they may be filled; this is a popular spot on spring and summer weekends. Be smart and courteous about parking.

Drought-diminished Devils Falls still waters a lush garden of moss and fern.

Grouse Falls is remote and inaccessible, but if you're up for a long drive through a fire-scarred landscape, it's worth the trip.

Grouse Falls

Plunging more than 500 feet into an inaccessible ravine deep in the wild, Grouse Falls would require a herculean scramble to reach, but a short, easy ramble through the woods once led to an overlook perched on the edge of the Grouse Creek ravine. The falls were visible across the void, a streak of white down a golden cliff in a wilderness that could, and has, swallowed explorers and gold seekers, and tormented firefighters. The 2022 Mosquito Fire, however, blew through much of the country surrounding the falls, which as of spring 2023 remained closed to public access. That said, waterfalls and wild-lands are eminently resilient, and, when deemed safe, they will open to visitors again.

Part of the Grouse Falls adventure is the drive to the trailhead. From westbound I-80 in Auburn, take the Auburn Ravine Road exit and head right to the junction with Foresthill Road. Follow Foresthill Road for 12.5 miles to the junction with Mosquito Ridge Road in Foresthill. Turn right onto Mosquito Ridge Road and wind 19.2 miles to the junction with Peavine Road/FR 33. Turn left onto the gravel Peavine Road and go 4.6 miles to the junction with FR 33, with parking for about five cars. Turn left onto the rougher gravel road and go 0.5 mile to the trailhead, with parking for about ten cars. While the last half mile can be traveled in a passenger car, conditions might warrant a high-clearance vehicle. Before you go, check in with rangers by calling (530) 492-5631.

Jenkinson Lake Falls

The waterfall on Park Creek, which feeds into sprawling Jenkinson Lake, is just one of many pleasant diversions along the long trail that loops around the reservoir in the Sly Park Recreation Area. The 25-foot whitewater spill lands in a clear pool, where you can wet your feet or take a swim, depending on the season. The pool is surrounded by a smooth rock outcropping, perfect for sunning and picnicking. Dark woods crowd the slopes surrounding the fall, lending a fairy-tale ambience to the spot.

Jenkinson Lake's north shore is fairly well developed, but the south shore—the waterfall is on this side—feels rugged and remote. You can pick up the trail at any point, but if you begin at the Stonebraker boat launch and picnic area, you'll not only enjoy an easy, 4.2-mile out-and-back hike to the waterfall, but also be treated to great lake views, a viewing platform with interpretive signs describing the different species of bats in the park and the annual ladybug migration in spring, and plenty of places where you can drop waterside for a rest, a snack, or a swim. To reach Sly Park from Sacramento, head east on US 50 for about 50 miles to Pollock Pines. Exit onto Sly Park Road and continue for 4.2 miles to the recreation area entrance on the left.

The falls on Park Creek are a nice diversion in the popular Sly Park Recreation Area.

San Francisco Bay Area

Most of the falls in the Bay Area are seasonal and best viewed in winter and late spring, when rains have saturated the hillsides and runoff flows into streams and creeks. The North Bay, and particularly Marin County, brings in the prize for the most waterfall hikes, while Uvas Canyon, in the South Bay, takes home a ribbon for the greatest concentration of falls on a single trail loop. San Francisco is the obvious hub of the region, with San Rafael the major city in the North Bay, Oakland in the East Bay, and San Jose in the South Bay. A web of major highways, including US 101, I-80, I-680, and I-280, link Bay Area cities, parks, and waterfall hikes.

Wild sweet pea blooms along the trail to Cataract Falls (hike 38).

36 Sugarloaf Fall

An easy loop in a Wine Country open space park leads through meadowland and woodland to a seasonal cascade near the headwaters of Sonoma Creek.

Height: 25 feet

Beauty rating: ★ ★ ★ ★

Start: Sugarloaf Ridge State Park day-use trailhead

Distance: 2.0-mile loop and spur

Difficulty: Easy

Hiking time: About 1.5 hours

Seasons/schedule: Year-round; sunrise to sunset

Fees and permits: An entrance fee is charged.

Trail contact: Sugarloaf Ridge State Park, 2605 Adobe Canyon Rd., Kenwood, CA 95452; (707) 833-5712; www.sugarloafpark.org

Canine compatibility: No dogs permitted on trails.

Trail surface: Dirt service road and singletrack

Land status: Sugarloaf Ridge State Park

Nearest town: Kenwood

Other trail users: None

Maps to consult: USGS Kenwood CA; park map available at the entrance kiosk and online

Water availability: Water is available in the campground and at the visitor center

Amenities available: Restrooms and an information signboard at the trailhead. Picnic sites, a campground, and a visitor center are nearby. The park is also home to the Robert Ferguson Observatory, which houses several telescopes and is open on a limited basis.

Cell service: Okay at the trailhead; marginal in the canyon

Trail conditions: The trails are well maintained.

Finding the trailhead: From CA 12 in Kenwood, head east on Adobe Canyon Road. Travel 4.7 miles up the scenic roadway, passing the park boundary sign, to the entry kiosk. The parking area is 0.1 mile past the kiosk on the left. Trailhead GPS: N38 26.279' / W122 30.862'

The Hike

Sugarloaf Fall is tucked in a verdant canyon on the lower slopes of Bald Mountain in the northern Sonoma Valley. It's a pretty little seasonal cascade, strengthened by winter rains and typically dry by late summer, with a pool at its base and a thick green canopy overhead.

Hiking directly to the fall is a relatively straightforward affair, but it would be a shame to limit your visit to this beautiful regional park. One aspect that sets the park apart is its astronomical focus: Not only is it home to the Robert Ferguson Observatory and its telescopes, it also features a Planet Walk, a moderately difficult hike that scales the solar system to walking distance. Another unusual feature: Sugarloaf Ridge is operated by Team Sugarloaf, a nonprofit that took over operation of the park when it was threatened with closure by a statewide funding scandal in 2012. The park is also twice-burned, first in the 2017 Nuns Fire and then again in the 2020 Glass Fire.

The Canyon Trail leads directly down to the fall from near the entrance station, but a pleasant loop that incorporates a bit of meadow and some nice views down the

Sonoma Creek cascades from its headwaters in Sugarloaf Ridge State Park to the valley floor.

valley toward the vineyards of Kenwood is described here. Begin by hiking up the broad Stern Trail, which cruises through grassland liberally peppered with wildflowers in the spring and burnished gold in late summer and fall. This graded, gravel, walk-and-talk stretch also features great views down Adobe Canyon toward Kenwood.

Leave the Stern Trail for the narrow Pony Gate Trail, dropping through more grassland to the junction with the Canyon Trail. You'll remain on the Canyon Trail for the remainder of the hike, dropping first through an open oak woodland and then down onto the park road. Cross the road to the sign on the creek side and continue to descend through woods with a more riparian flair, with an occasional maple in the mix of oak and bay laurel, and an understory thick with ferns and poison oak.

The trail parallels a seasonal stream as it drops into the canyon. The clear and well-used trail to the waterfall branches left (south) off the main Canyon Trail at 1.3 miles. Scramble down a final stretch to the pool at the waterfall's base; the cascade rumbles over large rocks at the head of the narrow, dark-green dell.

To return to the trailhead, retrace your steps to the junction of the Canyon Trail with the park road. Turn right onto the park road and follow it up, past the entrance kiosk, to the trailhead parking area.

Miles and Directions

0.0 From the parking lot walk down the park road toward the entrance kiosk to the junction with the Stern Trail/Bay Area Ridge Trail. Turn right onto the dirt service road and begin a moderate climb.

0.6 At the junction with the Pony Gate Trail, turn left and follow the singletrack down through the grasses.

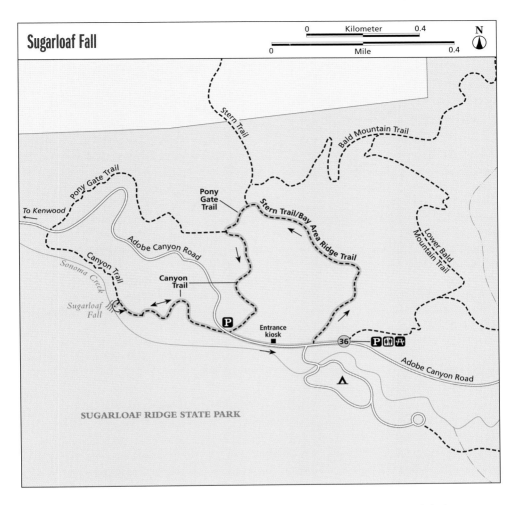

0   Kilometer   0.4

0   Mile   0.4

N

Stern Trail

Bald Mountain Trail

Pony Gate Trail

Pony Gate Trail

To Kenwood

Stern Trail/Bay Area Ridge Trail

Lower Bald Mountain Trail

Adobe Canyon Road

Canyon Trail

Sonoma Creek

Canyon Trail

Sugarloaf Fall

P

Entrance kiosk

36 P

Adobe Canyon Road

SUGARLOAF RIDGE STATE PARK

0.75 At the junction go left onto the Canyon Trail. Cross a streamlet that flows only in the wet season.

1.1 Drop into the parking area for the Canyon Trail alongside the park's access road. Cross the roadway and pick up the trail, which drops into the ravine cradling the creek.

1.3 At the unsigned trail junction, turn sharply left on the well-used trail that descends toward Sonoma Creek.

1.4 Reach the waterfall. Take it all in, then retrace your steps to the park road.

1.7 Turn right and follow the park road toward the entrance station.

2.0 Arrive back at the trailhead.

Option: To make a slightly longer loop, you can follow the Pony Gate Trail past the junction with the Canyon Trail, continuing downhill for 0.8 mile to the park road. Cross the road and head downhill about 25 yards to the Canyon Trail. Follow the Canyon Trail uphill to the falls in 0.2 mile, then continue up the Canyon Trail to the upper road junction and trailhead. Total distance is about 2.6 miles.

37 Carson Falls

A hike to this seasonal waterfall features superlative views of Mount Tamalpais. The waterfall flows through the breeding ground of the rare foothill yellow-legged frog, which may be seen clinging to rocks in the pool at the base.

Height: 150 feet

Beauty rating: ★★★★

Start: Azalea Hill/Pine Mountain trailhead on the Fairfax-Bolinas Road

Distance: 3.8 miles out and back

Difficulty: Moderate

Hiking time: About 2 hours

Seasons/schedule: Year-round; sunrise to sunset

Fees and permits: None

Trail contact: Marin Municipal Water District, 220 Nellen Ave., Corte Madera, CA 94925; (415) 945-1180 (ranger) or (415) 945-1400 (customer service); marinwater.org

Canine compatibility: Leashed dogs permitted.

Trail surface: Dirt fire road and singletrack

Land status: Marin Municipal Water District

Nearest town: Fairfax

Other trail users: Mountain bikers, equestrians

Maps to consult: USGS Bolinas CA; Marin Municipal Water District/Mount Tamalpais Watershed trail map available online at marin water.org/DocumentCenter/View/160

Water availability: None

Amenities available: Parking in small lots adjacent to the Fairfax-Bolinas Road

Cell service: Good outside the canyon; sketchy near the falls

Trail conditions: The Pine Mountain fire road is a favorite of mountain bikers. Be prepared to share the trail.

Finding the trailhead: From the junction of Broadway and Bolinas Road in downtown Fairfax, head west on Bolinas Road (which becomes the Fairfax-Bolinas Road) for about 3.8 miles to the parking area at the top of the hill above the Meadow Club golf course. If you reach the steep descent toward Alpine Lake, you've gone too far. Parking for about twenty cars is located across the road from the Pine Mountain trailhead at the base of Azalea Hill. Trailhead GPS: N37 57.834' / W122 37.511'

The Hike

Carson Falls, on the west-facing slope of Pine Mountain, is surrounded by coastal oak savannah and open to a baking summer sun. Semiarid as the season creeps into summer and drying to a trickle by August, the waterfall's setting is lovely, even if the flow, especially in drought years, is less than spectacular.

For a spring wildflower display, Carson Falls can't be beat, with the rolling grasslands erupting in lupine and poppy as the days grow longer. The hike to the falls boasts spectacular views south and west across the woodlands of the Marin Municipal Water District's watershed to Mount Tamalpais, reclining in perfect profile and especially spectacular when the fog begins to spill over the ridges. On clear days views

Waterfall to mossy streak: Carson Falls shows the effect of prolonged drought.

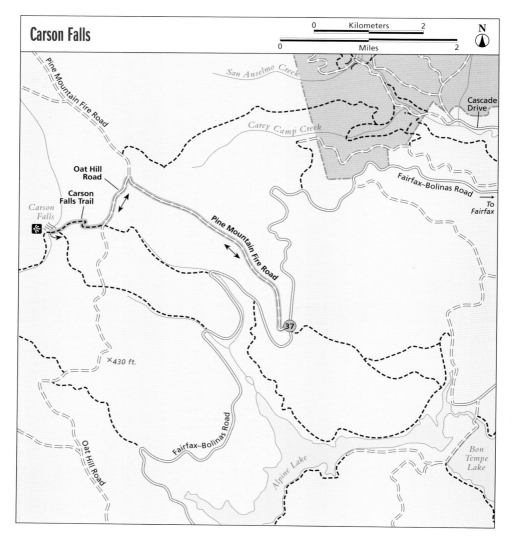

Kilometers
0   2

0   Miles   2

N

San Anselmo Creek

Cascade Drive

Carey Camp Creek

Pine Mountain Fire Road

Oat Hill Road

Fairfax–Bolinas Road

Carson Falls Trail

To Fairfax

Carson Falls

Pine Mountain Fire Road

37

×430 ft.

Oat Hill Road

Fairfax–Bolinas Road

Bon Tempe Lake

Alpine Lake

open north beyond Pine Mountain to Loma Alta and Mount St. Helena, and south-east across sprawling San Francisco Bay to Mount Diablo.

The fall itself spills down a narrow rocky canyon near the headwaters of Little Carson Creek, tumbling over several benches before a final 40-foot drop into a small pool. The pool is where you might be able to spot the foothill yellow-legged frog. Though the falls may be dry by midsummer, which is just about when the hike up the exposed Pine Mountain Fire Road becomes a sunbaked slog, the pool may hold water for weeks longer, and the frogs may be spotted into August.

Begin by climbing the broad Pine Mountain Fire Road. Popular with mountain bikers, the route is wide enough to accommodate all users. Stay right and aware: Cyclists typically warn you of their approach, and the crunch of their tires on the rocky road may give them away, but they move swiftly on the downhill. I'd call this a walk–and–talk stretch, except that it's relatively steep, so heavy breathing may preclude conversation.

You'll know you're nearing the top of the climb when you reach a telephone line that zigzags across the road several times. At this point the ascent mellows and the descent begins. At the junction with Oat Hill Road, with a sign pointing to Carson Falls, go left. The descent continues to a saddle, where a serpentine rock outcropping rises greenish-gray among the grasses. At the trail junction in the saddle, pick up the Carson Falls Trail.

The trail winds briefly through grassland and then drops via four switchbacks through oak woodland into the Little Carson Creek canyon. Emerge from under the oak canopy at a trail Y. The right path leads to rock outcroppings looking down onto the fall and out across the forested ridges of Mount Tam's watershed. The left trail crosses a bridge over the stream and then descends to overlooks on the opposite side of the canyon.

Though the Little Carson Trail continues, linking to other routes within the watershed to create long loops, the waterfall overlooks are the turnaround. Explore, and then return as you came, enjoying the views on the walk down the Pine Mountain Fire Road.

Miles and Directions

0.0 Begin by walking across the Fairfax-Bolinas Road from the parking area. Pass the gate and head up the Pine Mountain Fire Road.

0.7 Meet the telephone line, which crosses the road several times.

1.2 At the junction turn left onto the Oat Hill Road and continue downhill.

1.5 In the saddle go right onto the Carson Falls Trail.

1.9 Reach the overlooks for Carson Falls. Return as you came.

3.8 Arrive back at the trailhead.

38 Cataract Falls

A challenging but spectacular trail leads up along Cataract Creek, passing a series of waterfalls as it climbs from Alpine Lake to Laurel Dell.

Height: A series of small waterfalls, some 20 to 25 feet tall

Beauty rating: ★★★★

Start: Trailhead on Fairfax-Bolinas Road just beyond Alpine Dam

Distance: 4.6 miles out and back

Difficulty: Strenuous

Hiking time: About 3 hours

Seasons/schedule: Year-round; sunrise to sunset

Fees and permits: None

Trail contact: Marin Municipal Water District, 220 Nellen Ave., Corte Madera, CA 94925; (415) 945-1180 (ranger) or (415) 945-1400 (customer service); marinwater.org

Canine compatibility: Leashed dogs permitted.

Trail surface: Dirt, stone stairs

Land status: Marin Municipal Water District

Nearest town: Fairfax

Other trail users: None

Maps to consult: USGS Bolinas CA; Marin Municipal Water District/Mount Tamalpais Watershed trail map available online at marinwater.org/DocumentCenter/View/160

Water availability: None

Amenities available: Limited parking and information signboards at the trailhead; picnic sites and restrooms at Laurel Dell

Cell service: None

Trail conditions: This popular, sometimes crowded route features steep sections not for the weak of knee. Parking is limited at the trailhead proper; if no spots are available, park carefully on the shoulder of the Fairfax-Bolinas Road.

Finding the trailhead: From downtown Fairfax at the junction of Broadway and Bolinas Road, head west on Bolinas Road (which becomes the Fairfax-Bolinas Road) for about 8 miles to a hairpin turn just beyond the Alpine Lake Dam. Trailhead GPS: N37 56.193' / W122 38.280'

The Hike

Given sufficient rainfall, any number of ephemeral cascades can be found in the steep gullies of the Mount Tamalpais Watershed. But few carry the notoriety of the falls found along the Cataract Trail, which parallels Cataract Creek above Alpine Lake, one of five reservoirs on the mountain's flanks. Artfully combining switchbacks with stone and wooden staircases, the challenging trail traverses steep slopes between the lakeshore and Laurel Dell—1,000 feet of elevation change shaded by redwoods, bay laurels, and oaks, lush with sword and bracken fern, and glowing with moss.

The upside-down route begins innocuously, traversing easily above the shoreline of the biggest reservoir in the Tamalpais watershed. The first staircase is less than a half mile into the hike, and it's all uphill from here. Some of the stairsteps have significant rises, but in general they mitigate the climb, as does the sound of the creek flowing alongside, whether a tinkle, a rumble, or a roar. Overlooks at switchbacks along the lower part of the climb allow climbers to take breaks with views.

Cataract Falls spills down a long ravine on the slopes of Mount Tamalpais.

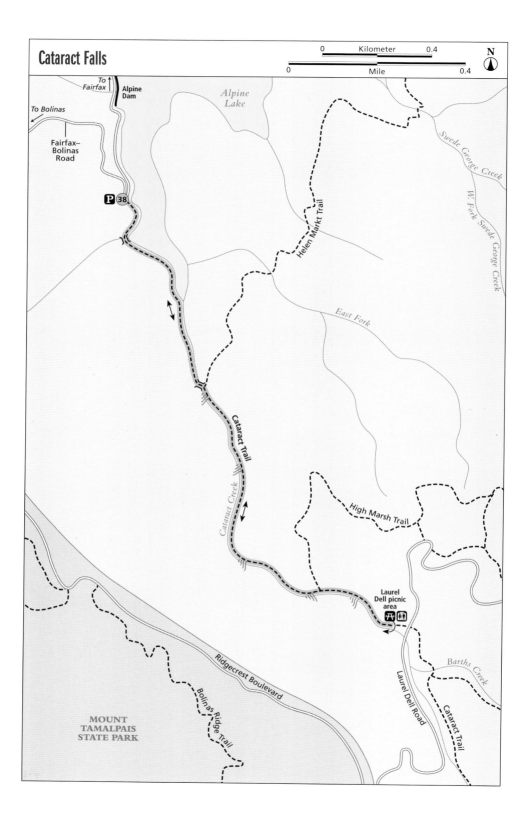

Cataract Falls

Kilometer

0   0.4

Mile

0   0.4

N

To Fairfax

Alpine Dam

Alpine Lake

To Bolinas

Fairfax–Bolinas Road

P 38

Swede George Creek

Helen Markt Trail

W. Fork Swede George Creek

East Fork

Cataract Trail

Cataract Creek

High Marsh Trail

Laurel Dell picnic area

Ridgecrest Boulevard

Bolinas Ridge Trail

MOUNT TAMALPAIS STATE PARK

Laurel Dell Road

Barths Creek

Cataract Trail

At about 1 mile the route crosses the creek via a split-log bridge. Round a switchback, pass a Cataract Trail marker, and take a break by stepping off the trail to enjoy a 10-foot plunge into a clear pool; in warm weather, water flows permitting, this is a nice place to dip your feet.

Above the pool the trail becomes a moderate streamside ramble bordered by primordial sword fern, the creek dancing from pool to pool alongside. Another set of staircases, the first arcing around a rock outcropping and the second featuring a metal rail, lead up to a second pool plunge, this one about 25 feet high. Take another break; then climb another staircase and round more switchbacks to yet another short fall and pool, this one reached via a staircase that breaks right from the main trail.

Beyond the junction with the High Marsh Trail, the Cataract Trail mellows. It's a short jaunt to the turnaround at Laurel Dell, with picnic sites, restrooms, and other amenities. Take a break in the dell, and then retrace your steps to the trailhead. It's all downhill, but take care on the descent, especially in wet weather, as the steps and trail surface may be slick.

Miles and Directions

0.0 Start at the gated trailhead, heading gently uphill along an arm of Alpine Lake.

0.1 Cross the bridge over a side stream.

0.3 Arrive at the first set of stairs and begin the relentless but lovely climb.

0.6 Cross a bridge over a second feeder stream.

0.75 Pass a couple of switchbacks offering overlooks of small cascades.

1.0 Cross Cataract Creek on a split-log footbridge. Round a switchback, pass a signpost, and reach an overlook of a 10-foot-high plunge into a pool.

1.7 Climb a staircase around a rock outcropping and a second staircase with a metal rail, and reach a 25-foot plunge into a pool.

2.0 A staircase breaks off the main trail to the right, down to another short fall and pool.

2.1 At the junction with the High Marsh Trail, stay right on the Cataract Trail.

2.3 Reach Laurel Dell. This is the turnaround; retrace your steps.

4.6 Arrive back at the trailhead.

Option: More than 130 miles of trails and fire roads lace through the Mount Tamalpais Watershed, allowing hikers to piece together a number of longer hikes and loops that include the Cataract Trail. Download the trail map and customize a longer route as time and fitness permit.

39 Alamere Falls

A long, lovely coastal ramble leads to Alamere Falls, which drops directly onto Wildcat Beach in the Point Reyes National Seashore.

Height: 50 feet, with shorter cascades above

Beauty rating: ★★★★★

Start: The Palomarin Trailhead

Distance: 13.0 miles out and back

Difficulty: Strenuous due to distance

Hiking time: About 8 hours

Seasons/schedule: Year-round, sunrise to sunset

Fees and permits: An entrance fee is charged.

Trail contact: Point Reyes National Seashore, Bear Valley Visitor Center; (415) 464-5100; www.nps.gov/pore

Canine compatibility: No dogs allowed on this trail.

Trail surface: Dirt roadway, singletrack

Land status: Point Reyes National Seashore

Nearest town: Bolinas

Other trail users: None

Maps to consult: USGS Double Point CA; Point Reyes National Seashore map available at the Bear Valley Visitor Center and online

Water availability: None

Amenities available: Restrooms, trash cans, and information signboards at the trailhead. The parking area fills early on weekends; additional parking is available along the gravel access road. If possible, carpool to the trailhead to prevent congestion.

Cell service: Marginal; don't count on it.

Trail conditions: The Palomarin Trail is well maintained and popular. If walking with a group, proceed single file when passing other trail users. Many cliffs and bluffs in Point Reyes National Seashore are composed of friable rocks and are quite unstable. Rockfalls and slumps occur regularly, so visitors should stay at least 10 feet away from the edges and bases of cliffs. Due to the crumbly nature of the rocks, climbing within the seashore is discouraged. This route leads past the unsanctioned use trail to the top of the falls. Climbing down to the beach is strongly discouraged to avoid injury. The park website notes Alamere Falls is the site of "numerous search-and-rescue operations each year."

Finding the trailhead: From Point Reyes Station in West Marin County, drive south on CA 1 to Olema. From Olema continue 9 miles south, toward Bolinas and Stinson Beach. Where the road forks at the Bolinas Lagoon, stay right on the unsigned Olema-Bolinas Road into Bolinas. Travel 1.3 miles to the stop sign at Horseshoe Hill Road; stay left (southbound) on the Olema-Bolinas Road. At the junction with Mesa Road, turn right and follow Mesa Road for 4.5 miles to its end at the Palomarin Trailhead, passing the Point Reyes Bird Observatory at 3.9 miles. Trailhead GPS: N37 56.038' / W122 44.822'

The Hike

Alamere Falls, like a wild rose, displays its remarkable beauty without reservation but is prickly and difficult to reach. When engorged with winter rains, the waters run muddy and swift, tumbling over a series of terraces before taking the final plunge onto Wildcat Beach, and filling the air with a turbulent roar that harmonizes with the

Alamere Falls is one of the few falls in Northern California that spills directly onto a beach.
NPS Photo

surf pounding the strand. While the postcard view of the falls is from the beach—and can only safely be reached by hiking along the beach—several options exist. I love the hike from Palomarin, passing Bass Lake, and that's what is described.

The route begins by climbing the short staircase adjacent to the restrooms and going left onto the broad Coast Trail. Pass the trail to Palomarin Beach and continue through a stand of eucalyptus. Then the route follows the contours of the coastline, weaving inland through gullies and out onto the bluffs overlooking the ocean. After a mile or so, the path climbs steeply up and inland. Round a couple of sweeping curves, ascend past a steep, rocky ravine, pass through a cleft between the two hillsides to a saddle . . . and the climb is done.

From the saddle, drop to the Lake Ranch Trail junction, which breaks off to the right (northeast). Stay left on the Coast Trail, passing a series of ponds and vernal pools as the trail drops to Bass Lake. A footpath to the lakeshore breaks off to the left before the Coast Trail begins to climb away from the water through a mixed ever-green forest.

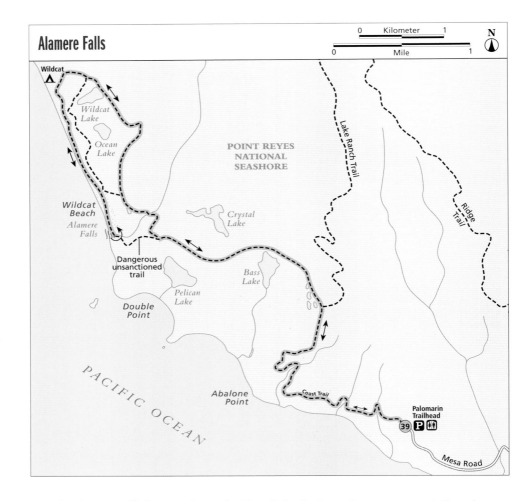

Alamere Falls

The Coast Trail flattens above the Bass Lake basin and arcs westward. Pass the closed trail to Crystal Lake, and the woodlands give way to coastal scrub. Pelican Lake lies cupped in a bowl below and to the left (west), and a snapshot of the ocean can be seen through a V-shaped break in the bluffs.

The easy descent continues, shaded in spots by thickets of broom and scrub, and the sounds of the nearby surf are carried up to the trail by the wind. Pass an unmarked social trail that breaks off to the left toward the Double Point Overlook. The unsanctioned, unmaintained use trail to Alamere Falls branches off to the left (west) about 100 feet beyond. I've hiked this path in the past and agree with the park service's assessment: Hikers should avoid using it for all the good reasons cited on the website—dangerous cliffs, trampling habitat, etc.

Thick brambles of coyote brush encroach on the eroded singletrack trail and Alamere Creek runs through the willow-choked basin to the right. The track heads downhill and, given both the ruts and pitch, is deceptively difficult. Reach the brink of the falls and the path is no longer deceptively difficult—it's plainly so, skittering down an eroded cliff, a hands-on affair that's not for the hiking neophyte. At trail's end, terraces misted by the adjacent cataracts overlook both the ocean and the cascades. *Do not attempt to climb down to the beach from here.* The bluffs are subject to erosion, and in the wake of a 2015 tragedy at nearby Arch Rock and other injuries and rescues, it's plainly just a bad idea.

To continue to the base of the falls, remain on the Coast Trail bound for Wildcat Camp. You'll pass Ocean Lake and Wildcat Lake along the way, along with connections for the Ocean Lake Loop. Remain on the Coast Trail at the junctions. From Wildcat Camp, drop down onto the beach and walk south to the falls (about 3 miles round-trip, best accessible at low tide). Water is everywhere—washing the sand, tumbling from the cliffs, cascading through channels. When you can tear yourself away, retrace your steps back to the trailhead.

Miles and Directions

0.0 Start at the Palomarin Trailhead, climbing the stairs next to the restrooms and turning left onto the Coast Trail.

0.1 At the junction with the Palomarin Beach Trail, stay right on the Coast Trail.

0.6 Cross the first footbridge.

1.4 Cross the second footbridge.

1.6 Round a switchback and head uphill and inland.

2.25 At the junction with the Lake Ranch Trail, stay left on the Coast Trail.

2.75 Pass Bass Lake.

3.2 Pass a closed trail, remaining on the Coast Trail.

3.75 Pass the narrow, unsanctioned trail to the top of Alamere Falls. Remain on the Coast Trail.

5.5 Reach Wildcat Camp, passing Ocean Lake and Wildcat Lake along the way. Descend to Wildcat Beach. Turn left and walk south toward the falls.

6.5 Arrive at the base of Alamere Falls and take it all in. Retrace your steps to the trailhead.

13.0 Arrive back at the trailhead.

Option: Alternative routes to the base of Alamere Falls can begin at either the Bear Valley or Five Brooks trailheads and are all-day or overnight affairs. Mileages from either starting point are in the 17- to 18-mile round-trip range, depending on how you design your route. Most often, hikers begin at Bear Valley, head out to Arch Rock on the coast, and pick up the Coast Trail heading south. The interim goal is Wildcat Camp; from there, timing for low tide, follow Wildcat Beach to the base of the waterfall. Consult a park map to plan your trek and check with rangers about trail conditions and conditions on the beach before setting out.

40 Castle Rock Falls

Follow forested trails past weirdly sculpted rock outcroppings to a waterfall that plunges 80 feet down a sheer face near the headwaters of Kings Creek.

Height: 80 feet

Beauty rating: ★ ★ ★ ★

Start: The trailhead on the west side of the parking lot

Distance: 2.6-mile lollipop

Difficulty: Moderate

Hiking time: About 2.5 hours

Seasons/schedule: 6 a.m. to sunset

Fees and permits: A day-use fee is charged.

Trail contact: Castle Rock State Park, 15000 Skyline Blvd., Los Gatos, CA 95033; (408) 867-2952; www.parks.ca.gov. Portola and Castle Rock Foundation, 59 Washington St. #107, Santa Clara, CA 95050; www.portola andcastlerockfound.org.

Canine compatibility: No dogs allowed.

Trail surface: Dirt singletrack, roadway

Land status: Castle Rock State Park

Nearest town: Saratoga

Other trail users: None

Maps to consult: USGS Santa Cruz CA; park map available at www.parks.ca.gov

Water availability: None

Amenities available: Pit toilets, trash cans, and information signboards

Cell service: None

Trail conditions: The trail is popular and can be crowded.

Finding the trailhead: From I-280 in Cupertino, take the CA 85 exit and head south on CA 85 to the Saratoga Avenue exit. Go right (south) onto Saratoga-Sunnyvale Road and continue for 2.4 miles to CA 9/Big Basin Way. Go right (west) on CA 9 for 7.3 miles to Skyline Boulevard/CA 35. Turn left (south) on Skyline Boulevard and travel 2.6 miles to the park entrance on the right (west).

Alternatively, from CA 17 in Los Gatos, take the Bear Creek/Black Road exit. Follow Montevina Road east for 0.3 mile to Black Road. Turn left onto Black Road and travel for 4.4 scenic, winding miles to Skyline Boulevard. Turn right (north) on Skyline Boulevard and go 3.7 miles to the park entrance, which is on the left (west). Trailhead GPS: N37 13.825' / W122 05.762'

The Hike

From the overhanging tafoni faces of Castle Rock to the observation deck jutting out over Castle Rock Falls, at the head of Kings Creek, the scenic destinations on this tour are enchanting.

Castle Rock, the park's high point, is more a palace for forest gnomes than for fairy-tale princesses. Perched on the crest of the Santa Cruz Mountains, its sandstone faces host a honeycomb of holds, shallow caves, and, on dry sunny days, crowds of rock climbers. Dense forest surrounds the rock and nearby sandstone outcroppings, creating an intimate setting for both climbers and hikers. Pull up a piece of the stone apron that surrounds the base and enjoy the athletic showmanship.

Castle Rock Falls, sapped by drought, as seen from the overlook platform.

If you seek views and cascades, head downhill and downstream from the rock, following the historic Saratoga Gap Trail to Castle Rock Falls. From the falls observation deck, views open across the ridgelines and forested hollows of the Santa Cruz range, with exposed rock outcroppings jutting from the canopy on the nearest slope to the north and vistas of the fire scar left behind by the CZU Lightning Fire in 2020. Climbing routes lie on either side of the cascade, which stains a long slab diving into the Kings Creek watershed.

The trails linking the rock and the falls cruise through a dense woodland of pine and oak, with very little sunlight filtering through. Mosses cling to the boulders lining the trails—at least to those faces that aren't used by climbers—and deadfall jams the creek above the falls. On a foggy day the atmosphere is primordial, with the slightest wind shifting the boughs overhead and rocks looming out of the woods suddenly, like giant trolls.

The elevation change from the trek's high point at Castle Rock to its low point at Castle Rock Falls feels significant, but the descent (and ascent) is not particularly

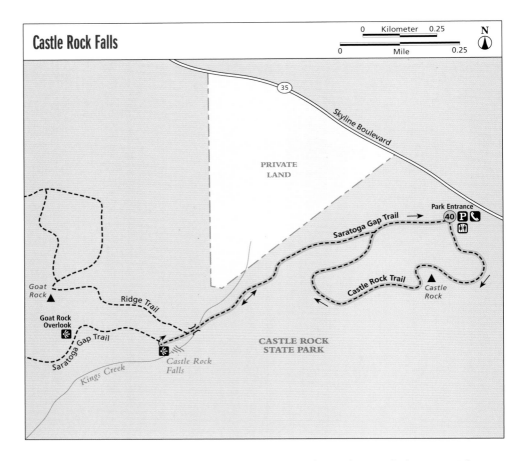

strenuous. Slopes are moderate and easily tackled by hikers who watch their pace. The observation deck is a perfect place to take a break and have a snack before tackling the climb back to the trailhead.

Miles and Directions

0.0 Start by heading left (south) and uphill on the trail to Castle Rock. A trail sign directs you up on the forested singletrack.

0.2 At the trail junction above the Isabella Soria and Nina Bingham Memorial Grove, go right on the Castle Rock Trail, now a dirt road. Rock formations dot the forest to the left (southwest).

0.3 Arrive at Castle Rock, which rises to the north of a large clearing. A trail marker points the way to Saratoga Gap Trail. The singletrack curls around the base of the rock, passing caves where climbers hang like bats while they contemplate their next moves.

0.5 At the trail sign, switchback right and downhill toward the Saratoga Gap Trail. Trail signs keep you on track for the next half mile, as climbers' trails branch off the main route.

1.0 Cross a series of little wooden bridges to the intersection with the Saratoga Gap Trail. Go left on the Saratoga Gap Trail toward Castle Rock Falls.

1.5 Cross a bridge to the junction of the Saratoga Gap and Ridge Trails. Go left on the Saratoga Gap Trail to Castle Rock Falls.

1.7 Arrive at the falls overlook. After checking out the cascade and the views, retrace your steps.

2.4 At the junction of the Saratoga Gap and Castle Rock Trails, stay left (east) on the Saratoga Gap Trail, which ascends past a cavernous rock. Ignore the climbers' trail that leads to the rock.

2.6 Arrive back at the trailhead.

41 Big Basin Redwoods Waterfalls

A varied trail loop links Big Basin Redwoods's main attraction, Berry Creek Falls, with the two equally stunning but less visited falls that lie upstream. Silver Falls flies over a relatively sheer cliff into a small pool, while Golden Cascades tumbles over tiers near the apex of the loop.

Height: 60 feet (Berry Creek Falls); 50 feet (Silver Falls); 50 feet (Golden Falls)

Beauty rating: ★★★★★

Start: The Skyline to the Sea Trailhead at the site of the old park headquarters

Distance: 12.3-mile lollipop

Difficulty: Strenuous

Hiking time: About 7 hours

Seasons/schedule: Year-round; 8 a.m. to sunset

Fees and permits: An entrance fee is charged. Reservations are required.

Trail contact: Big Basin Redwoods State Park, 21600 Big Basin Way, Boulder Creek, CA 95006-9064; (831) 338-8860; www.parks.ca.gov

Canine compatibility: No dogs allowed on trails.

Trail surface: Dirt singletrack

Land status: Big Basin Redwoods State Park

Nearest towns: Saratoga; Los Gatos

Other trail users: None

Maps to consult: USGS Santa Cruz CA; park map available online and at the park visitor center

Water availability: None, though that may change as post-fire recovery continues

Amenities available: Restrooms, trash cans, and information signboards at the trailhead

Cell service: None

Trail conditions: Big Basin Redwoods State Park was heavily impacted by the 2020 CZU Lightning Complex Fire. Potential hazards include falling trees, slides during the rainy season, and hidden stump holes.

Finding the trailhead: From CA 85 in Saratoga, take the Saratoga Avenue exit. Go right (southwest) on Saratoga Avenue through town; Saratoga Avenue becomes CA 9. Continue on CA 9/Big Basin Way for about 7 miles to the junction with Skyline Boulevard/CA 35; cross Skyline to continue on CA 9 toward the state park. Travel another 14 miles to the junction of CA 9 and CA 236. Stay right on CA 236 into the park. Continue on CA 236 for about 9 miles to the park headquarters and trailhead. Trailhead GPS: N37 10.311' / W122 13.329'

The Hike

This long loop, which takes in Berry Creek's three waterfalls before curling back toward home, pushes the limits of a day hike, but for hardy hikers who want to see what lies above lovely Berry Creek Falls, it's worth the effort. Just be sure you allot enough time to complete the whole loop in the span of a short winter's day, if that's when you choose to make the trip.

The other factor that may affect how you walk in Big Basin Redwoods State Park is the state of trails following the devastation wrought by the CZU Lightning

Golden Cascades is the last in line along a hike to waterfalls in Big Basin.

Complex Fire, which ignited in August 2020. Much of the park was closed for almost two years after the fire, which torched nearly 90,000 acres in the Santa Cruz Mountains, including 97 percent of the park's acreage, and destroyed crucial amenities. Reopening was happening in stages as of fall 2022, and the route to the falls remained closed at that time. This description assumes that, as is often the case in the wake of wildfire, the basics of the hike will likely remain the same. But things may also change. The route to Berry Creek Falls was well signed prior to the wildfire, but route finding may be less obvious in its wake. Access to trails and their level of accessibility may change as well, so check with rangers before setting off on the hike.

While conditions in the park are drastically different than they were before the fire, the good news is many of the old-growth redwoods survived the blaze. Its cascades endure as well, including the whitewater fan of 60-foot Berry Creek Falls, the prime waterfall attraction, and a pair of equally stunning falls on a path less traveled. Silver Falls flies off a 50-foot cliff and lands in a dark pool; the trail leading up along the cliff face follows a narrow, spray-washed staircase etched into the dark stone. The

Prior to the CZU Lightning Complex Fire in 2020, the waterfall hike through Big Basin skirted close to Silver Falls, with a wire-rope railing providing sketchy security on the mist-slick steps.

Golden Cascades are a short distance above and beyond, slipping down two tiers of lower-angle slabs with a hint of gold color in the rock.

The loop starts with a long meander down the Skyline to the Sea Trail to Berry Creek Falls. The cascade spills into a box canyon shaded by redwoods and crowded with ferns and moss; at less than 10 miles out and back, this is the turnaround point for many hikers. But the other two falls are an easy climb above, and then the Sunset Trail, which rounds out the lollipop, rolls along the upper reaches of the forested ridges back to the crest.

Begin at the site of the former park headquarters, which were destroyed in the fire. Cross Opal Creek and then head left (downstream) along the creek on the Skyline to the Sea Trail. The Skyline to the Sea Trail breaks sharply right, crosses a drainage, and begins the relatively short climb over the ridge. At the junction on the ridge crest, take the Skyline to the Sea Trail down the Kelly Creek drainage. Pass the junctions with the Sunset Connector Trail and the Timms Creek Trail as you descend. In the rainy season, moisture puffs up mosses that shrivel in the summer, and ferns, redwood sorrel, and trillium, along with other woodland flora, unfurl in season. The trail winding down the canyon incorporates stone steps to mitigate occasional steep sections and negotiates ravines that run with seasonal streams.

The long downhill ends with a crossing of Kelly Creek. Hike up and over into the Berry Creek drainage to Berry Creek Falls, a fine place for a break before beginning the long trek back to the trailhead.

From Berry Creek Falls, a brief climb along the stream leads to Silver Falls. Another short meander leads from Silver Falls to the Golden Cascades, a more sprawling set of falls that fans out over warm-hued slabs. Another staircase, along with switchbacks, leads out of the Berry Creek drainage above the falls and to the junction with the Sunset Trail, the return route. This trail rolls through folds in the ridgeline above the Kelly Creek drainage. Pass the top of the Timms Creek Trail and continue to the Sunset Connector Trail, which drops back to the Skyline to the Sea Trail, closing the loop. Retrace your steps from here.

Miles and Directions

0.0 Start on the Skyline to the Sea Trail.

0.3 At the trail junction, go right on the Skyline to the Sea Trail and begin to climb.

1.0 Reach the crest of the ridge and a trail junction. Go right and down on the Skyline to the Sea Trail.

1.5 At the junction with the Sunset Connector Trail, stay left on the Skyline to the Sea Trail.

3.4 Reach the Timms Creek Trail junction; stay left on the Skyline to the Sea Trail.

4.2 A rock outcropping offers a great viewpoint of the canyon. Drop down a stone staircase.

4.3 Cross Kelly Creek, then climb to the junction with the Berry Creek Trail. Go right on the Berry Creek Trail.

4.5 Pass a switchback and drop down to cross Berry Creek below the falls.

Big Basin Redwoods Waterfalls

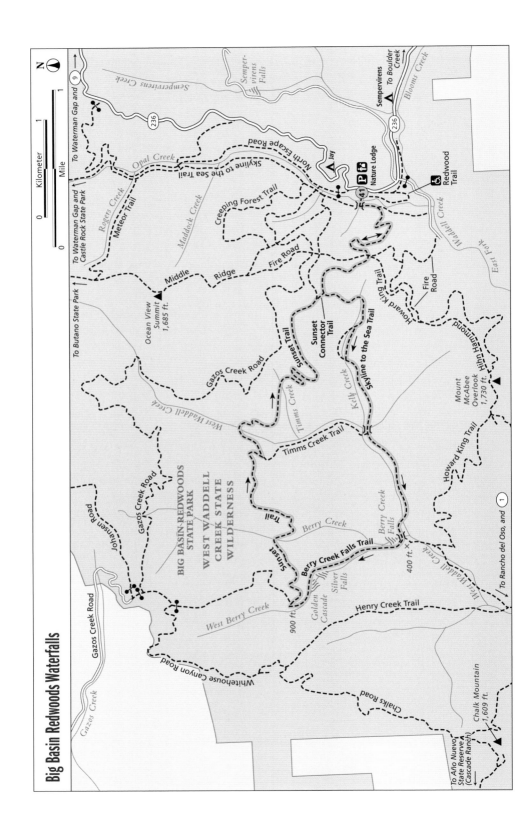

N

| 0 | Kilometer | 1 |
| 0 | Mile | 1 |

4.8 Reach the Berry Creek Falls overlook. Take in the falls, then make your choice: You can retrace your steps back to the trailhead to complete a 9.6-mile out-and-back trek, or you can complete the waterfall tour by continuing up the switchbacking singletrack, as described below.

5.2 Cross Berry Creek above Berry Creek Falls.

5.8 Arrive at Silver Falls. Climb the exposed section of trail up the cliff, skimming close to the funnel at the top of the falls.

6.2 Reach the two-tiered Golden Cascades. Switchbacks and steps lead away from the falls, gaining elevation quickly.

6.4 Arrive at the junction with the Sunset Trail. Turn right, heading east on the footpath.

8.4 At the junction with the Timms Creek Trail, stay left on the Sunset Trail.

9.8 In the open saddle stay right on the Sunset Trail, dropping toward the Sunset Connector Trail.

10.8 At the junction go right on the Sunset Connector Trail. The connector ends on the Skyline to the Sea Trail; from here retrace your steps to the trailhead.

11.3 Reach the ridge crest and begin the final descent toward the trailhead.

12.3 Arrive back at the trailhead.

Option: Big Basin Redwoods State Park is also home to Sempervirens Falls, a 20-foot spill on Sempervirens Creek and an easier destination for those seeking a fall but unable or unwilling to take on the challenges of getting to Berry Creek Falls or doing the waterfall loop. To reach these falls from the former park headquarters, pick up the Sequoia Trail, which parallels the park road south and then east, before curling north to follow Sky Meadows Road and Sempervirens Creek north to the falls. The round-trip distance is about 3 miles.

42 Uvas Canyon Falls

Saturate the Bay Area with a couple of good rains, and Uvas Canyon practically blossoms with falls, cataracts, and cascades.

Height: Six named falls, the shortest being Little Falls at about 5 feet and the tallest being Lower Falls at about 40 feet

Beauty rating: ★★★★★

Start: Trailhead in the day-use parking lot

Distance: 2.7-mile lollipop

Difficulty: Easy

Hiking time: About 2 hours

Seasons/schedule: Year-round; 8 a.m. to sunset

Fees and permits: An entrance fee is charged.

Trail contact: Santa Clara County Parks, Uvas Canyon, 8515 Croy Rd., Morgan Hill, CA 95037; (408) 779-9232; www.sccgov.org/sites/parks/parkfinder/Pages/UvasCanyon.aspx

Canine compatibility: Leashed dogs permitted.

Trail surface: Paved roadway; dirt roadway and singletrack; stone and wooden steps

Land status: Uvas Canyon County Park

Nearest town: Morgan Hill

Other trail users: None

Maps to consult: USGS Loma Prieta CA; maps available at the park and online

Water availability: Water is available in the campground.

Amenities available: Restrooms, picnic sites, information signboard, campground

Cell service: Sketchy but possible

Trail conditions: Reservations are required and can be secured online. The route is popular and well maintained.

Finding the trailhead: From San Jose head south on US 101 into Morgan Hill. Take the Bailey Avenue exit and head right (west) on Bailey Avenue for 3.2 miles to McKean Road. Turn left (south) on McKean Road (which becomes Uvas Road) for 6 miles to Croy Road. Turn right (west) on Croy Road for 4.4 miles, passing through the private Sveadal community, to the park's day-use parking lot. Trailhead GPS: N37 05.069' / W121 47.573'

The Hike

The surprise of Uvas Canyon is that a local park can boast a cluster of destination-worthy waterfalls. Making a comparison to Yosemite is a big stretch, but it's the only other place in NorCal where such a concentration of falls can be found in a compact setting. The scale is vastly smaller, and this canyon is smothered in oaks, bay laurels, ferns, and moss—no soaring granite domes. But douse the Santa Cruz Mountains in a good rain and head up the Waterfall Loop, and you'll pass cataract after cascade after waterfall after cataract. It's really fun.

The Uvas Canyon falls are hitched to year-round Swanson Creek. The park's Waterfall Loop takes in five of the named falls in this park; this description also includes a short out-and-back trek to Lower Falls. A seventh waterfall, Triple Falls, is located in a neighboring canyon.

Little Granuja Falls is one of six named cascades along the Waterfall Loop in Uvas Canyon.

Begin at the trail sign in the Black Oak picnic area. Arrows indicate the Waterfall Loop to the left and right as you face the sign, which is slightly confusing. To take the loop in a counterclockwise direction, matching the interpretive guide (downloadable from the park website), go right, walking down the paved road. Pass the junction with the trail to the Lower Falls (described later), climb a flight of stone steps, cross the bridge, and pass diminutive Granuja Falls. This is just the beginning. . . .

Follow the broad trail uphill, staying right at the two junctions (both lefts leading back to the parking area). The broad walk-and-talk track heads up alongside spring-fed (and, ideally, rain-swollen) Swanson Creek, which rumbles to the left. The side trail to Black Rock Falls breaks right at 0.7 mile. Climb a rustic set of stone steps into the side canyon to check out the sheet, which pours about 30 feet down the eponymous black rock face. Round a switchback near the falls' base and follow the path back to meet the main loop trail. Continue uphill to a flat area. The trail to Knobcone Point breaks to the right, and a few feet beyond is the side trail to Basin Falls, also to the right. A short out-and-back walk leads to the base of this 25-foot spill, in a side canyon like Black Rock Falls before. Upper Falls is to the left, on Swanson Creek, a tiered spill tumbling about 20 feet.

Uvas Canyon Falls

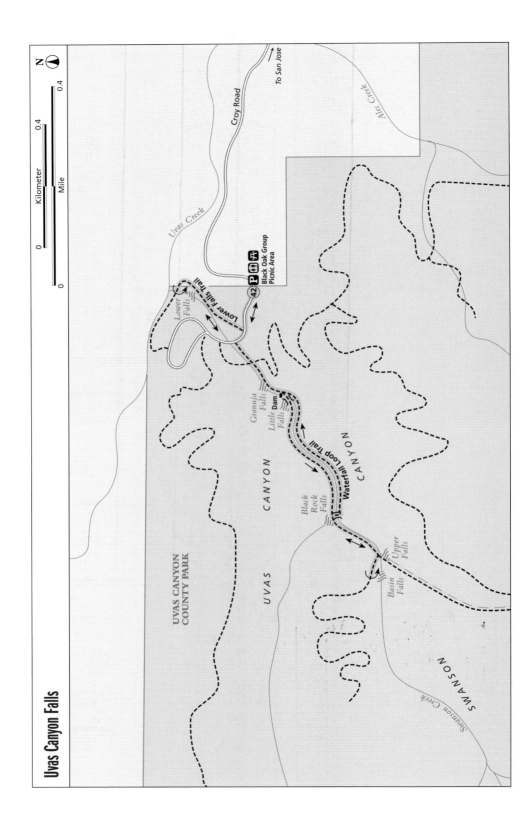

The path back to the start of the loop follows the opposite side of Swanson Creek, reached via a bridge opposite the turn to Black Rock Falls. Cross the bridge and head downstream, now close to the watercourse, which tumbles over a series of short drops. Pass Little Falls and continue down to the remnants of a concrete dam just above the first bridge. Water levels permitting, rock-hop across the stream to gain the bridge and close the loop; the alternative is a scramble over the steep face above the dam and down to the bridge.

Back at the junction with the Lower Falls Trail, head down the wooden stairs and follow the narrow track that skims the hillside above the creek, again heading downstream. The trail descends to a flat area, climbs around a mossy rock outcropping, and drops down a steep staircase to the base of Lower Falls, which plunges about 30 feet over a low point in an eroded cliff. This locale is the most open along the route, with the denuded earth of the cliff face forming a small open bowl in the oak forest. Should the sun be shining and the day warm, this makes an inviting place to picnic and, stream flows permitting, hang out in the water.

Retrace your steps to the trailhead.

Miles and Directions

0.0 Begin by walking up past the restrooms to the sign in the Black Oak picnic area. Go right on the paved park road.

0.1 Pass the junction with the trail to Lower Falls. Stay straight on the Waterfall Loop, climbing the stone steps and crossing the bridge.

0.2 Pass Granuja Falls. Stay right at the trail junctions that follow.

0.3 Cross the bridge below the dam, staying on the Waterfall Loop.

0.6 At the junction with the Black Rock Falls side trail, turn right and head up to the falls. To continue, climb the switchback and follow the path that parallels the main route.

0.7 Back on the main route, head right and uphill.

0.8 Pass the Maple Flat picnic area.

0.9 The Knobcone Point Trail breaks sharply right. Basin Falls is also to the right, up a short side trail. Upper Falls is to the left, in the main canyon. Explore, then retrace your steps to the junction with the Black Rock Falls side trail.

1.2 At the junction turn right, head around a switchback, and cross the bridge to reach the return route on the other side of Swanson Creek.

1.4 Pass Little Falls and cross a bridge.

1.6 At the dam rock-hop across the creek and regain the main trail, closing the loop. Cross the bridge and descend the stone steps.

1.8 Turn left onto the Lower Falls Trail.

1.9 At the junction stay straight on the Lower Falls Trail.

2.2 Cross a flat area, climb around a mossy rock outcropping, and descend a steep staircase.

2.3 Reach the base of Lower Falls. Retrace your steps.

2.7 Arrive back at the trailhead.

Honorable Mentions

Bouverie Falls

Charged by rainfall in the Mayacamas Mountains, this 100-foot ribbon waterfall is a headliner in this well-tended nature preserve in Glen Ellen. The seasonal falls received a boost after an earthquake punched the bedrock in such a way that streams in the North Bay region, including Stuart Creek, were recharged in the midst of the dry season and drought. Things were a little less productive following the 2017 Nuns Fire, which blew through 75 percent of the 535-acre Audubon Canyon Ranch Bouverie Preserve, destroying much of its infrastructure, including the falls overlook.

Bouverie Falls flows year-round, but access to the waterfall has been curtailed by wildfire.

You can join a docent-led hike to the falls: depending on the route the docent chooses, the out-and-back or looping walk will total about 4.5 miles. To learn more and to reserve a spot for a guided hike, contact the preserve at https://egret.org/preserves_bouverie.

Marin County Waterfalls

Marin County has been dealt a generous hand when it comes to seasonal waterfalls, and many of these are neighborhood treasures. Such is the case with **Cascade Falls** in Fairfax: It happens to be the waterfall I grew up with. It didn't take long to get from home into what was then called Elliott's property, splash through the ford of San Anselmo Creek to the base of Repack (a famous downhill mountain-bike run), then bushwhack through fern and poison oak to the cascade itself. Today the journey to Cascade Falls, 40 feet high and reached via a 1.8-mile out-and-back hike through Elliott Nature Preserve, part of the Cascade Canyon Open Space Preserve, is considerably more civilized. The tricky part is trailhead parking (it's sparse), and making sure you can cross the creek, not only because of flows but also to protect spawning steelhead.

The waterfall on Cascade Creek dried out come summertime, but it is a nice destination when swollen by winter rains.

The trail to Dawn Falls laces through redwood groves on the slopes of Mount Tamalpais.

Reaching **Dawn Falls** may be your goal, but Mount Tamalpais, Marin County's Sleeping Lady, is the dominant feature on this 3.8-mile hike. Views of the summit dominate at the outset, and even as the summit of the Lady slips from view, the dense oak and laurel forest that makes up her gown is all-encompassing. The 30-foot-high falls are tucked along Larkspur Creek in Baltimore Canyon, one of the mountain's deep green folds, and are fed by seasonal rainfall and dry by midsummer. The loop hike links the Southern Marin Line Fire Road, the Dawn Falls Trail, and the Barbara Springs Trail, but there are plenty of options for further exploration on Mount Tam. While you are exploring Mount Tam and environs, you can also check out Cascade Falls in Mill Valley (same name; different town), reached via a short walk via streets and trail from downtown.

Stairstep Falls is tucked away in an overgrown crevice in Marin County's beautiful Samuel P. Taylor State Park. Reaching the hidden 40-foot waterfall involves an easy 2.8-mile out-and-back hike linking the Devil's Gulch Trail, Bill's Trail (which may close in heavy rain; check with the park about status before visiting), and the Stairstep Falls Trail. The falls are on a side stream feeding Devil's Gulch, which flows into Lagunitas Creek, an environmental success story where coho salmon now spawn in winter. The falls themselves are slender, toppling from step to green step, hemmed in by steep walls overgrown with sword fern, poison oak, and moss, with a thick canopy of oak, madrone, bay laurel, and Douglas fir interwoven overhead. Stairstep is seasonal, by midsummer thinning to a trickle that is seen more than heard. The Devil's Gulch trailhead is 1 mile northwest of Camp Taylor. Parking for about twenty-five cars is on the west side of the road; the trailhead is across Sir Francis Drake on the east.

The stream that feeds Stairstep Falls empties into Lagunitas Creek, which supports a rejuvenated seasonal salmon run.

When it's not sapped by drought, Indian Valley Falls is a nice destination in its eponymous open space preserve.

A pleasant, 2.9-mile lollipop winds through oak woodland to the seasonal, 25-foot **Indian Valley Falls** in Novato's Indian Valley Open Space Preserve. The loop trail leading past the falls is a pleasant immersion in a pocket of oak woodland bordering quiet subdivisions. Two other Marin County Open Space parks in Novato feature short hikes to seasonal waterfalls, both best just after heavy rains. **Pacheco Creek Falls,** a seasonal cascade about 25 feet tall, is in the Pacheco Valle Open Space Preserve; **Fairway Falls** (aka Arroyo de San Jose Falls and Buck Gulch Falls) is in the Ignacio Valley Open Space Preserve, adjacent to the Indian Valley preserve but not linked by a trail. Fairway's first fall, about 30 feet high, is an easy half-mile walk from the trailhead. Other cataracts are farther up the creek.

San Francisco Waterfalls

San Francisco encompasses more than a bustling financial and shopping district: It's also home to Yerba Buena Gardens and the **Martin Luther King Jr. Memorial Waterfall,** an inspirational man-made diversion in the heart of the city. The 20-foot-high, 50-foot-wide sheet of water that washes over the stone-and-glass memorial to the civil rights leader radiates power, peace, and hope. You can take a short tour of the park and the Yerba Buena Center for the Arts if your focus is the falls, but downtown is at your feet, so wander at will.

Exploring Golden Gate Park—a 3-mile-long linear swipe of green space linking San Francisco's city streets to Ocean Beach and the Pacific Ocean—is a pleasure whether you live in the city or are just visiting. The park's amenities are plentiful:

Visits to the Martin Luther King Jr. Memorial Waterfall and Huntington Falls incorporate urban hikes in San Francisco.

strolling through the Japanese Tea Garden and the Conservatory of Flowers; taking in the exhibits at the de Young Museum and the California Academy of Sciences; and wandering through redwood groves, rhododendron dells, botanical gardens, or grassy meadows. **Huntington Falls,** 110 feet high and reached via a 1.4-mile double loop starting from the Stow Lake boathouse, with the option to hike to the top of Strawberry Hill, from where the falls spring, is one highlight among many, and an easy escape from big-city busyness.

Let your favorite paper map or map app be your guide to reach either or both of these falls, either on foot or bicycle, via public transit, or by car.

Seasonal **Brooks Creek Falls** can't be reached directly, but a nice 2.5-mile loop hike through coastal San Pedro Valley Park on the San Francisco Peninsula offers unimpeded views of the narrow 175-foot ribbon, a striking splash of white amid green scrub when swollen with rainfall. When the falls dry up in summer, the stained cliff still draws the eye, a streak of dark amid scrub dried by the season. When it's hot inland, fog and moist ocean breezes regularly cool the heights and hollows of Montara Mountain, the park's centerpiece. The hike also offers some interpretation of Spanish colonial history, white colonial history, and natural history. The park is located in Pacifica; visit www.smcgov.org/parks/san-pedro-valley-park.

East Bay Waterfalls

The seasonal **Abrigo Falls,** about 25 feet tall, is reached via an easy 3.2-mile out-and-back walk on the Abrigo Valley Trail. It's no stunner, only viable in a wet winter, and is best viewed through a screen of thick foliage from the trail. Listen for the waterfall as you climb a short, steep pitch past Camp Wee-Ta-Chi. You'll find, as I did with many hikes to less-than-stellar seasonal waterfalls, that hiking Abrigo Falls is not

A hike to Abrigo Falls is not so much about the waterfall as the gorgeous park surrounding it.

so much about the destination as getting there. Briones Regional Park offers great walking through rolling, grass-covered hills, and if you hitch your tag of the falls into a nice loop—like a 4.2-mile lollipop connecting Abrigo Falls Trail to the Briones Crest, where panoramic views open eastward onto Mount Diablo, the Carquinez Strait, Suisun Bay, and the Sacramento River delta—a walk in the park will be well worth your time. Complete the loop by following the Briones Crest Trail to the Mott Peak Trail, and then descend from Mott Peak back to the Abrigo Valley Trail. Visit www .ebparks.org/parks/briones for more information and directions.

They don't call it Mount Diablo for nothing. This iconic peak, the highest point on the east side of the San Francisco Bay Area, is lovely to look at, but the mountain's temperament, like its geologic origins, can be volcanic. It lures you in with wildflowers and waterfalls, then wallops you with devilishly steep trails that, in rainy weather, can devolve into boot-sucking mud. **Diablo Falls** are tucked in a steep canyon along Donner Creek. Because I did the hike in a drought, I can't personally vouch for the falls, but reportedly a cluster of rain-fed 20- to 30-foot plunges can be seen from the Falls Trail. You'll climb about 1,300 feet in about 3 miles to reach the waterfall area, and depending on the route you choose, the hike will take 3.5 to 5 hours to complete. From the visitor center in Clayton, I linked Oak Road to Murchio Road to Donner Canyon Road, then humped up to the junction with Cardinet Oaks Road, which linked via more steep, switchbacking climbing to the Falls Trail. The falls area is about 0.5 mile from the junction. Set your pace and slog on. For more information, visit www.parks.ca.gov or www.mdia.org/geologic-guide-falls–trail-loop.

Navigate the steep slopes of Mount Diablo to reach its seasonal waterfalls.

*Follow an easy
trail winding
through the steep
canyon contain-
ing Alameda
Creek to Little
Yosemite Falls.*

Alameda Creek steepens and gathers speed as it is funneled through the steep-walled Little Yosemite canyon in Sunol Wilderness Regional Preserve, forming a series of rolling cascades of varying heights known as **Little Yosemite Falls.** There are two ways to view the cataracts: You can simply follow the Camp Ohlone fire road out and back (about 2.5 miles total), or follow a 3.3-mile loop through a picturesque grassland dotted with serpentine rock outcroppings and archetypal oaks. The longer route, linking the Indian Joe Nature Trail and Canyon View Trail, tops out with an easy traverse that offers excellent views in three directions before dropping to the boulder-tossed waterway and the Camp Ohlone Road. For more information, visit www.ebparks.org/parks/sunol.

Monterey and Big Sur

One of California's most photographed waterfalls is in Big Sur . . . but then again, a number of postcard-perfect destinations lie along the dramatic coastline that stretches from Monterey to Lucia. This is one of the few places in the state where driving from trailhead to trailhead is as pleasurable as the hiking itself. Monterey, Carmel, and Pacific Grove offer all the amenities, with Big Sur a more rustic destination. The waterfalls all lie along scenic CA 1.

McWay Falls (hike 44).

43 Pfeiffer Falls

The trail to Pfeiffer Falls explores the interface of oak woodland and redwood forest on the Big Sur coastline.

Height: 60 feet
Beauty rating: ★★★★★
Start: Pfeiffer Falls/Valley View Trailhead near the Big Sur Lodge
Distance: 2.0 miles out and back
Difficulty: Moderate
Hiking time: About 1.5 hours
Seasons/schedule: Year-round; 8 a.m. to sunset
Fees and permits: An entrance fee is charged.
Trail contact: Pfeiffer Big Sur State Park, 47225 CA 1, Big Sur, CA 93920; (831) 667-1112 or (831) 667-2315; www.parks.ca.gov
Canine compatibility: No dogs permitted on this trail, but they are allowed on leash on other park routes.

Trail surface: Pavement, dirt singletrack
Land status: Pfeiffer Big Sur State Park
Nearest town: Big Sur
Other trail users: None
Maps to consult: USGS Big Sur CA; map available in the park brochure and online
Water availability: Water is available at the trailhead.
Amenities available: Restrooms, information, trash cans, picnic sites, camping facilities, and a lodge and cafe
Cell service: Marginal; don't count on it.
Trail conditions: The trail is popular and well maintained.

Finding the trailhead: From Carmel follow scenic CA 1 south for 27.5 miles to the signed entrance to Pfeiffer Big Sur State Park on the left. Finding parking can be problematic on busy spring and summer weekends. This route begins at the paved, signed trailhead in the parking lot at the Big Sur Lodge; your route at the outset may vary depending on where you are able to park. Trailhead GPS: N36 15.067' / W121 47.177'

The Hike

Dramatic redwood groves, which flourish in the fog-shrouded ravines of Big Sur, bookend the trail to Pfeiffer Falls. The route begins in a stand of massive trees: The shade is thick, footfalls are muffled by a dense carpet of needles, and Pfeiffer Creek flows through to its confluence with the Big Sur River. Trail's end is in another redwood stand, equally quiet and also bisected by the creek, with a 60-foot waterfall adding drama to the scene.

Between the redwood groves the route climbs across a slope cloaked in oak woodland, the trees low and gnarled, throwing a spindlier shade across the landscape and allowing a thick chaparral, including coyote brush and poison oak, to thrive. Buckeyes, with their fragrant blooms, are among the first trees to leaf out in spring, and the smooth, deep-burgundy bark of manzanita splashes color onto the gray and brown landscape.

Pfeiffer Falls splashes into a redwood-shaded pool.

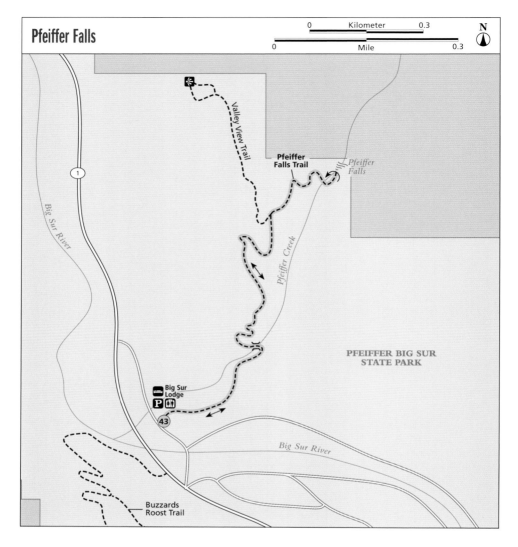

Kilometer
0   0.3

Mile
0   0.3

N

Valley View Trail

Pfeiffer
Falls Trail

Pfeiffer
Falls

1

Big Sur River

Pfeiffer Creek

PFEIFFER BIG SUR
STATE PARK

Big Sur
Lodge

P

43

Big Sur River

Buzzards
Roost Trail

Depending on where you park, you may travel a different route to the formal trailhead. From the restaurant at the Big Sur Lodge, a signed, paved path climbs gently to the trailhead proper. Beyond the information sign, wire rails usher you through the redwoods to the bridge across Pfeiffer Creek and then up onto the Valley View Trail. A short, switchbacking climb leads into the oaks, offering views of the Big Sur valley.

The Valley View and Pfeiffer Falls Trails diverge at the top of the climb: Go right on the path to Pfeiffer Falls. The trail traverses the hillside, with views opening inland across the tops of the redwoods and onto the steep slopes of the Santa Lucias.

A switchbacking descent leads into the redwood grove at the base of Pfeiffer Falls. Bear left on the path, climbing briefly to the overlook rocks at the base of the fall. The waterfall is tiered, the middle section a sheet of whitewater when the creek is fully charged. Crane your neck to see the upper tier, high on the mountainside. Retrace your steps.

Miles and Directions

0.0 Start at the signed trailhead next to the Big Sur Lodge restaurant. Follow the pavement across the park road.

0.2 Reach the formal trailhead, where there is an information signboard. Head into the redwoods on the wide dirt track.

0.3 Cross the bridge and bear left onto the Valley View Trail.

0.8 At the junction go right onto the Pfeiffer Falls Trail. The Valley View Trail heads left.

0.9 Descend switchbacks to a bridge in the redwoods.

1.0 Reach Pfeiffer Falls. Retrace your steps.

2.0 Arrive back at the trailhead.

Option: If you'd like to take in more vistas of the Big Sur valley and coastline, head up on the Valley View Trail. The rough singletrack continues climbing through the chaparral, passing benches along the way. The trail dead-ends at a lofty overlook; look north up the coastline, with the Santa Lucia Mountains forming an impressive rampart in the east and the world flattening into the Pacific in the west. Return as you came.

44 McWay Falls

The signature waterfall on the Big Sur coast, McWay Falls will not disappoint.

Height: About 80 feet

Beauty rating: ★★★★★

Start: Waterfall Overlook Trailhead in the day-use area parking lot

Distance: 0.8 mile out and back

Difficulty: Easy

Hiking time: Less than 1 hour

Seasons/schedule: Year-round; 8 a.m. to sunset

Fees and permits: An entrance fee is charged.

Trail contact: Julia Pfeiffer Burns State Park, Big Sur Station #1 / 47555 CA 1, Big Sur, CA 93920; (831) 649-2836; www.parks.ca.gov

Canine compatibility: No dogs allowed on trails.

Trail surface: Crushed granite

Land status: Julia Pfeiffer Burns State Park

Nearest town: Big Sur

Other trail users: None

Maps to consult: USGS Partington Ridge CA; park map available at the park's entrance station

Water availability: Water is available at the trailhead.

Amenities available: Restrooms, trash cans, information, picnic sites, and camping facilities

Cell service: Marginal; don't count on it.

Trail conditions: The trail is massively popular and can be crowded. Be courteous to other trail users. Do not attempt to reach the beach at the falls; the cliffs are dangerous.

Finding the trailhead: From Big Sur follow scenic CA 1 south for about 11 miles to the signed entrance to Julia Pfeiffer Burns State Park on the left. The park is 38 miles south of Carmel. The bend in CA 1 above McWay Cove is often congested with cars parking alongside the highway and using a secondary trail to reach the falls overlook. Trailhead GPS: N36 09.570' / W121 40.107'

The Hike

McWay Cove, and the wisp of a fall that spills into it, is iconic. Waterfalls that spill directly onto Northern California beaches are few and far between, and each has a spectacular seaside setting. But McWay, with its inaccessible crescent of sand and rugged Saddle Rock forming a protective break from the sea, stands apart. That it would become the focal point of an equally spectacular seaside home is no surprise: From the overlook among the foundations of the Waterfall House, the vistas are mesmerizing and inspirational.

A short, well-maintained, and well-traveled crushed granite trail leads from the day-use parking area to the waterfall overlook. Pass through the pedestrian tunnel under CA 1 and then turn right on the overlook trail, traversing the chaparral-coated slope above the cove. The path to the left leads up through a stand of eucalyptus to CA 1, providing access to visitors who've parked alongside the highway. The waterfall comes into view as the trail curves gently westward, the spill arcing out from the tree-topped cliff face and freefalling onto the beach below.

Slender McWay Falls is a main attraction along the Big Sur coast.

The turnaround is at the overlook. Surrounded by the remnants of the Waterfall House, interpretive signs describe both the human and natural history of the park, including a synopsis of the life of namesake Julia Pfeiffer Burns, who spent all her days on the Big Sur coast, and of Helen Hooper Brown, the heiress who, with her husband, purchased Saddle Ranch in 1924 and built the house on the point, along with a funicular rail line to get to and from the site. There's also a description of the massive slide that took out CA 1 just north of the park in 1983; debris from the slide makes up the beach upon which slender McWay Falls makes landfall. The slide scar is still visible.

When you've taken it all in—if that's possible in a single visit—return as you came.

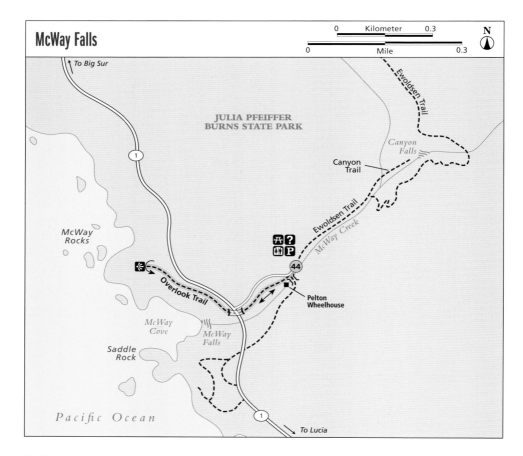

McWay Falls

Miles and Directions

0.0   Start by descending the staircase and heading right on the Waterfall Overlook Trail. Pass the trail that leads left to the Pelton wheelhouse.

0.1   Pass through the pedestrian tunnel.

0.4   Reach the waterfall overlook. Retrace your steps.

0.8   Arrive back at the trailhead.

Option: As you near the trailhead on the return from the McWay Falls overlook, take a right turn onto the path leading down to the Pelton wheelhouse. The trail leads through a bower of willow down to the wheelhouse, where you can check out the wheel, sometimes called a "hurdy-gurdy," and read about how it was used to generate electricity from McWay Creek, which descends steeply enough out of the Santa Lucia Mountains to provide power for Saddle Ranch. The side trip will add about 0.1 mile to the hike.

45 Limekiln Falls

Leave the thunder of the Pacific surf behind on an easy trail that leads into the steep coastal canyon that hosts Limekiln Falls.

Height: 100 feet
Beauty rating: ★★★★
Start: Limekiln Trailhead in the day-use parking area
Distance: 2.0 miles, including a side trip to the kilns
Difficulty: Moderate due to creek crossings
Hiking time: About 1.5 hours
Seasons/schedule: Year-round, 8 a.m. to sunset
Fees and permits: An entrance fee is charged.
Trail contact: Limekiln State Park, 63025 CA 1, Big Sur, CA 93920; (805) 434-1996; www .parks.ca.gov. The park is managed by Parks Management Company; for reservations and information, contact https://campone.com.

Canine compatibility: No dogs permitted on trails.
Trail surface: Dirt
Land status: Limekiln State Park
Nearest town: Big Sur
Other trail users: None
Maps to consult: USGS Lopez Point CA; park map available at the entrance station and online
Water availability: Water is available in the campground.
Amenities available: Restrooms, trash cans, picnic sites, camping, and information
Cell service: None
Trail conditions: The park was heavily impacted by the Dolan Fire in 2020. Check with the park to ensure trails are accessible.

Finding the trailhead: From Big Sur follow scenic CA 1 south for 24 miles to the signed turnoff for Limekiln State Park, on the south side of the Limekiln Bridge. The park is about 52 miles south of Carmel. Follow the entrance road for 0.1 mile to the entrance station, pay the fee, and park in the day-use parking area. Trailhead GPS: N36 00.625' / W121 31.108'

The Hike

The Santa Lucia Mountains have an arid feel, washed in warm winds that dry out the grasses earlier in the season than farther north. The weather and fuels are the kind that spawn wildfires, like the 125,000-acre Dolan Fire, which swept through Limekiln State Park in 2020. Still, if you slip back into the folds of the mountains, you'll find moist ravines where redwood groves, ferns, and mosses thrive. Limekiln Falls is the prime attraction in one of these canyons.

The waterfall is a major draw, but the park's namesake limekilns, in the neighboring ravine, are equally engaging. The limestone deposit in the canyon was fed into the four towering metal furnaces that still stand alongside the trail in a dark hollow; the lime purified by fire in the kilns was shipped north and used to make concrete. The operation lasted for only three years in the 1880s, according to park literature, and aside from depleting the deposit, the processing also consumed the surrounding redwood forest. What stands in the hollows now is second growth but still statuesque.

Above: Abandoned limekilns hunker in the forest near Limekiln Falls.
Below: Limekiln Creek rambles alongside the trail to Limekiln Falls.

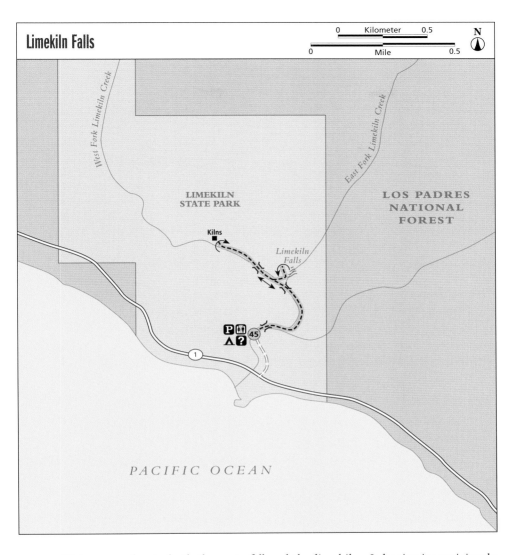

0   Kilometer   0.5

0   Mile   0.5

N

West Fork Limekiln Creek

East Fork Limekiln Creek

LIMEKILN STATE PARK

LOS PADRES NATIONAL FOREST

Kilns

Limekiln Falls

45

1

PACIFIC OCEAN

This route takes in both the waterfall and the limekilns. It begins inauspiciously, passing through the park's linear campground, which survived the Dolan Fire. Cross the bridge over Limekiln Creek, however, and development slips away, as does the roar of the sea, overtaken by the sound of water flowing in Limekiln and Hare Creeks.

The trail forks immediately on the far side of the bridge, with the right fork leading up Hare Creek and the left following Limekiln Creek. Stay left, following Limekiln Creek and passing through memorial groves. Cross a second bridge and then bear right at the trail junction and cross the creek yet again, heading up the east fork of Limekiln Creek toward the falls.

The Falls Trail crosses the east fork several more times as it climbs toward the destination: Be prepared to do some keen balancing on rocks and wet logs or to get your feet wet—and be especially cautious when the flows are high. The last ford deposits you on the south side of the creek. Follow the path up to the overlook, where views of Limekiln Falls, cascading over a 100-foot cliff, are unimpeded. Take it in, then retrace your steps to the trail junction above the second bridge.

After wringing out your socks, turn right onto the Limekiln Trail and hike up into another stunning redwood grove, this one studded with tall, round, metal structures that are reminiscent of the helmets worn by the Knights Who Say Ni in *Monty Python and the Holy Grail*. Check out the massive kilns, with their brick-lined mouths, and then retrace your steps to the trailhead.

Miles and Directions

0.0   Start by walking from the day-use parking area up the road through the linear campground along Limekiln Creek.

0.1   Cross the bridge at the end of the camp to the trail Y. Go left on the trail along Limekiln Creek.

0.4   Cross a second bridge. The trail continues about 150 yards farther to another trail Y; go right to follow the trail to Limekiln Falls. The trail drops across the creek.

0.7   Arrive at the falls overlook. Retrace your steps to the junction above the second bridge.

1.0   Back at the junction, turn right onto the Limekiln Trail.

1.1   Cross yet another bridge, proceeding up the north side of the west fork of Limekiln Creek.

1.3   Reach the four massive, antique limekilns. Retrace your steps.

2.0   Arrive back at the trailhead.

Honorable Mentions

Garland Ranch Falls

A lovely 2.6-mile lollipop loop through a popular park strung along the Carmel River leads to this seasonal, 70-foot waterfall. The multiuse trails in Garland Ranch Regional Park are wide, well-groomed, and shared by hikers, bikers, dog walkers, and equestrians, so the park can be a busy place. The large meadow hosts a long loop

Well-maintained trails lead to the waterfall in Garland Ranch Regional Park.

alongside the Carmel River, with the ridgelines of the Santa Lucia Mountains rising to the south. This loop takes in everything but the ridgelines, coursing through the meadow, arcing up to the fall, and cruising through oak woodlands at the base of the mountains. The fall is best viewed after winter rains have revitalized the watershed, an event that causes ferns to explode from the woodland floor and mosses to fatten up and display their most vivid greens. For more information, visit www.mprpd.org/garland-ranch-regional-park.

A hike in Garland Ranch Regional Park is as much about views and ambiance as about waterfalls.

Canyon Falls is the wallflower waterfall in Julia Pfeiffer Burns State Park.

Canyon Falls

Less than a mile from the more popular (and more crowded) McWay Falls in Julia Pfeiffer Burns State Park, Canyon Falls dances down a narrow gorge that seems a world away. Follow McWay Creek downstream, and you can witness its final descent into the sea. Follow McWay Creek upstream, and you can watch it tumble 60 feet down a steep gorge crowded with redwoods. The 1.2-mile out-and-back route is within the burn scar of the Dolan Fire, which blew through the area in 2020, and has been closed due to hazards including mudslides and hazardous trees. For more information, visit the park site at www.parks.ca.gov.

Yosemite

When it hits a landscape peppered with cliffs, what's a river to do? It must go with the flow; it must fall. In Yosemite National Park, the creeks and rivers taking that fall are epic. Most everything you'll need to support your waterfall explorations can be found on the Yosemite Valley floor, from camping to upscale accommodations at the historic Ahwahnee Hotel. Nearby towns include Groveland, Mariposa, and Wawona; highways leading into the park include CA 120/Big Oak Flat Road (coming from the north), CA 140 (coming from the west up the Merced River valley), and CA 41/Wawona Road (linking the valley to Wawona).

A perpetual rainbow arcs across the base of Vernal Fall (hike 50).

46 Wapama Falls

The thrill of a hike to Wapama Falls is the stretch of trail that leads right through the fury. A boardwalk winds through the boulder field that catches the Wapama spill and swirling mist.

Height: 1,400 feet

Beauty rating: ★ ★ ★ ★ ★

Start: Hetch Hetchy trailhead

Distance: 5.2 miles out and back

Difficulty: Moderate

Hiking time: About 3 hours

Seasons/schedule: Year-round, sunrise to sunset. The access road may be closed in winter if snowy/icy conditions warrant. Slippery, icy conditions may be present on the trail in winter.

Fees and permits: An entrance fee is charged.

Trail contact: Yosemite National Park, Public Information Office, PO Box 577, Yosemite, CA 95389; (209) 372-0200 (dial ext. 3, then 5); www.nps.gov/yose. The website is extensive and should be every visitor's first stop for information on the park.

Canine compatibility: No pets allowed on trail.

Trail surface: Dirt service road, dirt singletrack, boardwalk

Land status: Yosemite National Park; Hetch Hetchy Valley

Nearest town: Groveland

Other trail users: Horse packers

Maps to consult: USGS Lake Eleanor CA; Yosemite National Park map available online and at the park entrance station

Water availability: None

Amenities available: Parking and information signs at the trailhead

Cell service: None

Trail conditions: While popular, trails in Hetch Hetchy Valley are less crowded than in Yosemite Valley. Be courteous to other trail users.

Finding the trailhead: From CA 120/Big Oak Flat Road 1 mile west of the Big Oak Flat Entrance to Yosemite National Park, take Evergreen Road toward the Evergreen Lodge and Hetch Hetchy. Follow Evergreen Road for about 7.2 miles to the stop sign at the junction with Mather Road and continue right on Evergreen/Hetch Hetchy Road. Pass the Yosemite National Park entrance station and continue to the parking area/trailhead at O'Shaughnessy Dam, which is a total of 15.9 miles from the junction with CA 120. Trailhead GPS: N37 56.754' / W119 47.297'

The Hike

When fed by snowmelt, the destination is visible from the trailhead. Wapama Falls appears big, white, and relentless from a viewpoint on O'Shaughnessy Dam, but the distance minimizes its power. The sound and fury in Wapama becomes thrillingly apparent as you close in: The roar strikes you first, rumbling around the rock face on the final approach. Climb onto the boardwalks at the base of the falls, and the mist and noise envelop you. Round the bend to near trail's end and crane your neck; the genesis of the spill is more than 1,000 feet above. The beauty, intimacy, and ferocity of this waterfall are unparalleled.

Wapama Falls thunders into the boulder field at its base, then cascades into Hetch Hetchy Reservoir.

All that said, Wapama Falls is out of sight for much of the hike. Instead, the route showcases the spectacular Hetch Hetchy Valley and Reservoir. Legendary Yosemite champion John Muir waged his final conservation battle for this valley, taking on the city of San Francisco, which was rebuilding and burgeoning in the wake of the 1906 earthquake and firestorm. The City by the Bay had targeted Hetch Hetchy as the perfect place to sequester a secure water supply, regardless of the fact that the valley was within the boundaries of Yosemite National Park. The city won: Today water from Hetch Hetchy travels 167 miles downhill to San Francisco, powered by gravity. The controversy over flooding the valley has never entirely died out, and to this day wildland activists hope to drain the reservoir and restore what Muir called "one of nature's rarest and most precious mountain temples."

I am far too young to know what Hetch Hetchy looked like in Muir's day, but I can say that it remains a tremendous, evocative landscape.

Three waterfalls lie along the Wapama Falls Trail. Wapama Falls flows year-round; smaller Tueeulala Fall peters out as the summer season progresses; and Rancheria Falls lies farther up-valley, accessible via a 13-mile round-trip hike (best done as an overnight).

Wapama Falls

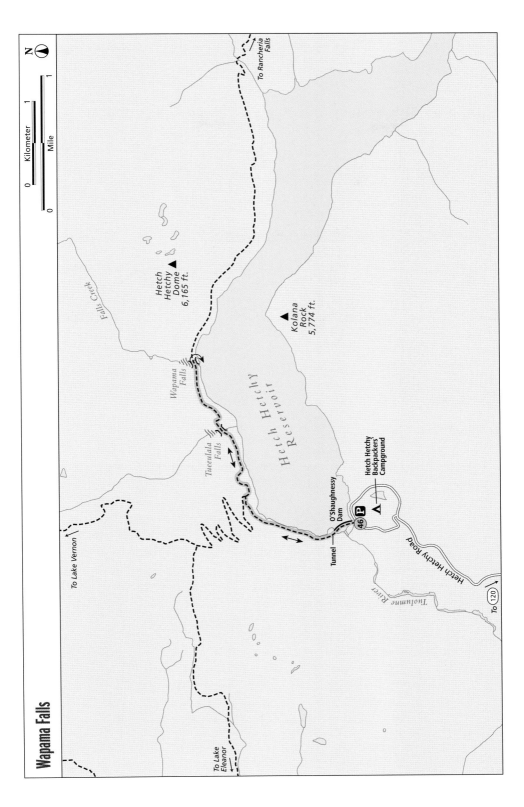

The route begins on the O'Shaughnessy Dam, authorized by the Raker Act in 1913, completed about ten years later, and blockading water for San Francisco by the mid-1930s. Looking down into the narrow canyon beyond the dam face, you might see powerful jets discharging from outlets into the Tuolumne River. The dominant feature to the east, rising from the water, is Kolana Rock, topping out at 5,774 feet, nearly 2,000 feet above the surface of the reservoir (depending on the water level).

On the other side of the dam, the trail passes through a long, dark, damp tunnel, emerging nearly 0.2 mile beyond in the shade of the valley wall. The path gradually narrows from road width to singletrack, climbing via pavement and stairs to a trail junction. Stay right on the signed path to Wapama Falls, Rancheria Falls, and, eventually, the Yosemite Valley.

From the junction the route drops down and across a granite apron with great reservoir views. The granite may be wet in early season; in fact, depending on the time of year and the quantity of snowmelt, much of the trail may be waterlogged. Stay left on the trail at about 1.5 miles and then veer right to cross more sunny slabs. Depending on the temperature, the shade of a stand of ponderosa pines at 1.9 miles will be welcome.

Tueeulala Fall is at about 2.1 miles, but it may be little more than a black streak on the cliff face in late season or in drought years, even though neighboring Wapama Falls may be in full force. Swing up stony switchbacks and then drop onto the bridges that span the jumbled rock apron at the base of Wapama Falls. You'll want to walk to the very edge of the last footbridge to take in the entire spectacle.

Miles and Directions

0.0 Start by crossing O'Shaughnessy Dam.

0.2 Enter the tunnel.

0.4 Emerge from the tunnel and traverse above the reservoir shoreline.

0.8 Cross a seasonal stream.

1.1 At the trail junction stay right on the signed trail to Wapama Falls. A left takes you to the Beehive, Laurel Lake, and Vernon Lake.

2.1 Cross the footbridge at the base of Tueeulala Fall.

2.6 Reach the boardwalks below Wapama Falls. Take it all in, then return as you came.

5.2 Arrive back at the trailhead.

Wapama Falls plummets from clifftop to reservoir in the storied Hetch Hetchy Valley.

47 Bridalveil Fall

Drive into the Yosemite Valley proper, and Bridalveil is the first fall you'll see, spilling over the shadowy cliff wall nearly opposite El Capitan. While many visitors simply stop alongside the road to view the waterfall, a short paved trail leads closer to its base.

Height: 620 feet
Beauty rating: ★★★★★
Start: Bridalveil Fall trailhead
Distance: 0.5 mile out and back
Difficulty: Easy
Hiking time: Less than 1 hour
Seasons/schedule: Year-round; sunrise to sunset. Slippery, icy conditions may exist in winter.
Fees and permits: An entrance fee is charged. A reservation system to visit Yosemite Valley is in place; visit www.nps.gov/yose/planyourvisit/reservations.htm for more information.
Trail contact: Yosemite National Park, Public Information Office, PO Box 577, Yosemite, CA 95389; (209) 372-0200 (dial ext. 3, then 5); www.nps.gov/yose. The website is extensive and should be every visitor's first stop for information on the park.

Canine compatibility: Leashed dogs permitted.
Trail surface: Pavement
Land status: Yosemite National Park
Nearest towns: Yosemite Village; El Portal
Other trail users: None
Maps to consult: USGS El Capitan CA; park map available online and at park entrances
Water availability: None at the trailhead
Amenities available: Restrooms and trash cans. An abundance of amenities—from gift shops to restaurants to tent cabins and more—not to mention the basics, such as restrooms, water, and trash cans, are available farther up the road in Yosemite Valley.
Cell service: Marginal; don't count on it.
Trail conditions: The trail is popular and congested. Be courteous to other hikers.

Finding the trailhead: From El Portal take CA 140 east into Yosemite Valley via the Arch Rock entrance station—or find your way into the valley via CA 120/Big Oak Flat Road or CA 41/Wawona Road. Take Southside Drive (one-way) to the signed junction with Wawona Road/CA 41. Turn right onto Wawona Road and then turn immediately left into the signed parking area for the Bridalveil Fall trailhead. There is a large lot, and overflow parking is available alongside Wawona Road. Trailhead GPS: N37 42.988' / W119 39.076'

The Hike

When Bridalveil Fall is fully charged, its spray washes over viewers gathered on the tiered platforms at trail's end. Expect to jostle with fellow hikers for the best camera angles during late spring and early summer, when the valley begins to clog with seasonal tourists. But regardless of whether the overlook is teeming or empty, the up-close views of the fall, the roar of its descent, and the thrill of its proximity will satisfy any waterfall aficionado.

Bridalveil Fall plunges toward the valley floor.

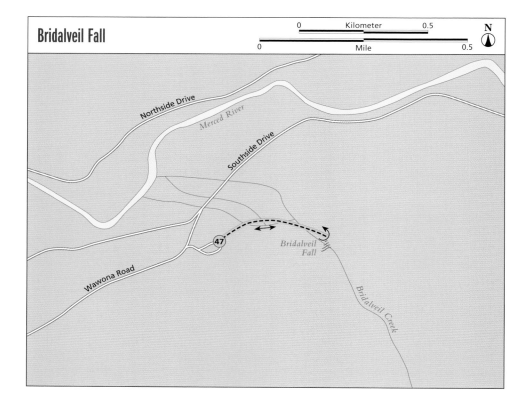

Later in the year Bridalveil Fall fades away to a gentler mist, though it flows year-round. Even when thinned by summer heat, however, the fall is still an iconic gateway element of the Yosemite Valley.

The trail is short and simple. From the trailhead follow the paved path up to a trail Y. Stay right on the signed route, climbing relatively steeply alongside a segment of Bridalveil Creek to the small overlook. Gaze upward at the long, slender spill of fall; then, if it's early in the season, turn around and look across the valley at Ribbon Fall, which drops more than 1,600 feet from the cliff top west of El Capitan to the valley floor. Return as you came.

Miles and Directions

0.0 Start on the signed paved trail at the east end of the parking lot.

0.1 At the Y stay right on the signed path to Bridalveil Fall.

0.25 Reach the overlook. Retrace your steps.

0.5 Arrive back at the trailhead.

48 Illilouette Fall

Follow the Panorama Trail past classic views of Half Dome to a sheltered overlook of one of Yosemite's more remote falls.

Height: 370 feet

Beauty rating: ★★★★★

Start: Panorama Trailhead at Glacier Point

Distance: 5.4 miles out and back

Difficulty: Strenuous

Hiking time: About 3 hours

Seasons/schedule: Late spring, summer, and early fall, when the Glacier Point Road is open. Sunrise to sunset. If you're winter-travel savvy and up for winter camping, you can venture out on the trail year-round.

Fees and permits: An entrance fee is charged. A reservation system to visit Yosemite Valley is in place; visit www.nps.gov/yose/planyourvisit/reservations.htm for more information.

Trail contact: Yosemite National Park, Public Information Office, PO Box 577, Yosemite, CA 95389; (209) 372-0200 (dial ext. 3, then 5); www.nps.gov/yose. The website is extensive and should be every visitor's first stop for information on the park.

Canine compatibility: No dogs allowed on trail.

Trail surface: Dirt singletrack

Land status: Yosemite National Park

Nearest towns: Yosemite Village; El Portal and Wawona

Other trail users: Horse packers

Maps to consult: USGS Half Dome CA; park map available online and at park entrances

Water availability: Water is available at the trailhead.

Amenities available: Restrooms, a cafe and gift shop, trash cans, maps, and information signboards

Cell service: Marginal; don't count on it.

Trail conditions: This lovely trail is popular but generally not swamped with hikers.

Finding the trailhead: From El Portal take CA 140 east into Yosemite Valley via the Arch Rock Entrance Station—or find your way into the valley via CA 120/Big Oak Flat Road or CA 41/Wawona Road. Take Southside Drive (one-way) to the signed junction with Wawona Road. Turn right onto Wawona Road and follow it for about 9 miles, through the tunnel and up to the junction with Glacier Point Road (open late May to Oct or Nov, snow permitting). Turn left onto Glacier Point Road and follow it about 13 miles to its end in the Glacier Point parking lot. Despite its expansiveness, this lot fills quickly in high season and can be clotted with buses. You may need to park at Badger Pass Ski Area. The trailhead is opposite the visitor center and gift shop. Trailhead GPS: N37 43.633' / W119 34.507'

The Hike

Just about every waterfall in Yosemite National Park could be called bucket list. For Illilouette Fall it's not only because of the fall itself—which, don't get me wrong, is spectacular—but also because of the journey. The trail's not named Panorama for nothing.

The Panorama Trail leads to an overlook of Illilouette Fall and offers spectacular views of Half Dome and other Yosemite landmarks along the way.

Illilouette Fall

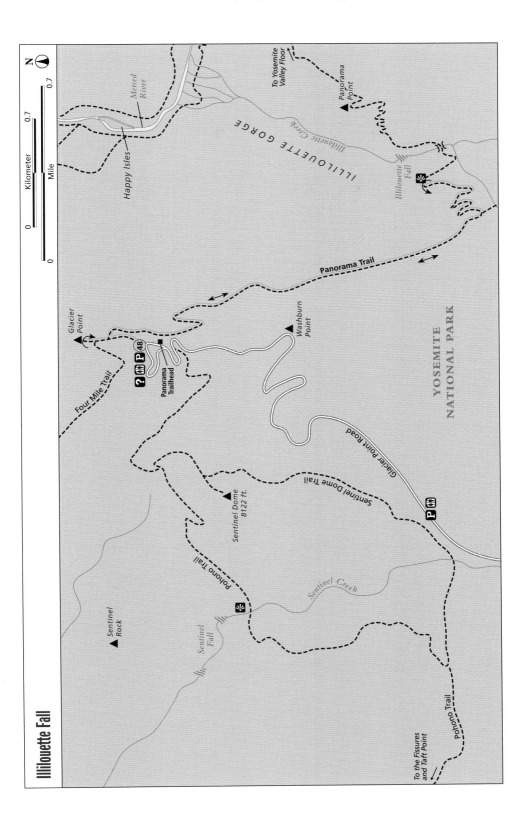

As you traverse southeast from Glacier Point into Yosemite's backcountry, views open in an arc before you. First, from Glacier Point, vistas drop through Yosemite Valley to El Capitan and the Brothers, Yosemite Falls and the Royal Arches, and North Dome. Farther along, Half Dome dominates the front-country, and then the eye is drawn down to Vernal and Nevada Falls in the Merced River Gorge. White-capped summits, sharp and shining in the sun, mark the skyline: Watkins, Hoffman, the Echo Peaks, and more.

The hike to Illilouette Fall starts and ends at storied Glacier Point, where touring the often-packed paved paths that lead out to the various vista points shouldn't be overlooked. With any luck you'll visit on a less busy day, when you can find a spot along the trail and thrill in the edge-of-the-void views. The out-and-back route described here incorporates that tour at the outset. Be sure to check out the information signboards, which describe McCauley's Mountain House and the Glacier Point Hotel, which burned in 1969, and identify landmarks in the foreground and on the horizon.

Pick up the signed Panorama Trail, directly opposite the gift shop, and set off on the relatively gentle downhill run toward Illilouette Creek and Illilouette Fall. The route switchbacks down through stands of evergreens settled on the landscape with parklike precision. Within half a mile the woods end and the trail ramps with relative gentleness (for Yosemite) across a scrubby mountainside. Pockets of trees and tall deciduous shrubs thrive in shallow gullies carved by seasonal streams, but none are thick enough to screen the amazing views. If hiking on a hot day, however, be sure to carry lots of water, bring a hat, and wear sunscreen. Half Dome dominates the views for the first mile or so, and then the shadowy canyon cradling Vernal and Nevada Falls comes into play.

The one and only trail junction is just beyond the 2-mile mark; head left on the trail signed for Illilouette Fall, Nevada Fall, and the valley floor. While still in the scrubland, views are dead-centered on Half Dome. Cross a streamlet and then drop into the woodlands surrounding Illilouette Creek. The overlook, which is the turnaround for this hike, is at a break in the trees directly opposite the Illilouette Fall.

The fall runs year-round. When fully charged, it plunges off the cliff into the shadowy gorge below; later in the season, when the flow mellows, Illilouette Creek drops about 30 feet into a pool and then splinters and falls hundreds of feet into the gorge, crashing into a steep, narrow cleft where the sun seldom shines. Trees shelter the rock slabs at the overlook, but depending on the time of day and time of year, those rocks may bake in the sun. If you want to check out the top of the falls, continue down the path and cross the creek.

From the overlook retrace your steps to the trailhead. It's all uphill from here. Though never painfully steep, the hike back is a slog with phenomenal views. Set your pace, stay hydrated, and enjoy.

Miles and Directions

0.0 Start with a tour of the paved paths on Glacier Point at the gift shop.

0.3 Complete the Glacier Point loops at the signed Panorama Trailhead opposite the gift shop. Head left on Panorama Trail, staying left at the Y and climbing briefly before traversing into trees.

0.5 Leave the trees for the long traverse down toward the Illilouette Creek drainage.

2.1 At the trail junction at a switchback, go left on the signed trail to Illilouette Fall, Nevada Fall, and the Yosemite Valley. The trail to the right leads to Mono Meadows, Buck Camp, and other points in the backcountry.

2.6 Cross a seasonal creek in the woods.

2.7 Round a switchback and arrive at the Illilouette Fall overlook. This is the turnaround; retrace your steps. (You can also drop another tenth of a mile or so to cross the creek near the top of the fall.)

5.4 Arrive back at the trailhead.

Option: You can continue past Illilouette Fall on a moderately strenuous one-way day hike to the valley floor. The route takes in a section of the John Muir Trail, includes views of Nevada Fall and Vernal Fall, and, depending on the trail you chose, incorporates the stairs of the Mist Trail. The route negotiates a significant uphill section between Illilouette Creek and the John Muir Trail. And don't discount the difficulty of the final downhill run: The Mist Trail can be brutal on the knees. The one-way distance is about 8.5 miles.

49 Yosemite Falls

An easy paved trail leads to the base of Lower Yosemite Fall, where Yosemite Creek completes its dive onto the valley floor. Reaching views of Upper Yosemite Fall involves a more demanding hike and features outstanding vistas of iconic Yosemite Valley cliffs and walls.

Height: 2,425 feet total (1,430 for the upper fall; 675 for the middle cascade; 320 for the lower fall)

Beauty rating: ★★★★★

Start: Shuttle stop 6/Lower Yosemite Fall Trailhead near Yosemite Village; shuttle stop 7/Camp 4 for Upper Yosemite Fall

Distance: 1.0-mile loop (Lower Yosemite Fall); 3.0-mile out-and-back (Upper Yosemite Fall viewpoint); 7.5-mile lollipop to link the two

Difficulty: Easy (Lower Yosemite Fall) to strenuous (Upper Yosemite Fall)

Hiking time: 1 hour for Lower Yosemite Fall; up to 4 hours for lower fall and viewpoint; all day to top out

Seasons/schedule: Year-round; sunrise to sunset, for Lower Yosemite Fall. Upper Yosemite Fall is a challenge once the snow begins to fly, but if you're winter-travel savvy, you can give it a go.

Fees and permits: An entrance fee is charged. A reservation system to visit Yosemite Valley is in place; visit www.nps.gov/yose/planyourvisit/reservations.htm for more information.

Trail contact: Yosemite National Park, Public Information Office, PO Box 577, Yosemite, CA 95389; (209) 372-0200 (dial ext. 3, then 5); www.nps.gov/yose. The website is extensive and should be every visitor's first stop for information on the park.

Canine compatibility: No dogs allowed on trails.

Trail surface: Pavement and dirt (Lower Yosemite Falls); dirt, switchbacks, stone staircases (Upper Yosemite Falls)

Land status: Yosemite National Park

Nearest towns: Yosemite Village; El Portal

Other trail users: None

Maps to consult: USGS Half Dome CA and Yosemite Falls CA; park map available online and at park entrances

Water availability: Water is available in Yosemite Village and throughout the valley.

Amenities available: Restrooms, trash cans, shuttle stop, and information signboards. An abundance of amenities—from gift shops to restaurants to tent cabins and more—not to mention the basics, such as restrooms, water, and trash cans, are also available elsewhere on the Yosemite Valley floor.

Cell service: Marginal; don't count on it.

Trail conditions: The trail to Lower Yosemite Fall is popular, paved, and crowded, but lovely. The trail to Upper Yosemite Fall is steep, popular, and exposed. Use proper trail etiquette and common sense on both routes.

Finding the trailhead: The Lower Yosemite Fall Trailhead can be reached from a number of nearby valley attractions in Yosemite Village or at Yosemite Lodge; the trailhead for this route is at shuttle stop 6/Lower Yosemite Fall, located between the two. The Upper Yosemite Fall Trailhead is at shuttle stop 7/Camp 4, located along Northside Drive west of Yosemite Village and Yosemite Lodge. Limited day-use parking is available at the camp, along Northside Drive, and at Yosemite Lodge; parking fills quickly in the high season. Trailhead GPS: Shuttle stop 6/Lower Yosemite Fall Trailhead: N37 44.768' / W119 35.536'; shuttle stop 7/Camp 4: N37 44.768' / W119 35.536'

The Hike

One of the park's premier attractions in spring and early summer, Yosemite Falls features three tiers that drop more than 2,400 feet from rim to valley floor. The upper fall is the tallest at 1,430 feet; the middle cascades are the most difficult to see; and the lower fall, at 320 feet, attracts the hordes—for good reason. The paved path to the lower fall leads into the spray itself when the flows are at their peak, and the experience is sublime.

From the trailhead the paved Lower Yosemite Falls Trail heads north, toward the falls, passing benches and interpretive signs that describe one of Yosemite's nineteenth-century accommodations, James Hutchings's boardinghouse. As you'll discover as you continue reading the interpretive plaques alongside the pleasant, wandering route, Hutchings hired a young John Muir to work in his sawmill in the valley, sparking a career that would alter the ethos of wilderness preservation in the West. Muir would go on to fight for preservation of Yosemite as a national park, and to cofound the Sierra Club, still a potent wilderness advocacy organization.

Stay right at the junctions as you continue toward the lower fall, enjoying forest and meadow watered by a peaceful stretch of Yosemite Creek. The path climbs to a junction with the Valley Loop Trail; go left toward the falls.

When the waterfall is raging, the mist hits before you reach the bridge that spans its rock-tumbled base. The bridge is broad, but this section of the route is commonly congested. The slowed pace allows more time with the spectacular sights.

Beyond the waterfall the paved route continues past the Spider Caves (on the right). At the Y stay right on the broad path, passing benches and interpretive signs as the trail loops back toward the restrooms near the shuttle stop/trailhead. You can end the hike here or continue along the Valley Loop Trail past Yosemite Lodge and into Camp 4, where the trail to Upper Yosemite Fall begins. A parallel dirt track cruises through the woods above the roadside, leading past a monument to the Ahwahneechee people, and boulders where climbers learn or hone their techniques.

The trail to Upper Yosemite Fall, given its steepness, doesn't attract quite as many visitors as the trail to the base of the lower fall, but it still sees plenty of traffic. An alpine excursion not suitable for those who don't like exposure, the trail climbs the south-facing wall of the valley, past Columbia Rock, to an overlook (this route's turnaround point), and then on to the top of the fall on the rim. You can break it down any way you choose: You can also turn around at Columbia Rock, or continue past the falls overlook turnaround to the top of the upper fall, as weather, daylight, and stamina permit.

The signed Upper Yosemite Falls Trail begins behind Camp 4, haunt of Yosemite big-wall climbers for more than half a century. If you've followed the Valley Loop Trail from Yosemite Village to the camp, you'll likely have passed climbers dangling from boulders alongside the trail, honing their skills. The trail itself is a devious Yosemite ascent, with sixty switchbacks carved into the mountainside leading up to the

Lower Yosemite Fall is a popular and often crowded destination on the valley floor.

Upper Yosemite Fall plummets from the valley rim.

Yosemite Falls

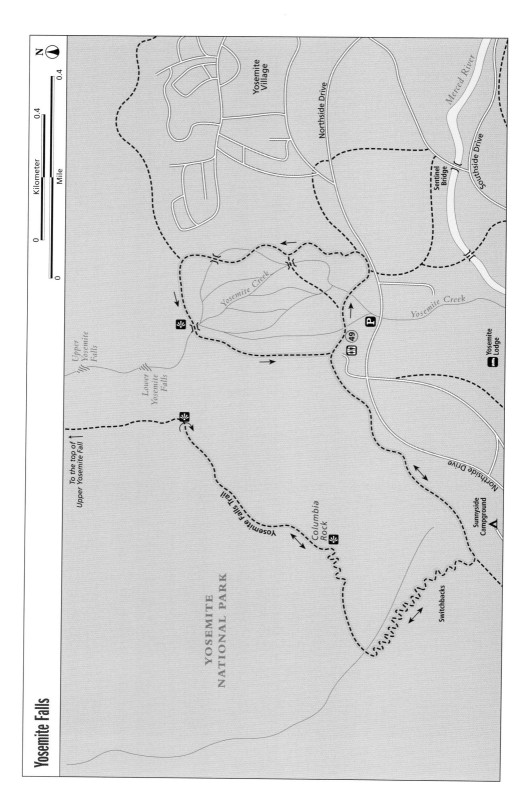

Columbia Rock overlook. No doubt the switchbacks ease the climbing (as the sign says), but this is not a trail for wimps. Thankfully the sharp, steep curves are shaded by an oak woodland.

The switchbacks are separated by longer traverses as the route nears the Columbia Rock overlook. A long stretch across an open slope leads up to the viewpoint, where vistas open east across the valley floor to Half Dome and the granite summits that surround it.

Columbia Rock is a turnaround option, but the Upper Fall overlook is the target, and it's only about 0.5 mile farther. Continue up a staircase carved into the slope, traverse around the mountainside, and then make a downhill run around switchbacks and through spring-fed gullies. A final curve, and the upper falls are in sight. The vista is thrilling: You won't be immersed in mist, but the suddenness of the waterfall's appearance and the thunder that it emits are guaranteed to thrill. This is the turn-around: Take it all in, then return as you came.

Miles and Directions

0.0 Start at the information signboard on the signed paved path; the first stop is Lower Yosemite Fall. Stay right on the paved path at the junction that follows.

0.2 Stay right on the paved path. The left path leads to an overlook.

0.3 Cross a boardwalk. At the junction with the Valley Loop Trail, go left to Lower Yosemite Fall.

0.6 Reach the base of Lower Yosemite Fall. Take it all in, then continue along the paved loop.

1.0 Close the loop near the restrooms at shuttle stop 6. You can end your hike here or pick up the Valley Loop Trail, heading right (west) on the paved path that follows Northside Drive past Yosemite Lodge to the trailhead in Camp 4 for Upper Yosemite Fall.

1.5 The signed Upper Yosemite Fall Trailhead is on the north (back) side of the parking area for Camp 4.

2.5 Reach the Columbia Rock overlook. Enjoy the magical views and then continue up the staircase toward the fall overlook.

3.5 Reach the Upper Yosemite Fall overlook. Take in the amazing view, then retrace your steps.

7.0 Arrive back at the Upper Yosemite Fall Trailhead.

7.5 Arrive back at the Lower Yosemite Fall Trailhead.

Option: The Upper Yosemite Fall Trail continues to the top of the upper fall, climbing switchbacks along the left (west) side of the cliff for a total of 2,700 feet. This is a challenging day hike, requiring both leg strength and lung power; it's 7.2 miles round-trip from the Camp 4 trailhead.

50 Vernal and Nevada Falls

The Mist Trail to Vernal Fall and Nevada Fall is one of Yosemite's most popular, for good reason. The storied staircase section of the trail follows the thundering Merced River to the top of spectacular Vernal Fall. The trail also serves up the best views of Nevada Fall, with the backward vistas of the whitewater plunge from the John Muir Trail pulling a close second.

Height: 317 feet (Vernal Fall), 549 feet (Nevada Fall)

Beauty rating: ★★★★★

Start: Happy Isles Trailhead in Yosemite Valley

Distance: 3.8-mile lollipop to Vernal Fall; 6.9-mile lollipop for Vernal and Nevada Falls

Difficulty: Strenuous

Hiking time: About 3 hours for Vernal Fall; about 5 hours for Vernal and Nevada Falls

Seasons/schedule: Year-round; sunrise to sunset. The Mist Trail is treacherous (and sometimes closed) in winter, when ice and snow preclude using the staircase.

Fees and permits: An entrance fee is charged. A reservation system to visit Yosemite Valley is in place; visit www.nps.gov/yose/planyourvisit/reservations.htm for more information.

Trail contact: Yosemite National Park, Public Information Office, PO Box 577, Yosemite, CA 95389; (209) 372-0200 (dial ext. 3, then 5); www.nps.gov/yose. The website is extensive and should be every visitor's first stop for information on the park.

Canine compatibility: No dogs allowed on the trails.

Trail surface: Pavement, dirt, granite, stone staircase

Land status: Yosemite National Park

Nearest towns: Yosemite Village; El Portal

Other trail users: Equestrians on the John Muir Trail

Maps to consult: USGS Half Dome CA; park map available online and at park entrances; just follow the crowd

Water availability: The best water you'll drink in Yosemite comes from the fountain at the bridge below Vernal Fall. It's as much about setting as taste. Water is also available at the trailhead.

Amenities available: Restrooms and information at Happy Isles (shuttle stop 16). An abundance of amenities—from gift shops to restaurants to tent cabins and more—not to mention the basics, such as restrooms, water, and trash cans, are available on the Yosemite Valley floor.

Cell service: Marginal; don't count on it.

Trail conditions: The Yosemite Valley floor is extremely popular, and all trails are likely to be crowded, especially in the summer season. Walk single file, keep right, and be courteous to all other trail users.

Finding the trailhead: The nearest parking for the Happy Isles trailhead is opposite the Upper Pines Campground at the east end of the valley floor. If parking is available (which may not be the case in the summer season), follow the roadside path south and east to the Happy Isles trailhead. If you find parking elsewhere in the valley, take the shuttle to stop 16. Cross the bridge to the trailhead on the right. Trailhead GPS: Upper Pines parking lot: N37 44.129' / W119 33.935'; Mist Trail at Happy Isles: N37 43.993' / W119 33.466'

Nevada Fall as viewed from an ascent along the Mist Trail.

The Hike

The Mist Trail is a bucket list hike. It's simply that good. It's steep and the footing can be treacherous, but the experience is quintessential Yosemite, full of granite and spray and views that soar heavenward. One of the most popular trails in Yosemite, it's often packed with people, so patience and courtesy are as necessary as good walking shoes. Take your time, walk single file, and stay right so faster hikers can pass. No need to rush—let the water do that instead.

The trail begins gently, following the relatively quiet Merced River through a boulder garden. But the river gains vigor as the trail gains elevation, starting within 0.1 mile of the trailhead. The ascent is unbroken from the base to the bridge below the falls but is mitigated by the river cascading alongside, whitewater crashing among boulders as it completes the final flight of the Giant Staircase.

The route flattens briefly at the Vernal Fall bridge. The waterfall is picture-perfect at this spot, framed in evergreens and backed by granite peaks. A water fountain and

Vernal Fall is the lower of two iconic falls on the Merced River.

The John Muir Trail offers great views of Nevada Fall.

restroom are on the far side of the bridge. This is a good turnaround point for those who aren't in shape; the length is 1.6 miles round-trip.

To continue to the top of the fall, follow the trail past a junction with the John Muir Trail, the return route. The pavement of the treadway is broken here, and the falls flicker in and out of view as you continue to climb.

Below the staircase ascent alongside the fall, several wide spots in the path allow you to pull aside and put on rain gear. What's generated by the fall when it's flowing full force hardly resembles mist; it can be drenching. Likewise, the mighty Mist Trail stairs—more than 600 of them—are perennially drenched. If the sight of the fall and the wind being sucked from your lungs by altitude aren't enough to slow your pace on the staircase, taking time to climb carefully will.

At the top of the fall, pause to take in the views from the sunny granite apron. The Merced appears calm above the cliff, gathering in the spectacular Emerald Pool before taking the plunge. Don't be fooled: This is a swift mountain stream, especially when swollen with snowmelt. Heed signs cautioning against wading and swimming. A railing near the top of the fall offers a great vantage point down the river valley, with a rainbow or two arcing in the mist and sunshine.

If you chose to turn around at the top of Vernal Fall, the best option for the downhill portion is to hook up with the John Muir Trail (also the return route from the top of Nevada Fall). Take the trail to Clark Point, which leads up from the top of Vernal Fall to connect with the Muir Trail, then follow the Muir Trail down to the junction above the Vernal Fall bridge (about 3.8 miles round-trip). From there retrace your steps to Happy Isles.

The Mist Trail to Nevada Fall continues beyond the apron alongside the now reasonably placid Merced, which fills the Emerald Pool and wets the Silver Apron. Social trails weave through the woods at the riverside; stay left of the restroom and follow the most obvious path. At the signed trail junction, stay left and proceed over the footbridge. The trail winds up a gentle incline through the forest.

Views of Nevada Fall open at a small granite overlook near the base of the 500-plus-foot cliff. In full swell it's a powerful sight, and the overlook makes a great rest stop before the next big climb. Set your pace and keep your head up as you gain altitude. This is not a brutal ascent, as switchbacks make the steepness tolerable, but it's stiff enough to elicit comments like "This is the longest 1.3 miles ever" from fellow hikers.

The trail tops out at a junction with the John Muir Trail, which leads to the top of the falls in one direction and farther into the Yosemite backcountry in the other. Turn right on the Muir Trail and walk out to the granite platform at the top of Nevada Fall, basking in views of Liberty Cap and the mighty Merced as it is funneled over the precipice.

To make the descent via the Muir Trail, wander over the slabs to the footbridge spanning the river and cross to the far side, following the trail gently downhill through the woods. Continue to a section etched into the canyon wall as you leave

Vernal and Nevada Falls

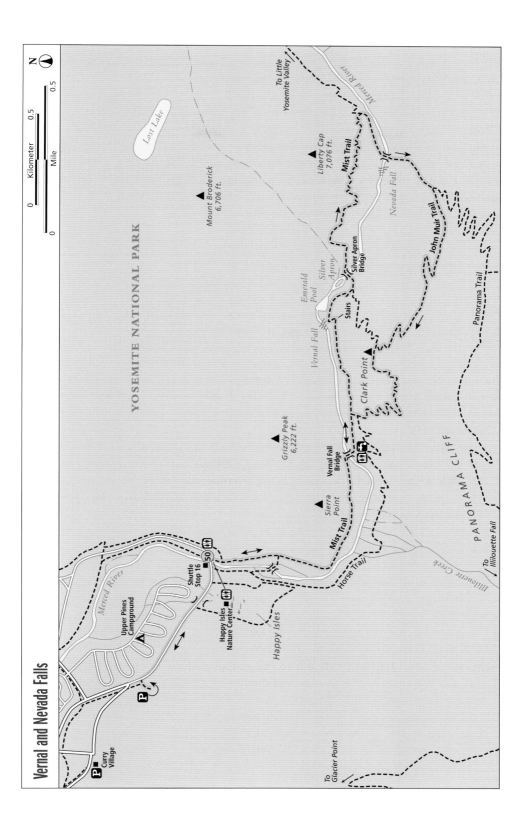

the Merced behind, where the granite face leaks moisture early in the hiking season. Turn around to take in views of Liberty Cap and Mount Broderick backing Nevada Fall. The exposure is exhilarating.

The Muir Trail presents a steady but moderate descent, with switchbacks and plenty of shade. Drop to Clark Point, where you can turn right to revisit the top of Vernal Fall or if you want to do laps. This loop continues on the Muir Trail, beginning a steeper descent toward the Yosemite Valley. Switchbacks ease the grade, as do views across the valley, but this can be a taxing section of trail for those with creaky knees. When you reach the junction with the Mist Trail above the Vernal Fall bridge, continue downhill, retracing your steps to the trailhead.

Miles and Directions

0.0   Start by taking the Mist Trail from Happy Isles.

0.1   Begin climbing up the paved path alongside the tumbling Merced River.

0.8   Arrive at the bridge below Vernal Fall. Water from the fountain on the far side of the bridge is delicious. Continue up the path, now on the other side of the river. (**Option:** If you're not going to the top of the fall, this is a good turnaround point for a 1.6-mile hike.)

1.1   At the junction with the John Muir Trail, stay left and riverside on the Mist Trail.

1.5   Ascend the Mist Trail stairs to the top of Vernal Fall. Take in the views, then continue on the most obvious path along the riverside, passing the Emerald Pool. Do not swim in the Emerald Pool; several people have died after being swept over Vernal Fall just downstream.

1.75 At the signed trail junction, go left on the Mist Trail to Nevada Fall.

1.9   Cross the footbridge.

2.25 Take in the view from the small granite overlook at the base of the fall.

2.9   Arrive at the junction with the Muir Trail and other backcountry routes at the top of the climb. Go right on the Muir Trail toward the top of the fall.

3.0   Reach the granite slabs at the top of Nevada Fall. Cross the footbridge over the Merced and begin your descent on the John Muir Trail.

3.5   At the signed junction stay right on the Muir Trail; the trail to the left leads to Illilouette Fall.

4.6   At the signed junction at Clark Point, stay left on the John Muir Trail. Long switchbacks break up the descent.

6.1   Reach the junction with the Mist Trail above the Vernal Fall bridge. Turn left and retrace your steps.

6.9   Arrive back at the Happy Isles trailhead.

Honorable Mentions

While the falls featured in this chapter are all located in Yosemite National Park, some of these honorable mentions are located outside the park and can be reached via Big Oak Flat Road/CA 120. And the Yosemite falls mentioned in this chapter, whether featured or listed as an honorable mention, barely scratch the surface of waterfall wonders in the park, including Waterwheel Fall and others in the Grand Canyon of the Tuolumne, Rancheria Falls in Hetch Hetchy, and more. You can learn more about all the waterfall wonders of Yosemite by searching online or contacting the park (www.nps.gov/yose).

Rainbow Pool

This waterfall is outside of Yosemite National Park, worth a visit if you happen to be entering via Big Oak Flat Road/CA 120. A brief hike leads down to a perfect pool fed by a 20-foot waterfall on the indefatigable South Tuolumne River. Sweet and easy, perfect for an outing with the kids, and sought after by early morning anglers, Rainbow Pool was once the focal point of a resort that burned in 1958. Now the site lies in the midst of the infamous Rim Fire of 2013, which torched about 257,000 acres (more than 400 square miles). The walk to the pool and back is less than 0.1 mile long. For more information search for Rainbow Pool Day-Use Area on the Stanislaus National Forest website at www.fs.usda.gov/recarea/stanislaus.

Rainbow Pool and its waterfall are an inviting stop along CA 120 outside Yosemite National Park.

Carlon Falls

Despite its proximity to Yosemite National Park and Hetch Hetchy, the route to 35-foot Carlon Falls is less traveled. An easy 3.3-mile out-and-back walk follows a peaceful section of South Fork Tuolumne River to a jumble of river rocks and the year-round cataract. The trailhead is located off Big Oak Flat Road/CA 120 on Evergreen Road, which leads to Hetch Hetchy. For more information search for Carlon Falls Trail on the Stanislaus National Forest website (www.fs.usda.gov/recarea/stanislaus).

Even when sapped by drought, Carlon Falls provides a cool turnaround point after a lovely woodland hike.

A hike to Foresta Falls leads through a fire-scarred landscape.

Foresta Falls

This year-round 50-foot waterfall and its upper cascades are surrounded by a haunting fire-scarred woodland. Reached via the hamlet of Foresta, located within Yosemite National Park's boundaries but not inside the valley, the wildlands surrounding the waterfall and town have burned or threatened to burn countless times over the years. A 1.8-mile hike leads down a closed dirt road winding through skeletal standing dead trees that groan when the wind flows through. Crane Creek runs alongside, offering views and access to the Foresta cascades and slides above the final plunge. The waterfall is at the bridge, dropping from about 50 feet above, fanning out across the dark slab, and then scattering in a mash of boulders and deadfall at its base. The year-round creek then rumbles under the bridge, through a cataract created by more deadfall on the downhill side. This is an upside-down hike, so be prepared for the uphill on the return; as a bonus, views of the cascades and slides are better on the way back. Visit www.nps.gov/yose for more information.

Cascade and Wildcat Falls

Cascade Fall (750 feet) and Wildcat Fall (700 feet) are Yosemite's gateway waterfalls. They are glorious when full with snowmelt, turning the heads of drivers following scenic CA 140 through the Merced Gorge toward Yosemite Valley proper. A quick stop at the Cascade Fall pullout and a short walk west link the two plunges, which can run year-round but fade to ribbons in late season. Visit www.nps.gov/yose for more information.

Left: Tucked in a shady cleft, the Cascades offer an introduction to Yosemite waterfalls.
Right: Viewing all of Wildcat Fall isn't easy to do, but sections of the cascade enliven the drive into Yosemite Valley.

Ribbon Fall

Heralded as the tallest uninterrupted waterfall in the United States, 1,612-foot Ribbon Fall slips down the cliff just west of El Capitan. With no trail leading to its base or to its summit, Ribbon Fall is best viewed from Bridalveil Fall or from the pullouts alongside the meadows on Southside Drive. Fed by Ribbon Creek, the ephemeral waterfall is just what its name implies: a ribbon of water streaking down one of the valley's steep ramparts that typically disappears just as the summer season in Yosemite kicks into full gear. Visit www.nps.gov/yose for more information.

Ephemeral Ribbon Fall is the highest unbroken waterfall in the United States.

Horsetail Fall is ephemeral both in terms of water and the February sunsets that fire it up.
SHAREALIKE 2.0; WIKIPEDIA COMMONS.

Horsetail Fall

You'll have to time this just right: Not only is Yosemite's 1,575-foot Horsetail Fall short-lived, but the window for viewing the spectacle of firefall is even shorter. For a few weeks in February, conditions permitting, this narrow fall catches the light of the setting sun just right and lights up like a flow of lava down the east face of El Capitan. The fall cannot be approached via trail but can be viewed from the El Capitan picnic area on the valley floor, west of Yosemite Lodge, or from points along Northside Drive. For more information visit www.nps.gov/yose.

Staircase Falls is one of Yosemite's remarkable ephemeral falls, descending the broken cliff face behind Curry Village.

Staircase Falls

Checking out 1,300-foot Staircase Falls does not require a significant hike. A walk through Curry Village reveals the lower part of the ephemeral spill, which runs in rivulets down the cliff face behind the tent cabins. A more impressive view of the falls, which scatter across the cliff face as an unnamed creek drops from near Glacier Point into the Yosemite Valley, can be had from the boardwalk in Stoneman Meadow, which begins opposite the road leading into Curry Village. The short walk through the meadow also offers great views of Half Dome and other Yosemite monoliths. For more information visit www.nps.gov/yose.

Views from the top of Sentinel Fall, near Sentinel Dome, take in iconic views of Yosemite Valley, El Capitan, and more.

Sentinel Fall

Though the tiers of 2,000-foot Sentinel Fall are best viewed from below, looking up from Sentinel Beach or other locations on the Yosemite Valley floor, a 4.8-mile loop hike takes you to the funnel at the top, as well as to the awesome 360-degree views from the summit of Sentinel Dome, which are colossal. The Cathedral Rocks, Half Dome, El Cap, the distant glacier-sculpted peaks and ridges of the High Sierra—a compass rose helps you name them all, including distant Mount Conness, Mount Ritter, and Banner Peak. For more information visit www.nps.gov/yose.

Chilnualna Fall

This year-round, 2,200-foot waterfall, composed of five cascades along more than 4 miles of Chilnualna Creek, is in the Wawona area of the park. You have options: You can view the first 700 feet or so via a 1-mile out-and-back hike near its base, or you can climb to the top cascade, following a trail designed by the same trail builder, John Conway. Conway constructed the devious yet brilliant switchbacking trail to Upper Yosemite Fall—a strenuous, 8.2-mile out-and-back day hike with an elevation change of 2,400 feet. For more information visit www.nps.gov/yose.

A drought-sapped Chilnualna Fall trickles into the shallow pool at its base.

Resources

Waterfall lovers have written guidebooks and created websites that provide abundant information on falls to visit in Northern California. Check them out.

Books

Brown, Ann Marie. *California Waterfalls*, 4th ed. Berkeley, CA: Moon Outdoors, 2011.

Danielsson, Matt, and Krissi Danielsson. *Waterfall Lover's Guide to Northern California*. Seattle, WA: Mountaineers Books, 2006.

Publications

Greene, Linda Wedel. Historic Resource Study. *Yosemite: The Park and Its Resources, vol. 1, Historical Narrative*. Washington, DC: US Department of the Interior/National Park Service, 1987. www.nps.gov/yose/historyculture/upload/greene 1987v1.pdf.

Websites

www.parks.ca.gov (Search for "waterfalls" and select "Wet Winter Strengthens Cascading Waterfalls in California State Parks.)

worldwaterfalldatabase.com

waterfallswest.com

www.world-of-waterfalls.com/california.html

hikemtshasta.com

visitredding.com

chicohiking.org

Hike Index

About the Author

Tracy Salcedo has written more than twenty-five guidebooks to a number of destinations in California and Colorado, including *Hiking Lassen Volcanic National Park* (3rd edition; winner of the 2020 National Outdoor Book Award for Outdoor Adventure Guidebooks), *Best Hikes Near Reno and Lake Tahoe*, *Best Rail Trails California*, and Best Easy Day Hikes guides to the San Francisco Bay Area, San Jose, Lake Tahoe, Reno, Sacramento, Denver, and Boulder. She's also written several books of essays about national parks in the West, including *Historic Yosemite National Park*, *Historic Denali National Park and Preserve*, *Search and Rescue Alaska*, and *Death in Mount Rainier National Park*. She lives with her family in California's Wine Country. You can learn more by visiting her website at laughingwaterink.com.

THE TEN ESSENTIALS OF HIKING

American Hiking Society

American Hiking Society recommends you pack the "Ten Essentials" every time you head out for a hike. Whether you plan to be gone for a couple of hours or several months, make sure to pack these items. Become familiar with these items and know how to use them. Learn more at **AmericanHiking.org/hiking-resources.**

 1. **Appropriate Footwear**

 6. **Safety Items** (light, fire, and a whistle)

 2. **Navigation**

 7. **First Aid Kit**

 3. **Water** (and a way to purify it)

 8. **Knife or Multi-Tool**

 4. **Food**

 9. **Sun Protection**

 5. **Rain Gear & Dry-Fast Layers**

 10. **Shelter**